# City of Lingering Splendor

大清國當今慈德端佑康頤昭豫莊誠壽恭欽獻聖母皇太后

The Dowager-Empress whose spirit still haunted Peking

# City of
# Lingering Splendour

A FRANK ACCOUNT OF OLD PEKING'S
EXOTIC PLEASURES

## JOHN BLOFELD

SHAMBHALA
BOSTON & SHAFTESBURY
1989

Shambhala Publications, Inc.
Horticultural Hall
300 Massachusetts Avenue
Boston, Massachusetts 02115

Shambhala Publications, Inc.
The Old School House
The Courtyard, Bell Street
Shaftesbury, Dorset SP7 8BP

9 8 7 6 5 4 3 2 1

First Shambhala Edition
Printed in the United States of America on acid-free paper
Distributed in the United States by Random House
and in Canada by Random House of Canada Ltd.
Distributed in the United Kingdom by Element Books, Ltd.

Library of Congress Cataloging-in-Publication Data
Blofeld, John Eaton Calthorpe, 1913–1987
City of lingering splendor : a frank account of old Peking's
exotic pleasures / John Blofeld.
p.    cm.
Reprint. Originally published: London : Hutchinson, 1961.
ISBN 0-87773-506-9 :
1. Peking (China)—Social Life and customs.   I. Title.
DS795.2.B56   1989                              89-101139
951'.156—dc20                                   CIP

Dedicated to the hermits,
scholars, youths and courtesans
who inspired these pages

*Lament for the Past*

What we have once known,
Is it forever ours?
These thoughts are mirrors of eternity.
Again the moon-white petals on my face,
Again the voice of the wise man
From the boat at evening, and the twisted branch
Etching the language of heaven upon the blue.
Again the poems in my hands, and all of life
An art, as it was in legend of old time.

What we have once known,
Is it forever ours?
O then comfort me!


*Taoist's Song*

Like the blue robe of a Presence,
A mist iridescent with jade and plum blossom,
Rustling with falling torrents,
Draperies in folds of dragons and crags,
Enfolds me, carries me, pervades me
In gusts of laughter as if I strode
From peak to peak in a vast embrace.

Ah, but this is my eternal friend,
My ancestor before I was born,
My counsellor, companion, and without him
I am not.

CLARE CAMERON

# Contents

# Illustrations

ILLUSTRATIONS

# Glossary

| | |
|---|---|
| *Hsienshêng (Elder-Born)* | Mr or Sir. |
| *Laoyeh (Old Daddy)* | Mr or Sir, used by subordinates. |
| *Taifu (Greatly Honourable)* | Dr (of Medicine). |
| *T'ait'ai (Exceedingly Exalted)* | Madam. |
| *Lao (Old)* | A prefix often used with the names of friends, servants, courtesans, etc., regardless of their age. |
| *Taoshih* | A Taoist adept. |
| *Tashihfu* | Maestro, meaning a chef. |

# Preface

This is the story of the joyful years I spent in Peking at a time before
the Second World War when many of her ancient traditions still
flourished, adding rich undertones and overtones to the gorgeous
colours of imperial architecture. The disciples of Mao Tse-Tung will
scarcely feel grateful for my eulogy of an era preceding the 'Red Dawn'
by some fifteen years; yet I am convinced there are still Pekingese
who, in the silence of their hearts, share my incurable nostalgia for a
way of life now vanished from the earth. Even non-Communist
readers may reasonably object that the gaiety, charm, good-living and
old-world fragrance of that era went hand in hand with wretched
poverty and many other human ills. True, but the human race has yet
to build up and maintain century after century an intricate, many-
splendoured civilization without cost in tears; nor have the Communists reached their present level of achievement without some
outpouring of tears, sweat and blood. High endeavour directed to
whatever end is always costly.

I suspect that for myself and other foreign admirers the greatest
of all Peking's charms was that, even as late as the nineteen-thirties, so
much of the ancient past was still vigorously alive within her walls. I
found her infinitely more satisfying than those cities where the
Pyramids, the Parthenon and the Colosseum remain only as dry husks
of civilizations long since passed away. Though constantly aware of
the dark shadows of poverty and illiteracy hovering close to the fading
gold and magenta of Peking's former imperial splendour, I was too
young and too eager for life to allow them to impair my happiness.
How many youths, magically transported through space and time to
Renaissance Italy, would forgo the pleasures offered by wealthy or
learned Florentines out of sympathy for the poor at their gates?
Compassion would prevent them from adding to the misery of those

13

without; it would scarcely restrain them from enjoying themselves at sumptuously laden tables set amid scenes of magnificence, or blind them to the charm of gay, witty and beautiful companions.

I arrived in Peking in 1934 and left after three exquisitely happy years to avoid being a helpless spectator of Japanese arrogance and brutality towards my friends. The war over, I hastened back to the city determined to live out my life there, but was compelled to leave it again—probably for ever—on the eve of the Red Army's triumphal entry. During that first visit, which forms the material of all but the last two chapters of this book, I earned my living by lecturing a few hours a week at one of the many universities and by giving private lessons in English. I have deliberately said little about these rice-bowl-filling activities, because in those days I always thought of myself as a student rather than a teacher and because the system of education had by then become so standardized as to have nothing uniquely Pekingese about it.

My age at the time of my arrival was twenty-two. I was young enough to respond eagerly to the sensuousness of those incredibly beautiful and, to me, exotic surroundings. Readers of my *Wheel of Life* need not be surprised by the unspiritual quality of some of the pleasures I enjoyed; I hope they will recall my frank statement that the erratic tide of my youthful strivings towards a spiritual goal reached a very low ebb under the impact of Peking's countless sensuous, aesthetic and intellectual charms. Moreover, though the present work is largely devoted to descriptions of banquets and lovely girls with specialized talents, I have also included some account of my contacts with the spiritual sides of Chinese life. Loving sincerity and hating cant, I cannot now pretend to have been other than I was.

While I was writing this book, a curiously revealing and quite unmeditated pattern took shape, as though of itself. It will be seen that, while the earlier chapters are much concerned with wine, women and song (or, more accurately, with feasting, courtesans and such trifles as fox-spirits), the later chapters show some traces of moral and spiritual development. This arrangement faithfully reflects the actual course of my Peking life. After sporting in the dazzling, foam-flecked shallows, I progressed very slowly into deeper waters where beauty was less fleetingly diverse.

Every incident set forth in these pages actually occurred; the characters on the other hand are sometimes real and sometimes composite. I have employed the methods of fiction only to reconstruct conversations or to refurbish settings fading from my memory. So all I have written records truthfully either what *was* or what easily *may have been.* As the single chapter concerning my post-war stay in Peking is only included to continue the stories of my friends of earlier years, I have said almost nothing of two events which happened in 1947 —my being accepted as a blood-brother by Chin P'ei-shan, Confucian scholar and Manchu nobleman; and my marriage to a Chinese lady, Chang Mei-fang; for neither of them was known to me before the war.

Having first lived in some other parts of China, I arrived in Peking already able to speak and read Chinese with reasonable fluency. To avoid tediousness, I have seldom done much to indicate in which of my two languages particular conversations took place, but wherever I am called John it may be assumed that the speaker was using English. My Chinese name is P'u Lo-Tao. The use of P'u Hsienshêng (Mr P'u) or of Hsienshêng (Sir) or Laoyeh (Sir) indicates that the conversation was in Chinese.

Life in a city of over a million inhabitants inevitably presents a bewildering number of facets. Others writing of Peking in those days have found plenty of different things to say. Personally, I went to China's ancient capital to saturate myself in all that remained of the traditional ways of life, so I chose my friends accordingly. Even the grossest of my pleasures (if the word 'gross' has any meaning at all in connection with so much beauty) were subtly blent with the rare loveliness of my surroundings. I spent my leisure now with courtesans or scholars (or both together), now with Taoist recluses or Buddhist monks—loving them all. Had I sought out politicians or sociologists or engine-drivers, no doubt I should have come to write a different sort of book, equally true to Peking but less so to myself.

JOHN BLOFELD

The Bamboo Studio
Bangkok

# I

# Twilight Amid Uneasy Splendour

WHEN after a lapse of several decades a man recalls the chief object of his youthful devotion, he seldom achieves simple truth. Blemishes are hidden by the purifying mists of time, charms exaggerated through his efforts to conjure warmth from long-dead embers. But as the object of my love was a living, breathing city to which whole centuries had brought their gifts of beauty, gaiety and voluptuous charm, there can be scarcely room for exaggeration. The attractions of a lovely mistress are necessarily limited and seldom retain their full power after long familiarity; whereas those of a city are inexhaustible, since a lifetime is much too short to discover them all.

It was my good fortune to live in Peking at a time when she was permitted to remain faithful to some of her centuries-old traditions. I can speak of her only as she was then, having seen nothing of her new guise as the capital of the Chinese People's Republic and second city of the Communist world. When I knew her, she was not even a capital, for Chiang Kai-Shek's Government had reduced her to the status of provincial town—she resembled a deposed empress, still clad in the remains of her imperial wardrobe, making ineffectual attempts to pose as an ordinary housewife.

Merely to pay Peking a fleeting visit was to be made aware of the breathtaking greatness of China's past. Though her castellated walls overshadowed plenty of hovels lacking even the merit of picturesque-ness, they also encompassed magnificent lotus-covered lakes and broad pleasure-gardens enriched by a wealth of gorgeously lacquered pavilions and groves of ancient trees. There were vast palaces looking deceptively squat beneath their heavy upward-sweeping roofs tiled with golden-yellow porcelain, and green- or blue-roofed temples with scarlet pillars and intricately painted eaves. Multi-roofed ceremonial archways spanned tree-lined boulevards running at right-angles to narrow, silent lanes with bronze-hinged scarlet gates set in otherwise featureless grey walls, enigmatically unrevealing. Behind these walls were flower-filled courtyards surrounding low curly-roofed buildings with coloured lattice doors and windows. I also loved the lanes of unpretentious shops beyond the Ch'ien Mên Gate, which divides the southern part of the city from the rest, shops from whose dim interiors came the sheen of precious silks, the rich glow of warmly coloured porcelain and the gleam of old-gold lacquer.

Though the citizens were more soberly clad than in the days of empire, they were still colourful by contemporary standards elsewhere. The ordinary people thronging the markets wore gowns or quilted jackets and trousers of almost every shade of blue, often with hints of white undergarments visible at the edges of their long sleeves and just showing above their high Manchu-style collars. The more leisured classes seen strolling along the boulevards or crossing the marble bridges in the imperial pleasure-gardens still clung to softly shining silken gowns, their colours pale or deep to harmonize with the seasons. There were also Mongols clad in maroon robes belted with scarlet or yellow sashes, their collars left open on purpose to reveal underjackets of yellow silk brocade; and Central Asian or Chinese Muslims distinguished by white turbans and thin silky beards. The Chinese girls come to market from the surrounding villages wore short jackets and wide trousers with bright floral patterns; small children were sometimes given scarlet clothes to ensure good fortune, many of the little boys being disguised as girls to deceive envious demons; and babies often wore hats and shoes fashioned like tiger-heads to endow them with health and strength. Though police and military uniforms had by then succumbed to modern drabness, some of the gendarmes still wore strapped to their backs swords with wide curved blades narrowing towards the hilt which made them colourful in another sense.

Peking's continental climate, too hot in summer and icy cold in winter, at least has the merit of extreme dryness; this ensures a Mediterranean clarity of sky and water, so that, except during the spring dust-storms or the brief summer rains, a brilliant unclouded arc of turquoise blue adds to the richness of the many-coloured temples, palaces and private courtyards. The progress of the seasons occurs with such extraordinary regularity that I came to think the dragons in charge of climatic phenomena must be deeply enamoured of bureaucratic precision. As to the respective merits of each season, the old

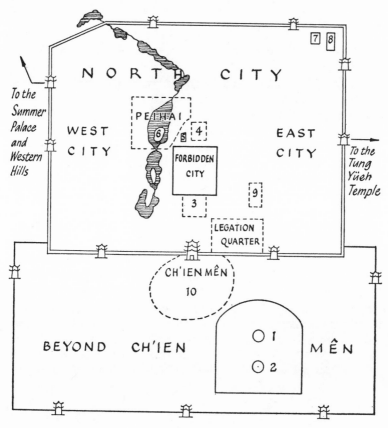

NORTH CITY

To the
Summer
Palace
and
Western
Hills

WEST CITY

PEIHAI

6

5 4

FORBIDDEN CITY

3

EAST CITY

To the
Tung
Yüeh
Temple

9

LEGATION QUARTER

CH'IEN MÊN

10

BEYOND CH'IEN    MÊN

○ 1

○ 2

7 8

1 Temple of Heaven
2 Altar of Heaven
3 Approach to the Forbidden City
4 Coal Hill
5 The National Library

6 Island and CHORTEN-crowned hill
7 The Temple of Confucius
8 The Lama Temple
9 The Tung An Market
10 Theatres, restaurants, willow-lanes

卍 City gate

scholars with their Taoistic feeling of kinship with nature could seldom agree. If spring brought appalling dust-storms now and then, it also clothed the naked limbs of trees with fresh young greens or with a mass of blossom—peach, apricot, plum, crab-apple and pear, followed in May by foaming cascades of lilac. In summer the sleepy lotus bloomed redly on lakes and palace moat, weeping willows bent to the water's edge and imperial peonies flaunted their unrivalled glory. In autumn chrysanthemums of more than a hundred varieties were set out in the courtyards or stood ranged in porcelain pots upon the pearwood stools within; the trees in parks and gardens put off their summer greens, replacing them with every shade of yellow, gold and red. When winter had set in, thick carpets of snow lay upon the upturned roofs and hid the sombre green of knotted cedar-trees; blue-grey ice covered the palace lakes, and an unearthly silence fell upon the lanes where a million pairs of felt-soled shoes moved soundlessly across the hard-packed snow.

In those days, though already a quarter of a century had passed since the last Son of Heaven had occupied the Dragon Throne, it was impossible to wander about the centre of the city without being reminded of the gay throngs of princes, courtiers, concubines and splendidly apparelled eunuchs and officials whose very names, features and idiosyncrasies were in some cases well remembered by my older friends. Their ghosts seemed always close at hand. Best-remembered of all was the enigmatic Tzŭ Hsi, who, as Empress or Empress-Dowager, had for some fifty years wielded, from behind the throne, supreme power over the largest nation on earth, and so impressed her personality upon the capital that she was everywhere regarded as its good or evil genius. Newly arrived foreigners were apt to imbibe details of her tastes in clothes, food or amusements and her methods of statecraft before they had discovered the names of half a dozen of the principal streets; for the Pekingese—even those born after her death in 1908— had an inexhaustible fund of stories about her. Many spoke of her with hatred, some with grudging admiration, a very few with love, but none with indifference. The heavy lacquered barges which now carried summer visitors across to the Five Dragon Pavilions to admire the giant lotus blossom had been Tzŭ Hsi's barges. The exquisite lakeside gallery, with its scarlet cloisters where I watched winter skaters come to warm themselves with spiced meat dumplings, had once been a favourite haunt of hers. The whole of the I Ho Yuan Summer Palace covering the slopes and environs of the Hill of Ten Thousand Years, which lies some miles beyond the city walls, had been built according to her plans. Its lakes and streams, with their humped bridges, the life-size brazen bull and the curiously ugly marble houseboat, had been shaped at her command. Some of the beautifully executed golden inscriptions proclaiming the poetic names of palace and temple halls were the talented work of Tzû Hsi's own hand. The Summer Palace theatre, where splendid spectacles had been enacted before the Son of Heaven and the imperial entourage, had been the scene of her operatic triumphs. Indeed, the history of all China had throughout two and a half reigns been inseparably linked to her.

If, as many people affirmed, Tzû Hsi's ghost still walked the precincts of the Forbidden City, it must have been because the troubles of her reign had pursued her beyond the grave. Perhaps she was still weighed down by memories of repeated foreign depredations, resulting in huge territorial losses and in the payment of crippling 'indemnities' exacted by the European Powers and their ally, Japan. Her reign had also been a time of internal ferment accompanied by perpetually smouldering rebellion. Then there had been those emperors, imperial concubines and countless others whom she had felt it desirable to imprison or put to death—but if ghosts can be as stubborn as autocratic old ladies, Tzû Hsi's spirit probably felt all these actions to have been fully justified.

The Empress-Dowager had recognized that if she allowed the gates to be opened even an inch to the flood-tide of Western ideas beating upon China's shores, traditional Chinese civilization would soon be swept from the earth. Though the ramparts she built or reinforced against this flood were too weak to stand for long, without them the end of all she cherished and admired would have come even sooner than it did. Besides, the losses of territory, wealth and prestige, due in part to her unyielding conservatism, might one day be repaired (as has now happened), but none of her republican successors has been able to enrich the world with anything of beauty comparable in size and magnificence to her inimitable Summer Palace, which stands to this day in all its perfection upon the Hill of Ten Thousand Years. Long may it remain!

The Peking I came to know so well had within living memory drawn the whole rhythm of its life from the imperial court. For centuries, stupendous wealth and luxury, displayed with the instinctive elegance and good taste of Chinese unspoiled by alien traditions, had been bringing to flower new arts and graces. Though I could not feel unqualified admiration for rulers to whom murder came more easily than breaches of good manners, I took full delight in the sunset glow of the splendour they had created. How different was their city from those, such as Shanghai, Hong Kong, Calcutta, Birmingham or Chicago, built on wealth and industry alone! In Peking so much that was excellent remained, quite apart from the palaces, pleasure-gardens, temples and imperial monuments; for the Pekingese as a whole still preserved some of the more inward qualities of the unique civilization of which they had become the last custodians. Urbanity, courtesy, a manner at once smiling and restrained; a preference for the pleasant tastes, sounds and colours that money could buy rather than for wealth itself; and an instinctive appreciation of beauty in art and nature—all these were commonly found at every level of Peking society, literate or not. Though degrees of refinement naturally varied with education and prosperity, even at the lowest level I saw nothing of the coarseness and boorishness usually associated with extreme poverty in large cities.

The general cheerfulness of the Pekingese was all the more remarkable in that so many of them had ample cause for being miserable. Misrule, civil war and foreign aggression were as familiar to them as the dust-storms of spring or the winter snow-blizzards. The living standard of about half the population was at least inadequate and in many cases appallingly low. Hunger and severe cold often caused not only suffering but death; and everyone alike must have been uneasily conscious of the ever-present threat of war. In spite of all this, to a newcomer acquainted only with the surface of the city's life, everything appeared as calm as the undisturbed reflections of magenta walls and ornamental turrets in the moat surrounding the Forbidden City; it took time to discover that this seeming placidity was deceptive. For, although Peking had been invested and captured by the armies of one warlord after another, there had never been such cause for alarm as during the apparently peaceful years of the mid-'thirties. Previously, even if some warlord had formed the impious wish to batter a way through the mediaeval ramparts, he could not have carried it out, for lack of artillery capable of doing more than deface the outer surface of those prodigious walls. Besides, the citizens had always been willing to surrender gracefully when strong enemy troops seemed impatient to lay aside their teapots and umbrellas in favour of rifles or broadswords with the intention of storming a gateway and rushing in to loot and burn. With well-understood emergencies of that sort they had known very well how to deal. The current threat to life and property was too sinister to be treated lightly. The Japanese, who three years earlier had seized the Manchurian provinces (collectively known as North-East China) in defiance of the League of Nations' protests, were like a pack of wolves crunching the bones of one victim before leaping upon the next. That Peking and the surrounding provinces had been selected for this fate was impossible to doubt, yet China's Central Government showed no signs of contemplating an attempt at rescue. Indeed, North China had already been forced to accept the status of a buffer region; it was only theoretically still a part of China, being already under the shadow of Japanese control. The only favourable circumstance was that the enemy had agreed for the time being to leave the region under the command of a northern general named Sung Ch'üeh-Yuan, whose persuasive air of docility towards the Japanese cloaked his genuine loyalty to his own country; but, lacking active support from Chiang Kai-Shek, he was powerless to offer more than brief resistance to an all-out attack.

A particularly galling result of Peking's being accepted by both sides as the centre of an ill-defended buffer state was that individual Japanese and Korean subjects of Japan found themselves virtually above the law. Of the thousands of such alien spies living within the city walls, only a few bothered to pass themselves off as Chinese citizens or bona-fide foreign residents. Worse than these contemptuous spies were the so-called *Ronin*—Japanese and Korean gangsters who roamed freely about the doomed provinces engaged in smuggling, dacoity and drug-peddling, secure in the knowledge that Chinese customs guards and policemen could be beaten up or even done to death with impunity. Their constant depredations made it sickeningly clear that Chinese sovereignty over the region existed only in name. Naturally the Pekingese looked forward to the future with uncertainty and dread. Though the old-style Chinese warlords had seldom won people's affection, their actions had at least been predictable; whereas the hated island dwarfs showed no signs of understanding the value of civilized restraint in dealing with a weaker enemy. They were not the sort of men who would agree to suspend hostilities on a rainy day, or give their opponents time to retreat with their baggage and waggonloads of officers' concubines intact, or be willing to retreat themselves when outnumbered! It was very sure that tactfully offered gifts of gold and delicacies would not persuade a Japanese general to keep his troops outside the city walls. However, in consequence of the Nanking Government's supine policy, there was nothing for the Pekingese to do but to make their last few months or years of freedom as enjoyable as possible, meanwhile bolstering their morale with vague hopes of some shift to the balance of international power occurring before the Japanese struck again.

Of the various foreign nationals within the city apart from Japanese and Koreans, the most numerous and least regarded were the White Russians. Stateless since the Russian Revolution, they had been driven by poverty and misfortune into leading more or less disreputable lives. Finding themselves unable to compete with the thrifty Chinese as labourers or shopkeepers, and lacking the capital or skills (including fluency in English) by which other foreigners earned good livings, the men were often forced to depend on what we should now call spiv-like activities; while numbers of the women became dance-hostesses and prostitutes or hovered on the fringes of those professions. One of the saddest sights in Peking was that of blowzy, middle-aged Russian women making hopeless attempts to appear young and alluring. By night, decked out in cheap, gaudy clothes, heavy make-up and imitation jewelry, they depended on the semi-darkness of the tawdry cabarets where they worked to hide their defects from all but those rare customers who counted a white skin more precious than the youthful chic of their Chinese competitors. Understandably, the Chinese treated these White Russians with contempt, not seeing that, whatever their faults, their unenviable position made them deserving of generous compassion. For the Chinese had endured too much humiliation at the hands of white nations (including Tsarist Russia) to have either liking or sympathy for Europeans in the mass; their affection was given only to individual Westerners with personal qualities of a sort they could love and *sometimes* even respect. I suppose that, from a Chinese, love was always easier to gain than respect, for almost every Chinese possessed an innate but courteously hidden sense of superiority to people of all other races. With the White Russians they discovered too little common ground for affection to arise easily; a race which for thousands of years had been bent on cultivating restraint and which therefore condemned violent displays of emotion (except at rare and terrible moments) could not be expected to comprehend the alternating gales of gusty laughter and unashamed bouts of weeping with which the exiles displayed their Russian souls. Similarly, it was impossible for the Chinese, constantly occupied with duties to preceding and succeeding generations, to sympathize with people capable of flinging away a month's earnings on one gloriously riotous evening regardless of the suffering which must ensue for themselves and their dependants. I was able to see many lovable qualities in both races, but I seldom risked trying to entertain my Chinese and Russian friends together. An evening spent in that way would have had scarcely any chance of success.

Apart from the Christian missionaries, of whom I saw and can recall almost nothing, the remaining Westerners in Peking fell roughly into two categories. The larger consisted of those diplomatic officials, bank staffs and employees of mercantile firms who lived stuffy lives within the walls of the Legation Quarter, guarded from dangers which had long ceased to exist by military detachments furnished by their respective countries. With their real enemies, the Japanese, they tended to live on terms of childishly trusting good-fellowship. The Legation Quarter's stout walls formed an iron curtain of the sort now familiar to the whole world, though naturally less hard to penetrate than its modern counterparts. Everyone was free to pass in and out at will and yet most inmates of the Legation Quarter led lives so detached from the currents of life swirling around them that they were always the last to know what was happening, if they ever came to know it at all. (For example, in 1948, only a month or two before the Red Army's bombardment of Peking's airfield ushered in the first stages of a siege that was to end in total victory for the Communists, there were foreign consular officers so ignorant of the opinions of every Chinese in the city that they still accepted Nationalist assurances that there was nothing to fear. Apparently they trusted the Government-inspired news in Nationalist papers as fully as the Singapore authorities had once trusted to their seaward-facing guns!)

The more amusing Westerners were those who in varying degrees loved Peking and who lived scattered about the great city free from the unwanted, anachronistic protection of walls and bayonets. For the most part they were Western counterparts of the Chinese literati —research scholars, university lecturers, writers and so on, with a sprinkling of painters and sculptors, together with a very few possessed of private means. British, German, American and French nationals predominated, the Germans being by far the most numerous of that small band of devoted scholars who intended to pass their whole lives in pursuit of Chinese studies. My own friends, though there were several foreigners among them, were principally Chinese. If my knowledge of literary Chinese had been deeper, I should have loved to sit at the feet of those elderly scholars who, after receiving a purely classical Chinese education, had passed high in the public examinations which in those days had formed the gateway to rank, riches and honour. I admired these old gentlemen with their unfailing courtesy, impressive manners, marvellously graceful gestures, deep learning and keen sense of humour—I admired them perhaps more than any class of human beings encountered before or since those days, but I was hopelessly unqualified to profit by the kind of teaching they wished to give me; to have spent many hours in their company would have given me a permanent inferiority complex. I preferred to seek the friendship and guidance of university dons then in their fifties or early sixties, for these people combined traditional and modern traits in about equal parts and understood the special needs of foreigners studying Chinese literature or philosophy at a relatively low level. Young students on the other hand, though with plenty of exceptions, struck me as undervaluing the greatness of their heritage; they were too onesidedly attached to the future, too anxious for China to progress along typically Western lines, too nationalistic and too fond of imagining China's future greatness in terms of military strength— though I doubt if any of them in those pre-war days envisaged such a sudden rise in international prestige as the Communists were later to achieve or realized that such radical changes could be brought about within the short space of ten years. Had they been gifted with fore-knowledge of these events, I think they would have been torn between elation and an inclination to shrink from the ruthlessness involved; for few of them were so iconoclastic as to wish for the destruction of *all* the old ways, including the gradual substitution of a roman alphabet for their ancient and beautiful Chinese characters. For the rest, I came to know several Taoists, Buddhist monks, actors, musicians, flower-girls and some of those delightfully courteous shopkeepers who bade you welcome even when they knew you would sit and chat for hours over the cups of jasmine-scented tea and cigarettes they provided, fingering their wares without much hope of being able to afford a single purchase. Some of them seemed to welcome the conversation of an appreciative pauper more than the generous but negligent custom of the very rich.

During my first few weeks in Peking I lived in a *kungyü*; that is to say I had a large room opening upon one of the inner courtyards of a huge mansion which had once belonged to a nobleman, but was now divided into sets of apartments run more or less like service flats in the West. This mansion consisted of some ten or more single-storey buildings ranged around courtyards of various sizes in which fantastic rockeries, clusters of porcelain flower-pots and handsome old fruit-trees remained from more opulent days. As with most Peking houses, the buildings were of grey brick with latticed paper windows set in frames of scarlet and green lacquer beneath eaves painted with vignettes of strange animals and birds surrounded by a uniform floral design in seven colours. Inside the principal rooms old carved wood-work encrusted with fading gilt contrasted with the simple furniture placed there by the later occupants.

After spending almost a month in the *kungyü*, I rented a small house of my own—the first of my several Peking dwellings. Each of them had charming details peculiar to itself, but the general arrange-ment was always about the same. The principal building faced south across a courtyard bounded by smaller buildings to east and west; there was also a southern wall centring upon the high, roofed gateway leading out into the lane. The relatively large southward-facing building, orientated to receive the maximum amount of sunshine in winter, was built in such a way that it could easily be converted into one, two or three living-rooms according to the requirements of the occupant; while bedrooms, kitchen, servants' rooms, storerooms and so on occupied the smaller buildings to east and west. The whole city of Peking, where the gates of the Forbidden City and those in the outer walls faced exactly towards the four main compass-points and where every wall ran precisely from north to south or east to west, had been laid out with such regard for symmetry that the words 'left' and 'right' were rarely used. Taxi-drivers and rickshaw-pullers would be instructed to turn north or south or to enter such-and-such a lane at the 'east mouth' or 'west mouth'; and when I supervised the hanging of a wall-scroll I would tell my servant to move it a fraction of an inch to east or west, never to left or right.

A particularly attractive feature of Pekingese houses was that they combined the privacy of a country cottage with the convenience of living in a large metropolis. In those days motor vehicles were few and scarcely ever seen in the residential lanes; so once you had entered a house and heard the heavy gates swing to behind you, the silence was so complete that the softest fluttering of the leaves on the courtyard trees could be enjoyed. Almost every courtyard contained one or more trees chosen either for the shade they afforded in summer or for the beauty of their blossom; if you looked down upon the city from one of the two artificial hills built just to the north of the Forbidden City you saw what appeared to be a forest walled in by the many miles of ramparts and broken only by the lofty porcelain roofs of the great palaces and temples.

Amusement was never hard to find, whatever the season or time of day. If I grew tired of wandering through the great throne-halls and residential quarters within the Forbidden City I could climb one of the two hills constructed centuries ago with the earth dug from a chain of artificial lakes and look down upon the yellow-gold and magenta buildings from above, or turn and admire the willow-bordered lakes set amid a forest of green boughs; or I could stroll about the pleasure-gardens with my friends and sip tea in exquisitely designed lacquer pavilions of which no two were ever the same, as they had been planned to attract glances from imperial personages already gorged with a surfeit of beauty. In winter the well-heated reading-rooms of the palatial Peking National Library offered refuge from the icy wind as well as the choicest and largest collection of volumes in all China, including thousands of works in English and other foreign languages. If I preferred a scene of cheerfulness and bustle, I could visit one of the huge covered markets or pass an hour or two at the Lung Fu Temple bazaar admiring flowers and potted plants or smiling at the more grotesque varieties of goldfish. The bath-houses to be found in every part of the city afforded their patrons several hours of relaxation; they provided not only hot water and expert massage, but also the solace of fragrant tea, hot buns, soft couches and idle conversation with chance acquaintances. If I wished to be astonished by something more subtle than the antics of the acrobats, conjurers and magicians who could always be found performing extraordinary feats in the locality known as the Heavenly Bridge, I could usually depend upon some Taoist adept to say or do something profound or startling; while Buddhist monks would gladly satisfy my erratic thirst for things more spiritual.

In the evenings I had a choice of restaurants offering so many specialities from every province of China that the total number of dishes available to anyone prepared to walk or ride half a mile must have amounted to several thousand. While luxuries such as bears' paws, fish-lips, camel's hump and so on had to be ordered in advance, it was always possible to get at short notice anything ranging from shark's fin and swallow's nest to common foods such as goose, duck, poultry, meat, fish, seafood, etc., blended with whatever vegetables, herbs, spices or edible weeds and fungi land and sea afforded. After dining with a few friends at one of these generally unpretentious-looking restaurants, I sometimes accompanied them to a theatre, either to enjoy the feast of music, colour and agility provided by the traditional opera-ballet (which, to tell the truth, I never learnt to appreciate properly) or else to see a modern realistic play strongly influenced by the techniques of Russian and English drama. If some of us were in the mood for more intimate amusements, we visited the flower-houses where there were pretty girls trained in a dozen different ways of pleasing men according to their mood, varying from sympathetic or witty conversation to the pleasures of 'clouds and rain'. They were talented courtesans rather than prostitutes; quite half their patrons came to them for entertainment almost as chaste as that provided by young ladies in an English drawing-room; but, of course, there were others who demanded more than that.

In addition to all these delights, Peking offered pleasures more difficult to describe because less tangible. They included, for example, the smell of chestnuts being roasted over a charcoal brazier casting its redness upon the snow, the sound of flutes carried across the water from a boat moored in the centre of a moonlit lake, the taste of steamed crabs seasoned with ginger sauce, the touch of silken sleeves against the wearer's naked arms, the sight of dazzlingly white herons standing motionless against the green darkness of temple pines, and the mingled pleasures of a weekend spent among the secluded groves and moss-covered temples of the Western Hills.

Today, like so many exiles from Peking, Chinese and foreign, I wander about the world grateful for whatever happiness I find and generally cheerful enough to pass for a contented man, but always with the conviction that nowhere else shall I find a life so satisfying to senses, heart, intellect and (for those who searched diligently) spirit as Peking offered everyone who loved and understood her well.

## 2

# Drum-girls Survive Confucius

'EXCUSE me; please wait. I am undressed.'
        'Never mind. It doesn't matter.'
        '*Please!*'
    Another misunderstanding, no doubt; but why should the old
gentleman describe himself as undressed when he wasn't? I had already
caught sight of him through the open doors of his study; they gave
directly on to the smooth-flagged courtyard where I stood waiting
for him, shaded from the afternoon sun by a tall oleander clump growing from a green earthenware jar. I had seen that he was quite smartly
dressed in a short summer jacket and loose trousers of fresh white
silk with an almost satiny gleam. Yet he had actually run from the
room as shyly as a young girl surprised in over-scanty négligé! When
he reappeared I understood. He was formally clad now in a high-
collared, ankle-length gown of pale dove-grey silk. As he hastened
towards me smilingly chattering the usual set phrases of welcome, his
body arched itself into a series of short bows, which I was careful to
return with the more elaborate sort suited to his age and station.
    'I'm sorry, Yü Hsienshêng, if I am disturbing you. The front gate
was ajar and, finding nobody about, I took the liberty of walking in.'
    'Quite right. Quite right. Did you notice my new goldfish? When
you are rested, we must have a look at them. I've just extended my
collection by adding three pair of phoenix-tails. Such beauties!'
    He glanced affectionately towards an inverted dome of glazed
earthenware surrounded by pots of mountain-ferns which stood near
the front gate. I turned to walk over immediately, but the movement
disconcerted him.
    'Just a little while, please. You must come in first. My wife will give
you tea.'
    Heavens, what a bad impression I was making on the old gentleman!

Within five minutes of my arrival I had twice offended against the proprieties, bumping my head against obstacles like those which sweep an Englishman's hat from his head when he enters a house or cause the vicar's daughter to endure hours of torture rather than ask her host the way to the bathroom. Two years in South China had clearly been insufficient preparation for me to cut a good figure in the eyes of elderly Pekingese still wedded to the smooth formality and intricate decorum of Confucian society. Though increasingly successful in keeping my Western impetuosity under control, I still had a lot to learn. (Indeed, the process of learning occupied the next several years. I grew accustomed to being rigidly formal upon some occasions, still formal but gracefully relaxed on others, and delightfully free and debonaire at the proper moments. In time I realized that the conservative Pekingese were not really more overburdened than my own country-men with rules of conduct—it was just that their categories of *done* and *not done* were, at least in superficial matters, so different.)

This was my second visit to the former Assistant Imperial Tutor, Professor Yü Shêng. On the day after my arrival in Peking, I had called with a letter of introduction from an old subordinate of his whom I had met in Kwangsi. The Tutor had bidden me return in a few days, promising he would introduce me to a relative who might be of use to me. Now, as on that first occasion, two porcelain bowls of jasmine-perfumed tea were brought into the study by a shy, soberly gowned lady who, after the briefest words of welcome, quickly retired as though to avoid the embarrassment of conversing with someone of whose background she knew nothing. She looked so nearly young that but for her plain gown I should have taken her for the Tutor's daughter. As it was, I assumed she was his second wife, until her nephew told me later that she had been married to the Tutor for thirty-five years, had borne him seven children and was already in her fifty-third year. Then I remembered how often a middle-aged Chinese woman's appearance is deceiving. Some well-to-do women retain their youthful looks and figures all through their thirties, forties and early fifties, undergoing scarcely any perceptible change from year to year; then, with dreadful abruptness, their smooth flesh falls away leaving them wrinkled and old. After a summer strangely prolonged, their autumn is brief and quickly swallowed up by winter.

While Yü Hsienshêng and I sat chatting over our tea, Madam Yü flitted in and out to replenish our bowls, appearing at the right moments with such promptness that I suspected her of observing us from a place of concealment. Presently my host pushed away his bowl and took me into the courtyard to admire his goldfish. Though almost an hour had passed, he had so far made no reference to the real object of my visit. The brown porcelain tank, formed like an inverted bowl, contained over forty fish comprising some sixteen varieties distinguishable by peculiarities of their lacy tails and fins, the shape of their heads and particolouring of their bodies. The most handsome were a pair almost six inches long with golden-red scales and jet-black tails sweeping out behind them like scarves of fine lace. Many of the fish seemed to me more grotesque than beautiful—nightmarish monsters with baneful, bulging eyes happily reduced to unfrightening proportions. My simulated enthusiasm must have sounded hollow, for presently Yü Hsienshêng exclaimed:

'Englishmen of course prefer dogs. It must be tiring and expensive to maintain a representative collection. I hope to acquire a hundred and eight varieties of goldfish and shall be able to house at least a pair of each in two or three tanks no larger than this one—but *dogs*!'

I explained that English dog-lovers rely on other people's dogs to satisfy their craving for variety and that only professional breeders attempt looking after more than 'two or three pairs'.

'And do you also breed sleeve-dogs?'

'I beg your pardon?'

'Sleeve-dogs, also called *Pa Kou*. In Manchu times they were bred in the palace—dogs perfectly formed but no larger than medium-sized rats. If a eunuch came running to herald the approach of the Lord of Ten Thousand Years they could be snatched up and hidden in the sleeve. Sometimes we used them like muffs. With hands clasped and hidden beneath our long sleeves, we warmed our fingers against their furry bodies, especially we scholars who needed supple fingers for our calligraphy. But forgive me; I must not forget to send for my young kinsman, Pao Hsienshêng. As I told you, he works for the English-language *Peking Chronicle*. Command him as you wish during your wanderings about our city; he will be grateful for the opportunity of conversing with you in English upon superior subjects.'

He had been prompted to speak of Mr Pao by the return from school of his youngest son. A fourteen-year-old boy in a blue school uniform and peaked cap had just come in from the street carrying a satchel. After saluting me with a profound bow and whispering the

Chinese word for uncle, he had hovered shyly in the background, too absorbed in the rare sight of a foreign guest to go right away and too respectful to join us without permission. Now his father beckoned him over and said:

'Kuo-Wei, run across to Sixth Auntie's place and tell Cousin Three we should like to see him.'

Though the words were spoken gently, I noticed that the boy obeyed instantly and even managed to look as if running an errand for his father were a pleasure. Perhaps it was. Meanwhile, the old gentleman felt it necessary to give me a warning.

'You will find that young Pao knows our city well and will be disposed to show you whatever you wish, but he is an impetuous youth who reads too much—I mean worthless books by writers like Turgeniev and Dostoievsky, none of whose characters, judging from the Chinese translations, know the value of restraint. Young Pao even claims to have fallen in love! Ha-ha! He talks about it constantly as though it were important—or novel! You must reprove him if he wastes your precious time with his nonsense.'

'Is he thinking of getting married?'

'Naturally he must marry soon. He's almost twenty-six and has been formally betrothed for seven years. His fiancée is not ugly and his family has already indulged him to the limit by letting them meet no less than four times, yet still he is being obstinate.'

'You mean he's found another girl?'

'Exactly. A drum-beater! Just imagine!'

'Drum-beater?'

'Yes, a female beater of drums!'

'I see.' I did not see, but preferred to wait for a more sympathetic explanation from the victim of this mysterious drum-beater's charms.

When he appeared, about half an hour later, we went back into the study to drink tea, with which all Chinese friendships are baptized and constantly cemented. I found him a pale, quietly handsome, elegant young man whose present languid manner failed to conceal his considerable nervous vigour. He was wearing a thin gown of sky-blue cloth over jacket and trousers of white silk. Talkative by nature, he had some difficulty in restraining his chatter before his elderly and formidable kinsman, who now and then glanced at him with an expression slightly contemptuous. An hour or so before dusk, the Tutor suddenly decreed that our exploration of the city must start auspiciously with a visit to the Temple of Confucius, which happened to be conveniently close at hand. Without doing anything so crude as to order us from his presence, he contrived to usher us to the front gate at a time of his own choosing, chattering the while of Confucius. His parting words were:

'Emperors have gone. Republican generals come and go, but our Chinese people rise or fall in accordance with how far we continue to live by the good sense and reasoned behaviour taught by the Sage. Now, as you, Hsienshêng, can see, we are falling headlong into plain barbarity. When you reach his temple you will probably find only herons for company.'

Waiting until we had bowed our way out through the lacquered gates into the lane beyond, my new friend exclaimed impatiently:

'Confucius! Why always Confucius? The past is past—mouldering bones in a dry gully. Who can revive them? Who wants to? Lu Hsün and Gorki—they are the sages of today. Marx, too, but less surely. Are you a Marxist, Mr Blofeld? No? Why should you be? You are from a wealthy country. I'm not one either. I believe in freedom, infinite freedom for the individual. Marx and Confucius were like brothers in their opposition to individual self-expression, just as Taoists and anarchists are united in their contempt for rules. Sometimes I think nothing really changes except the names of things. Am I right?'

Astonished beyond measure by this juxtaposition of lusty bomb-tossing anarchists with Taoists, whom I had visualized as frail hermits seated in solitary mountain pavilions composing poems to the moon, I remained speechless. Fortunately, Pao, though not talking for effect, did not really care much for other people's reactions to his constant flow of speech; for him speech was an antidote against indigestion caused by too much reading and thinking about matters outside the realm of his own experience.

Just then we came to the broad main road running straight north to the Anting Gate. Wide enough to allow for several lanes of modern traffic, it had been constructed centuries before the invention of cars, to accommodate the elaborate processions which used to form part of every imperial progress. In the old days, if the Emperor decided to set foot outside his palace, the whole route would be sprinkled with golden sand and the people warned in advance to hide their faces from the light of the sacred countenance on pain of death. Presently a procession of gaily caparisoned guards, musicians, eunuchs and officials, mounted and on foot, would escort the sacred palanquin with its curtains of imperial yellow-satin brocade and its great scarlet poles resting upon the shoulders of eunuchs in silken robes. To either side rode skilled archers, arrow fitted to bow in preparation to shoot dead any impious creature seen gazing through window, cranny or chink upon the august person of Heaven's Son.

Crossing this road, now crowded with the blue-hooded carts of peasants hurrying to pass the city gate before sunset, we entered some broad dusty lanes on its farther or eastern side. Before long there reared up in front of us a tremendously imposing mass of buildings which, according to Pao, was the second largest built-up walled enclosure in all that city of ten thousand walls. The porcelain roofs shone like jewelled surfaces against the fast deepening blue of the late-afternoon sky. This was the Yung Ho Kung or Palace of Eternal Harmony, known to foreigners as the Lama Temple. Built centuries ago to house an imperial prince, it had come to be the birthplace of a child who ascended the Dragon Throne under the reign-title of K'ang Hsi. Thenceforward, as a mere mortal would have risked his head by daring to preside over it, its dedication to an Immortal Being had become inevitable; so it was converted into a temple for the thousand or more Tibetan and Mongolian lamas inhabiting Peking. It was sad to find that this once splendid palace had been shamefully neglected. The crimson paint was peeling from the outer walls and tufts of grass, thrusting their way through the roof, had pushed the shining tiles all awry. In front of the principal gateway stood three Mongol laymen who were fingering their rosaries and muttering the preliminaries to their evening devotions in a singsong hum; they glanced at us incuriously without interrupting their mantric recitations. Like the temple itself, they looked both splendid and down-at-heel in their many-coloured but carelessly soiled garments of satin and dyed wool. Naturally, I longed to follow them into the temple to watch the lamas massed in the Great Hall intone their evening chants to an accompaniment of clashing cymbals and the boom of their deep-voiced horns.

'Mr Pao, may we not forget Confucius for today and go inside?'

'Please, not. It's an enormous place—a cathedral.' Then, glancing at his watch, he added quickly: 'The temple of Confucius is very close now and not too large for us to explore before dark.'

'I say, I do hope I'm not keeping you from something important.'

'Not at all. But it will be dark within the hour. Then we shall have dinner somewhere and, perhaps, take in some sort of typically Pekingese entertainment—a drum-show might amuse you.'

Too shy to pursue the interesting subject of drum-shows just then, I assured him I would gladly see whatever he recommended.

Yü Hsienshêng had guessed rightly. The Temple of Confucius was deserted except for an old caretaker. Far smaller than the Yung Ho Kung, it was still enormous, but so deeply enveloped in a cloud of silence that it seemed almost impious to disturb it. My immediate impression was one of grandeur tempered by austerity. I could see dark crimson halls and pavilions with heavy upward-sweeping roofs standing majestically in a park of very old cedars, with herons perched motionless among their branches. Strolling slowly towards the main halls, we passed rows of open-sided pavilions, each housing an upright slab of inscribed stone rising from the back of a giant stone turtle. To our left was a gallery sheltering hundreds of engraved slabs from which block-prints of the entire set of Confucian classics could be made; so that, even should the city with all its libraries perish in flames, the sacred teachings would be preserved for posterity.

With the sun already low upon the horizon and dusk gathering in the interiors of the halls, the severe simplicity of their appointments excited awe. There were no frescoes, no pictures, no statues, nothing but the wooden spirit-tablets of the Sage and his chief disciples, facing us across altars of blood-red lacquer. Few arrangements could have been more suggestive of unseen Presences. In one hall there was also a set of ancient stone percussion instruments. They reminded me that Confucius had regarded music as essential to the good government of the state. Who knows what melodies moved him to exalt it so highly even in the sphere of practical affairs? No certain knowledge of them has survived.

'When I was still a child,' said Pao, 'there used to be rites held in this hall, during which a troupe of boys in white ceremonial garments would dance here, waving their long sleeves to the music of strings and flutes. But that was many years ago. They are no more.'

'How disappointing!'

'Why so? The past is past. We in this city live too much among ghosts. Why use taxes for the perpetuation of outworn ceremonies when we are short of schools, clinics, hospitals and things like that? Not that the present government spends revenue on either. All the money slides gently into the officials' sleeves.'

One of Peking's many outer gates

A funeral procession

A corner in the Forbidden City

Finding Pao scarcely interested in my questions about the rôle of music in the Confucian system of government, I asked slyly:

'Talking of music, who exactly are those drum-girls we are going to see tonight?'

His eyes narrowed with amusement as he answered chidingly:

'I can see my uncle has been chattering. It shows, doesn't it, how little our Confucian elders respect the right to privacy of us young ones. Forgive me for saying so, but you've just dropped a slip. Isn't that what you call it?'

'I should think you mean a brick.'

'Ah, a brick. Earlier this evening I did mention a drum-show, but not drum-*girls*. Never mind. My uncle would think me a rude lout for pointing out your brick. A drum-show is a sort of musical story-telling which I am unsophisticated enough to enjoy more than Peking opera, quite apart from the drum-girls.'

'Ballads?'

'You might call them that—ballads with action and a drum.'

I fell silent. Drum-troupes could be discussed later. Meanwhile, looking around me, I felt glad to have begun my exploration of the city here in the Temple of Confucius, though an older guide more in harmony with its atmosphere would have suited me better. For around two millennia, the Chinese had subscribed not to one religion but to three. Confucianism had remained the central pillar to which Taoist nature-mysticism and the Buddhist doctrine of all-embracing Mind had clung like the gilded dragons twining round the pillars supporting a temple roof. There had always been Taoist adepts and Buddhist contemplatives uninterested in Confucianism, but the genius of the race had been moulded by diligent study of the Confucian classics. For here was a doctrine, not devoid of mysticism, but principally rooted in the affairs of *this* world and directed at the achievement of a harmonious society sustained by a stern sense of public duty and by personal morality, restraint and decorum. For close on sixty genera-tions, Confucianism had been the core of the imperial system, the root, stem and branches of all officially approved scholarship and learning. Eccentric Taoists might dream themselves into communion with the mountains and the moon; individual Buddhists might lose themselves in contemplation of the Divine Essence; but the race as a whole had preferred such Confucian virtues as a ruler's concern for his subjects and the people's loyalty to elders and superiors, coupled with the universal practice of benevolence, good faith and decently restrained behaviour. Only thus could Earth be brought into harmony with Heaven, and Man with both. Now, under the Republic, Confucianism was receding before a flood of political, sociological and scientific ideas imported from the West. Though the results might in some respects be encouraging, the break with the past and the consequent withering away of Chinese traditional civilization was beyond remedy.

By the time we emerged from the Hall of Classics on the west side of the temple, the gnarled cedars were dissolving into irregular patches of blue-black shadow, the engraved tablets and the giant stone turtles had merged into the darkness gathered beneath the roofs which sheltered them, and even the caretaker seemed to think it was time for us to go. A Pekingese of his generation could not inflict indignity upon visitors by ordering them out, but his purposeful coughing suggested that we ought not to keep an old man from his rice.

'The Kanmênti,' announced Pao unnecessarily, 'seems to think it is dinner-time. How about going to the Tung An Market for some *Suan Yang Jou?*'

'What's that?'

'Mutton, just mutton,' he answered laconically.

We rode side by side in two rickshaws along the wide road leading south. Few people were about and there were long intervals between the pools of yellow light shed by occasional street-lamps.

'It seems like the middle of the night.'

'In this part of the city, people seldom go out after dark, unless on their way to somewhere gayer. We have our night-life as you will see. In fact, my uncle's choosing me to be your guide shows how much he disapproves of me. As he is convinced that all foreigners indulge in disreputable pleasures, his sense of hospitality required him to find you a disreputable guide. Only a feast in some widely renowned restaurant or the reappearance on the stage of some star performer long absent from the city could tempt him out at night. Being a rich man, he does not need to be disreputable himself; he can afford discreet arrangements known only to his wife and servants.'

Entering the well-lighted Wang Fu Ching Street, our rickshaws set us down at the entrance of the Tung An Market. There was no room for vehicles amidst those acres of alleyways lined with stalls, small shops, restaurants and tea-houses. Good-natured crowds of loiterers and shoppers allowed us to push our way through them until, pausing only to buy a handful of toffeed grapes speared on sticks to eat after dinner, we reached a dingy doorway overhung by a black-lacquered board inscribed with three Chinese characters in gold. This otherwise unassuming entrance belonged to the Tung Lai Shun Restaurant, the very name of which—after more than twenty years—can still make me feel hungry. Like most good Chinese restaurants, the Tung Lai Shun offered a choice of not less than two hundred dishes, but most of its experienced customers seldom bothered to call for the menu. Like their fathers, grandfathers and great-grandfathers before them, as soon as they had sat down and wiped their faces with the hot scented towels brought to them at a run, they would give one brief order—*Suan Yang Jou.*

Experiences involving taste and smell are difficult to convey in words. Unless close comparisons offer themselves, no amount of description succeeds. *Suan Yang Jou,* though a French gourmet would be hard put to it to find adequate superlatives, was in one sense just boiled mutton! Upon the centre of the table was placed a sort of open samovar—a largish copper bowl pierced in the middle by a chimney stacked with red charcoal and with boiling water seething all around. Apart from this, there were several plates of raw mutton sliced wafer-thin, a tray containing about a dozen ingredients for mixing a sauce and, before each of us, the usual implements—bowl, porcelain spoon, and a pair of chopsticks. With the smile of a conjurer about to create living animals from a lump of mud, Pao spooned a selection of liquid sauce-ingredients into my empty bowl until it was about half full; and, after doing the same for himself, set about showing me what to do next. Lifting a mouthful of mutton slices with his chopsticks, he dipped them into the boiling water where, being so thin, they were done almost instantly; then, immersing them briefly in the spicy contents of his bowl, he carried them straight to his mouth. While I was copying him, a servant hurried forward with a pewter jar of mulled grain-spirit and a plate of salted pancakes straight from the fire—the Chinese equivalent of hot rolls. That was all. No meal could have been more simple to prepare or more delicious.

Most Chinese are hurt or even shocked by the bad manners of a guest who enjoys good food without remark. An appreciative diner-out should display curiosity regarding all sorts of relevant subjects—the native province of the cook, the composition of an unfamiliar dish, the source of its ingredients, the method of preparation, the effect of climate, season and weather upon their growth, and the province in which that particular style of cooking originated. Naturally such questions must not be fired off in cross-examination-style; they should arise spontaneously from genuine interest prompted by a wealth of culinary knowledge. I had learnt this civilized custom in South China and could generally hold my own at table, but what could be said about *Suan Yang Jou*, a dish cooked in the simplest fashion before my eyes? Fortunately, the talkative Pao did not wait for questions. He explained that three skills contributed to the Tung Lai Shun's masterpiece—the rearing of a special breed of sheep nourished on a selected diet and prevented from becoming either too fat or too lean; the cunning manner of slicing the meat; and the proper blending of the sauces by the customer himself.

During the meal the water gradually turned into a meat broth which, mixed with the remains of the sauce, provided a rich soup well suited to conclude a Chinese meal. To improve it, Pao ordered chopped heart of cabbage and some handfuls of bean-noodles to be thrown into the pot, but these were frills rather than an essential part of *Suan Yang Jou*. I noticed that, though our pewter wine-pot had been several times replenished and we had each presumably drunk about two dozen miniature bowls of Peking's famous or infamous *paikan*, neither of us was noticeably drunk.

'You see, John, the *paikan* neutralizes the richness of whole plate-fuls of meat; the meat softens the effect of an ocean of *paikan*. They are like a bridal pair, not to be separated!'

When the waiters had brought hot green tea to send the bridal pair to sleep and hot towels to wipe our perspiring faces, Pao showed the first stirring of impatience to be gone. Glancing at his watch, he began steering the conversation towards drum-shows. This gradual approach was curiously out of keeping with his usual *mo têng* ('modern') behaviour. That he did not spring to his feet crying 'Come on; let's go' illustrates a peculiarly tenacious trait of which even *mo têng* Chinese seldom wished to rid themselves. The essential graces contributing to the enjoyment of good food remained amid the ruins of many other ancient customs. As a Western artist, in hot revolt against civil usages in general, continues showing regard for the proper etiquette of attic and studio, so did the Pekingese rebels cling to the rules relating to the conduct of host and guest at table.

From the Tung Lai Shun to the tea-house where the drum-troupe gave nightly performances was only a few minutes' walk through the crowded alleys. Its unimposing doorway gave on to a narrow staircase leading apparently to a scene of carnage! From the upper storey came a sinister medley of terrifying noises. I seemed to hear female wailing rising to piercing screams, accompanied by dreadful thuds and the cracking of a whip-lash! However, Pao appeared to find all this quite normal. He led me upstairs without surprise or hesitation, and I followed him through a door into a place which, far from being sinister, was just a crowded Chinese tea-room. The patrons, all male with long-gowned scholars and coarsely jacketed working-men jumbled together, sat at square wooden tables littered with grey earthenware tea-bowls and husks of melon-seeds. Their eyes were fixed upon a tiny figure prancing on a low platform at the far end of the room, as though hypnotized by the prodigious volume and variety of sounds she was creating. Below the platform were clustered five or six other young girls who sat on low benches facing the patrons. If they had been sitting less demurely, I should have supposed them responsible for part of the noise; I could not believe such a medley of ferocious sounds emanated from just one girl who looked scarcely sixteen years old.

We sat down at one of several empty tables mercifully far back from the performer; and, while Pao was busy shouting in the waiter's ear enquiries about the kinds of tea-leaf available, I watched to see how that one little girl managed to make such a varied and powerful din. Never had I seen so lively a figure! Besides weaving through a series of astonishing attitudes and martial gestures with warlike facial expressions to match, she was perspiringly accompanying her 'ballad-singing' with two separate instruments! In one hand she flourished a wooden stick which served now for sword-like gestures, now to rain vigorous thwacks upon a drum fixed to a tripod level with her waist; with her left she wielded a pair of heavy wooden clappers, the sound of which I had mistaken for the cracking of a whip-lash. As for the sing-ing, it was so high-pitched and extraordinary (even to ears reasonably well attuned to ordinary Chinese opera) that she might have been one of those hapless mountain fiends who, concealing themselves in dismal caverns, wail forth disgust and horror at the frightfulness of their own hideous forms!

All this was merely my first impression. Gradually, as I grew more accustomed to such novel sights and sounds, I began finding in them unexpected attractions; rather as a lover of unspoiled nature, at first appalled by the metallic monstrosities of our age, may presently discover in them a grotesque sort of beauty. The girl's voice did have a metallic quality, at once harsh and exciting. Unable to understand the words, I set my imagination adrift upon the sound; it conjured up images of sheep huddling for protection from snow-blizzards moaning across the Mongolian grasslands, of young men dying in combat before the eyes of their keening lovers, of Sir Bedevere stalking towards the sedge-fringed lake with his armour clanging against the icy rocks, of the stately Morgan Lefay weeping as she pillowed on her lap the dying Arthur's head.

At last the song, if song it could be called, came to an end and was followed by a very long interval. There was no clapping; applause in the form of sporadic shouts of '*Hao! Hao!*' had already marked the high-points of the performance. Pao seemed unimpressed.

'They always put the less accomplished girls on first. This is one of the best drum-troupes in Peking and, by its standards, the girl we've just heard is a novice. Her gestures were good, but her voice is still underdeveloped. Those who applauded were people who liked the look of her—you know, face, figure, animation, that sort of thing.'

'May I ask about the girl your uncle so indiscreetly mentioned? Is she here?'

'You can just see the top of her head. There, the one leaning forward between the tall girl in peacock blue and the fattish one in pink. She is really good, so they'll keep her till almost the last.'

'Can't you go over to talk to her?'

His face fell.

'Something has happened. If I talk to her now, I may upset her and mess up her performance. By the way, what we've just heard was a long episode in which the girl had to take the part of five different characters. It's about the widow of a Chinese general who fell in love with a Mongol raider. After she had become his mistress, she learnt that he was the very man who had sliced off her husband's head. A poignant situation, yes?'

'What did she do then?'

'What could she do, except kill him? She used a hairpin on him, when he was asleep in her bed. Naturally our traditionalists have never ceased to laud her for a proper sense of duty to her husband's memory. To me it seems much more likely that she didn't care a single cash for her husband. The Mongol was a lover of her own choice; the Chinese general had been foisted on her by her parents; but, of course, her relatives would have put out her eyes rather than continue enduring a stain upon the family honour. What choice had she?'

Just then, a hard-faced, pock-marked old creature in dingy black came sidling up to our table. For some time I had been watching her weaving her way from one to another of the more opulent-looking customers. She moved at an awkward hobble on tiny feet which, according to an already obsolete custom, had been tightly bound some years before she reached the age of puberty so that the toes were squashed down under the sole. In her hand was an unpractically large black fan which she now and then flicked open for someone to look at. When my turn came, I saw that each of the segments was inscribed with a short column of Chinese characters written in gold ink. Pao, whose suddenly expressionless face conveyed his distaste for the sinister crone, looked across at me in silence.

'What's this?' I asked. 'I don't recognize some of these characters. Is it a poem?'

'No, it is not. You are looking at a double-sided fan which exactly symbolizes the real status of the drum-girls. The characters on this side relate to their art; they are the names of the lyrical and historical episodes which can be performed on request. But if you show the old woman even a flicker of interest, she will reverse the fan.'

'Meaning?'

'On the other side are the names of the drum-girls. They are all for sale. You can buy one for a night, a week, a lifetime, just as you choose or can afford.'

He waved the woman away and, as though the sight of her had been too much for his feelings, abruptly leant towards me and began pouring forth his troubles. The story as I see it now was almost banal, but it was told forcefully enough to arouse keen sympathy. Besides, it took on added colour from the performance of the next singer, not to mention the added suspense resulting from the long diversion she caused, for her high-pitched song made talking out of the question. While this singer, a tall girl in peacock blue, was wailing forth with dramatic accompaniment the ardours, passions, terror and pain of lovers torn asunder in some ancient war, she succeeded in pantomiming tenderness, ferocity and agony so effectively that I could almost *feel* the emotions tormenting my new friend. Deprived of these powerful romantic aids, his story would in any case have moved me, but perhaps not so deeply.

I gathered that, emotionally, Pao had until recently resembled most other Pekingese. Reserved and chaste towards women in general, he had never since reaching puberty felt inhibited from making love to girls belonging to the numerous classes of courtesan; though, on the other hand, he disdained the pleasures offered by straightforward prostitutes as boringly crude. He was inclined to defend this attitude towards courtesans as being conducive to the well-being of society; for in those days even youths caught by the spell of *mo têng* Western romanticism generally found the idea of seducing a chaste girl repugnant. Chinese girls were either good girls or bad girls; there could be no intermediate class. The bad girls were thought to perform the valuable function of making it easy for men to respect the chastity of all the others. Rigid chastity being regarded as inhuman and against *male* nature, few parents expected their sons to remain continent. Women, on the other hand, were born naturally chaste and, unless driven by misfortune into the ranks of courtesans and prostitutes, would undoubtedly come to their husbands as virgins and usually remain faithful to them or to their memories until death. All this was held to be axiomatic. Parents and even wives never doubted it; and probably few people of either sex worried much as to how this otherwise benevolent and salutary arrangement worked out in practice for the courtesans. Whatever misery some of them might have to endure was surely due to fate.

Anyway, Pao, who was fond of drum-shows in themselves, had now and then happened to amuse himself with one or other of the performers. Then, chancing to take out a girl called Kuei-Hsiang (Cassia Fragrance), he had suddenly stumbled upon an entirely novel experience—he had fallen in love! I realized that his uncle's scornful refusal to admit the novelty of this was due to confusion arising from incomprehension of the state of being in love. No doubt he had found some people sexually gratifying and others worthy of love in the exalted old-fashioned Chinese sense of that word, but that there could be more than a chance connection between the two could hardly have occurred to him. He must have thought this new-fangled talk of being *in love* was a Western barbarian euphemism for wanting to sleep with somebody—which, I suppose, is often but not always the case.

'You see,' Pao explained, 'falling in love is a luxury not permitted in our kind of family. Love is something you feel for parents, teachers,

A small pavilion in the Temple of Confucius

The lotus-filled moat around the Forbidden City

A fortress-like building guarding the approach to the throne-halls
of the Forbidden City

children and very close friends—also for a wife who has won it by years of devotion to your happiness and to the comfort of your parents. Otherwise, feelings for women are not thought worthy of that name. On your wedding night you go to bed with a woman you have never seen until that evening. You clutch her to you in the dark, a little because of your lust, chiefly to perform your family duty by begetting a child as soon as you can. By day, during the first months after the marriage, you feel ashamed to be caught talking to your wife or exchanging smiles with her. Apart from meal-times, when she serves you but does not eat with you, you hardly see her until bed-time. For the rest, if you are bored, you can always buy a girl's services for the night; or, if you prefer to remain spotlessly pure, you take a concubine or two.'

On Pao's first night with Kuei-Hsiang he had looked to her for no more than a charitable pretence of enjoyment and, perhaps, a few moments of excitement; but his own mood had been affected by having spent the afternoon reading some Chinese renderings of Shelley—the work of that gifted but neurotic scholar, Su Man-Shu, who could never make up his mind whether a Buddhist temple or a Japanese brothel was a better place in which to assuage the restlessness of desire. The tenderness induced by this mood had awakened a response in Kuei-Hsiang so touching that, the next morning, they had actually parted in tears. Thereafter, he had taken her out as often as he could afford the fee—which the old woman, seeing how matters lay, had gradually increased. About two months before I had come to Peking, Pao and Kuei-Hsiang had decided to elope to Shanghai, where jobs for journalists were abundant. Her only stipulation was that he must promise to send money to her parents now and then.

'Her parents!' I exclaimed. 'Why should she still care for them? Didn't you tell me they had *sold* her to the drum-troupe? How could she possibly forgive that?'

'They did sell her. She regards it as a special sign of their love and virtue.'

'*What!*'

'They are poor people with only a few *mou* of stony land and several children to support. They needed the money to help educate her brothers so that the two boys need not be half starved *all* their lives. It's entirely in the classical tradition, you know.'

'I see her point. But do go on.'

Before Pao's arrangements were complete, Kuei-Hsiang's enthusiasm for the elopement had suddenly and inexplicably waned. She had become morose, reticent and on the whole unwilling to go out with him at all. One evening she had been so curt and unfriendly that he would have left her of his own accord if he had not chanced to glance at a mirror and see her gazing at him from behind, eyes filled with affection and hopeless longing. But when he had turned towards her and made to embrace her, her face had hardened and she had angrily pushed him away.

'But why, why, why? Surely you have some idea?'

'I haven't. I've tried every way I know without getting a single clue. I know there's a Japanese officer interested in buying her, but she hates him and he won't be able to bother us once we have eloped down south. All I do know is that stinking old woman over there is behind it, though I am sure she suspects nothing of the planned elopement.'

'What are you going to do?'

'I'm going to talk to Kuei-Hsiang tonight. If she doesn't come out with me or doesn't tell me the truth when we are alone, I'm going to break with her. It must be one way or the other.'

We had to listen to ballads by several more girls before Kuei-Hsiang's turn came. Up to then, my efforts to get a good look at her face had failed. She had been sitting most of the evening with her head bent forwards and cupped in her hands, or in some other position which made it difficult for Pao's eyes to meet hers. When at last she did climb into full view, my first feeling was one of disappointment. Very young men prone to imagine magical allurements in the girls they love are inclined to expect them in the girls glowingly described by their friends; it always shocked me to discover that someone else's Venus looked no lovelier than the Misses Smith or Jones next door.

Kuei-Hsiang was certainly pretty, but far from resembling the mental image I had formed of her. Fairly tall, pleasantly rounded in the right places and otherwise slim, she wore a high-collared ankle-length gown of figured cloth above floppy trousers of pale green. Her hair, following the drum-girl tradition, was bound in two thick plaits which the vigour of her performance sent sailing out behind her. Her face, disfigured by heavy professional make-up, seemed a little too plump, but I admired the vivacity of her expressions and noted with pleasure her one mark of real beauty—a pair of lovely long classically slanting eyes. I had seldom seen their equal, for, contrary to Western belief, noticeably slanting eyes are by no means common even in China and Japan. The eyes of those splendid figures who leap about the Chinese stage owe their handsome slant to skilful make-up.

During Kuei-Hsiang's act, Pao sat bolt upright against the high back of his chair, watching in moody silence and sometimes drumming his fingers on the table. As soon as she left the platform, he muttered an apology and hurried over to her. Almost at the same moment, the old woman with the fan appeared from somewhere behind me and hobbled purposefully in his wake. Curious to discover where she had been standing out of sight for so long, I shifted my chair as though to ease my legs so that I half faced the previously empty tables behind. Now all were occupied. At one of them an undersized man sat alone, holding himself stiffly upright and appearing so different from the relaxed, cheerful people around him as to be somehow *cut off* from them —as much out of place as a naked sword lying across the family tea-table. Short, lightly built and clad in an ill-cut Western-style suit, ludicrously short at the wrists, he still managed to look dignified and impressive. Even the melancholy expression of strained attention upon his sallow face and the look in his eyes of a small boy about to cry could not detract much from this appearance of dignity. Another man dressed so unbecomingly and looking so woe-begone might have excited the sort of derision we accord to clowns. Not this man! His whole bearing chilled mirth. It was so very easy to imagine him striding about the parade-ground in a yellow uniform with a great sword clanking against his legs, conveying with his eyes alone: 'I am a senior officer in the Imperial Japanese Army. Do not presume to regard me as one of your despicable selves!'

I next turned my attention to the people occupying the tables around him. I saw at once that they were all deeply aware of his presence. Those sitting so that they faced more or less in his direction allowed their glances to slide past him, through him or over him exactly as if he did not exist, but in a manner calculated to make him feel the weight of their hatred and contempt. Judging from the frequent horror-stories carried to the city by people coming from Japanese-occupied territory in the north-east, he would one day make many of their countrymen pay a fearful price for this silent exhibition of contempt against which he had no present remedy.

Pao remained away from my table during the whole of the long interval; but as soon as the next girl mounted the platform he came back looking so white and unhappy that I was on my feet even before he gestured towards the door. He remembered to leave money on the table to pay for the tea, but did not manage to reach the door without bumping into one man and nearly jogging a tea-bowl from another's hand. Clearly something drastic had happened; I prepared to comfort him as best I could; but the opportunity never came. Though the market alleyways were by now deserted, the shops closed and the stalls either bare or occupied by sleeping apprentices wrapped in thin summer quilts, he avoided walking abreast with me, preferring to lag behind all the way to the gateway leading on to Wang Fu Ching Street. Then he caught me up and said briefly:

'Excuse my not seeing you home. I'll call a rickshaw for you and say good night. Be sure I'll come to see you very soon.'

Surprised and disappointed by this abrupt leave-taking, I was even less prepared for the surprise that followed. Just as I was getting into my rickshaw, I heard him engage another to take him to Ch'ien Mên Wai! At some other time, Ch'ien Mên Wai might have meant anywhere at all beyond the great central gate leading into the southern part of the city; but so late at night, with the shops shut, the restaurants closed and the operas drawing to their noisy climax, it clearly meant that Pao was bound for the lanes of 'flowers and willows' where people go only to enjoy the companionship of courtesans and the pleasures of 'clouds and rain'. That Pao should sometimes visit those lanes was not in itself surprising; but my Western mind was startled by the idea of a lover's seeking so unromantic a cure for a broken heart only ten minutes after the event. His uncle must have exaggerated the influence of the nineteenth-century Russians upon his character. I could not believe that any of Turgeniev's heroes would have been quite so prompt in seeking that particular remedy. Only the Chinese, whose romanticism is absorbed by such chaste objects as peonies, the autumn moon and the music of the wind in the pines, could display in human relationships such earthy realism. I did not know whether to be shocked or to admire him.

# 3

# A Solitary Eunuch and Some 'Flower-girls'

CAGED song-birds being taken out for their morning airing; bearded scholars seen for once without their robes, their baggy trousers tightly secured above the ankle to allow more freedom to weave with arms, legs and torso the tortuous patterns of Chinese eurythmics; younger men shadow-fencing, each with two red-tasselled swords; wild birds perched upon branches yellowed or bared by the autumn cold; and the first white frost melting on the grass—thus Central Park in October an hour or so after dawn. For the early-morning air was said to possess a magical purity from which song-birds, athletes and elderly men staving off the disabilities of age could all gain immeasurable benefits, while calligraphers and essayists who practised at that hour found the air conducive to the highest elegance of script or beauty of style.

It had become my occasional habit to begin the day with a walk in the park to observe all these things while increasing my appetite for breakfast; and, sometimes on the way home, I would pause near the park gate to buy half a dozen *shaoping*—salted sesemum-seed pastries straight from a pan spluttering on the hawker's charcoal brazier. It happened one morning during my first autumn in the city that I reached the gate just in time to see the last of the *shaoping* being handed to a jolly-looking old woman whose frost-reddened cheeks and sky-blue jacket made such a gay patch of colour that I readily forgave her. While I was still admiring her, footsteps approached me rather hesitantly from behind and someone enquired in English, with a Slavonic rather than a Chinese accent:

'Have you chanced to meet my friends?'

Mildly puzzled, I looked round to find a stranger in his late twenties, good-looking except for the over-virile blue-black of his smooth-shaven chin, and dressed with such elegance that at first I doubted whether he really belonged to the sad ranks of Peking's Russian émigrés.

'Well, that's a strange question,' I replied. 'As I haven't the pleasure of knowing *you*, how can I say for certain whether I've met any of your friends or not? What do they look like?'

He laughed, displaying two rows of small white teeth, so exquisitely formed that any pretty girl would have been proud to have them.

'Yes, it is right. How could you know them? They are—— Never mind. It is enough that they have gone, yes? They do not amuse me enough that I pursue them. You have leisure now?'

'Yes. That is, not really. I have to go home for breakfast.'

'Then I shall ask you directly. Do you enjoy to drink wine—the good red wine of Crim?'

'Probably I should enjoy it very much, but surely not at seven in the morning?'

Again he laughed, astonishing me by the contrast between his little girl's teeth and manly blueness of chin.

'No, you do not drink at seven in the morning, unless champagne or one small tumbler of very good brandy. I wish only for you to know I have Crim wine to sell—very cheap, very delicious. Here is my name-card. If you desire a dozen bottles, you will please to find my house on the north side of the east end of the lane. With how much pleasure shall I stay for you coming. Good morning, dear friend.'

He raised his hat with a somewhat affected flourish and abruptly turned back into the park.

At that time I was living in a small, typically Chinese house which I never recall without pleasure. It consisted of three modest buildings facing a courtyard whose principal glory had once been a pair of plum-trees of a kind famous for their wealth of blossom; but these were now so old that they seldom succeeded in putting forth anything more exciting than leaves. The main building comprised a single living-room of three *chien*, i.e. three times the area between two normally spaced parallel roof-beams. I used this as my dining-room and study. To the east of the courtyard lay a building containing the two-*chien* bedroom equipped with a brick sleeping-platform which could be heated from underneath during the bitter Peking winter, and a one-

*chien* bathroom housing a Soochow tub—a kind of Ali Baba jar in which I liked to sit cross-legged with hot water up to my neck. The opposite wing contained kitchen, servants' room and store-room, each of one *chien*. The heavy roofs were tiled with grey only a shade lighter than the grey brick walls; but there was plenty of once-vivid colour now softened with age, for the walls facing inwards to the courtyard served as frames for doorways and oblong windows of papered lattice-work all covered with fading scarlet and green lacquer; and the beams supporting the eaves bore stylistic floral designs, red, yellow, green and purple against a sky-blue background. Such a medley of gay colours in a setting of sober grey walls and roofs produced a cunningly contrived harmony of bright and dark.

The furniture was of dark polished wood, almost monastic in its simplicity and freedom from unnecessary ornament or curves. Though not beautiful Ming furniture of the kind which inspired the severer sort of 'Chinese Chippendale', it bore a relationship to it rather like that of a nobleman's rustic cousin. Lighting took the form of electric bulbs concealed in lanterns of transparent horn overlaid with paintings of imperial hunting scenes. These, together with the flat crimson chair-cushions, softened the furniture's severity. Throughout the year my servants remembered to supply both my rooms with flowers appropriate to the season. Hyacinths growing from a bed of pebbles and a sort of plum-blossom called *La Mei* proclaimed the approach of Chinese New Year (February). After that came assorted spring flowers, followed by the roses, peonies and asters of summer. Chrysanthemums with petals of many shapes, textures and colours hard to find elsewhere lasted through the autumn, and sprigs of winter plum appeared just as the last chrysanthemums withered.

I was looked after by a married couple known respectively as Lao Chao and Chao Ma. Between them they managed all the marketing, cooking, washing and housework, contriving to serve me not only with loyalty and affection, but also with a resourcefulness that very seldom, if ever, broke down. For example, once, at seven-thirty in the evening (about a year after the other events described in this chapter), six guests arrived in response to an invitation which had slipped my memory. As they were not intimate friends, I was aghast at the thought of having to confess a lapse so unflattering to them. Not so Lao Chao, who quietly signalled to me to behave as though they had been expected; and who, punctually at eight-thirty, produced a very adequate hot meal. It seemed miraculous, for all the food-shops in our neighbourhood shut early and, with my Chinese taste for fresh food, I hardly ever had much in the larder. Yet Lao Chao seemed almost offended when I told him later of my fear lest the guests discover what had happened.

'Laoyeh, why were you anxious? I sent Chao Ma out to borrow from the neighbours, a little here and a little there. It was not difficult.'

'But how could you manage to cook it so quickly?'

'Quickly, Laoyeh? None of the dishes was of the sort that needs elaborate preparation. I varied the textures by crisp-frying some things and soft-frying others, also by adding more or less soya-sauce, water or stock. I could not offer good dishes, but there had to be variety.'

My encounter with the vendor of Crim wines occurred months before that memorable dinner, but not before I had learnt to value my excellent servants; so when I reached home after my walk in the park, I was not at all prepared for the furious shouts of combat coming from within my gates.

'Thwack! Aaaaah! Thwack-thwack! Aiyah, aiyah! You devil! Your mother's—— Thwack!'

It was incredible. Worse than the shouts, insults, oaths and fierce panting was the sound of some wooden object now ringing upon the flagstones, now thudding dully against human flesh! Sure that my faithful servants were interposing their bodies and even their lives between my property and a band of robbers or deserters from the army, I beat upon the gate, shouting:

'Open up! Open up!'

Instantly there was silence, though by putting my ear close to the gate I could just hear the sound of laboured breathing. I had to shout again and again before dragging feet at last approached; then the inner bar was slowly withdrawn and the gate swung open. Keyed for instant action, I rushed in but could at first see nobody but a breathless Lao Chao, who was nervously fumbling with his disordered garments. Then, just as the first excited question rose to my lips, I found myself biting it back; a sudden glimpse of an angry Chao Ma slinking back into the kitchen with a broomstick still in her hand came just in time. Had the question been asked, poor Lao Chao would have been compelled to reveal his burden of shame at having been out-fought and beaten up by his wife! Without a word, I strode across to my living-room and shut the door. Thereafter, about twice or thrice a year,

I would come home to discover signs that a similarly unexplained quarrel had flared up between them, with the husband always coming off worst, but as I never again caught them in the act of fighting, I judged it wiser to say nothing. Nor, in spite of these rare discords, did I ever have cause to revise my opinion of them as two of the kindest people imaginable. I am sure Chao Ma only beat up her husband for what she conceived to be his own good; at all other times they behaved with a cheerful, affectionate regard for each other's happiness.

Immediately after that first fight, Lao Chao served me with my breakfast as though nothing extraordinary had occurred, except that, perhaps fearing a reprimand, he did not linger as usual to make sure I had everything I wanted. The breakfast consisted of thick rice gruel in a large blue and white bowl with a porcelain spoon to match, four saucers of condiments to flavour it and a plate of hot sausage-shaped *yiu t'iao*—the Chinese equivalent of breakfast rolls. I finished off the meal with a pot of pale amber-coloured jasmine tea, which the Northern Chinese prefer to any other kind, except in summer when the green tea called Dragon's Well is taken for its blood-cooling properties. Personally, I preferred, to either, the semi-fermented teas from Wu I Shan in Fukien and later obtained a supply of them from the south.

After breakfast, I had a couple of hours in which to dawdle through the preparation of a lecture which I was due to give at the university at eleven o'clock; it formed part of a course called Freshman English which even I was considered sufficiently qualified to teach. The English literature courses were given by Chinese professors who knew the subject many times better than I did, having read English at universities such as Oxford, Harvard and so on. I had fallen into the bad habit of leaving the preparation of my lecture-notes until the day they were needed, being reasonably sure that my mornings would be undisturbed by callers, and quite certain that the only noises I should hear from outside would be the musical cries of the hawkers and the notes of the various instruments by which they indicated what they had for sale. However, that morning was to be an exception. Hardly had I settled down to work when two visitors were announced. One was Pao and the other a tall, middle-aged, bearded Taoist recluse! I had never dreamt to see Pao in such company but, as he afterwards explained, Yang Taoshih was a distant connection of his; happening to meet him near my house, he had decided on the spot that a Taoist would be congenial company for me. The latter was an imposing figure dressed in a dark-blue robe of antique cut with enormous kimono-like sleeves; his long hair, worn in a topknot, protruded through a circular hole in the crown of his cap and was secured by a carved wooden comb. In other words he wore the sort of garb fashionable among Chinese scholars some five centuries ago!

I had met Taoist adepts elsewhere in China and generally found them over-fond of treating new acquaintances with elaborate ceremony and elegant turns of speech. These, though pleasantly picturesque, were difficult for a foreigner unversed in them to respond to without awkwardness. However, Pao's friend was, by the antique standards of his kind, almost simple and direct. Perhaps he did not care to cast the pearls of civilized behaviour before a crude barbarian from the outer rim of the Western Ocean. So, in little more than ten minutes, we managed to skip our way through the formulas of introduction, to exchange a sufficient number of preliminary compliments and even to get ourselves seated in good order. The Taoist, after only four or five professions that the honour was more than he could bear, allowed himself to be gently dragged to the 'highest' seat—a couch facing the doorway. Pao as usual sat where he pleased and I, mindful of the most elementary rule governing the behaviour of a youthful host, sat upright on the edge of a small stool placed just inside the door. When Lao Chao brought in the tea, the Taoist stood up and extended both hands to accept the bowl I offered him with both of mine, whereupon Pao began speaking in a style so unlike his ordinary casual manner that I suspected him of deliberate irony.

'Yang Taoshih [Taoist Yang], my young English friend here has long been thirsty for the pleasure of your acquaintance, for a knowledge of your fame reached his ears as soon as he arrived in our city. I have ventured to bring you together because, though I myself am too ignorant to appreciate the inestimable value of your transcendental studies and attainments, I can assure you that my friend, P'u Hsien-shêng, would like nothing better than to become your most fervent admirer and diligent disciple.'

Glancing quickly at the Taoist to see how he was taking this surely ironical speech, I saw that he was watching me keenly with an amused expression, as though interested in my own reaction. So I hastened to say:

'Last year I had the pleasure of becoming intimate with a Taoist scholar living in a secluded hermitage on a mountainous island near the mouth of the Pearl River, close to Hong Kong. His wisdom and conduct persuaded me that the study of the Tao [the Great Way] is deeply rewarding. Since then, I have always longed to meet other accomplished Taoists and today my wish is fulfilled. May I ask you, Yang Taoshih, what particular aspect of the Way you practise?'

I had secretly thought my speech elegant, to the point and sincere, but Pao burst out laughing and, giving his friend no chance to reply, cried:

'I am sure Yang Taoshih is disappointed in you already. Why, even an ignoramus like myself knows you should never ask a Taoist what he *does*. You must always assume that he *does not*! *Wu Wei*, the doctrine of accomplishing everything by scrupulously *doing nothing*, is the core of Taoist belief. Yang Taoshih, of course you agree with me?'

'I am sure,' answered the Taoist blandly, 'that P'u Hsienshêng has already achieved a profound understanding of the Great Way. His question was not wrongly put. *Wu Wei* means not non-action but the avoidance of unnecessary action; in other words, it implies acting only in response to the needs of the moment. A tree does not reflect: "Recently there has been too little rain, so I must compensate by drinking heavily when next it falls." Without forethought or after-thought, it drinks in as much as it needs when the opportunity arises. This is true conformity with the Great Way. It is as simple as that.'

'Oh,' replied Pao, still laughing. 'Perhaps trees may manage to stay alive that way; human beings would mostly die of thirst. Pray be careful to remain alive long enough to instruct my friend how to join you in the realm of phoenix-riding Immortals. As for me, I have done my duty by bringing you two together. From now on you will be able to pay each other long visits and diligently practise inactivity while I have to go on with the tiresome job of earning my living. So may we please talk now of simple, homely things which even I can understand?'

They did not stay much longer, because Pao was in a hurry, but before they left I received an invitation to visit Yang Taoshih as often as I wished in the Tung Yüeh Temple. While I was seeing them to the gateway, Pao lowered his voice to remind me of a dinner engagement for that night, adding cryptically:

'Though I cannot, like Yang Taoshih, offer you a phoenix to ride, you shall if you like indulge tonight in the sport of mandarin ducks.'

The last sentence, unintentionally spoken louder than the rest, was overheard by the Taoist, who, of course, understood the scarcely veiled reference to erotic pleasures. Putting his mouth close to my ear, he murmured:

'Mandarin ducks behave as their nature dictates. Our mutual friend here goes out seeking a banquet when he is not hungry. He has not learnt that every woman has a sword between her legs.'

Then he laughed softly and stepped into the lane.

.        .        .        .        .

The party that night was to be given by Professor Lee Wên-Liang, who, as Head of the Foreign Languages Department in the university where I was teaching, was my boss. An Oxford man belonging to a generation largely brought up in the traditional Chinese way of life, he was someone whose friendship I particularly valued because he knew so well how to interpret Chinese behaviour in terms which a Westerner like myself could understand. His only fault in this respect was his impatience with my occasional concern for the spiritual rather than the purely moral and aesthetic aspects of Chinese culture. For Buddhism and Taoism he cared nothing; a typical product of his class and generation, he reinforced the gentle Confucian agnosticism of his parents with the 'scientific' materialism current in the West during his Oxford days. His incomprehension of mysticism made him inclined to confuse genuine religious feeling with popular superstition, which he regarded as absurd for scholars, but useful as a means of disciplining the uneducated. In other matters he was urbane, tolerant and a firm individualist. Incapable of deliberate unkindness or dishonesty, he lived according to the moral standards of his fathers; only those people (usually Westerners) who are prone to regard sexual continence as the beginning and end of morality might hesitate to describe him as a man of exalted behaviour. His appearance was unremarkable. About fifty-five years old, with close-cropped grizzled hair, he usually wore a plain cloth gown which concealed the contours of a body as firm and vigorous as that of a man half his age.

As the autumn evenings were still warm, Professor Lee had selected a small restaurant in the Pei Hai or North Sea Park, loveliest of all the former imperial pleasure-gardens within the city walls: and second only to Tzû Hsi's Summer Palace some miles out along the road to the Western Hills. If the night were fine and there were no wind, we should be able to sit out and enjoy our dinner close to the margin of the lake.

Soon after dusk, and early enough to have plenty of time to spare, I made my way through the south gate of the park and strolled across the graceful marble-topped bridge leading to the *chorten*-crowned island which rises steeply from the lake to a height of several hundred feet. Above me I could see the white *chorten*, a great bottle-shaped Tibetan-style pagoda, glimmering faintly against the star-lit autumn sky; its pale radiance was only just perceptible, yet it drew my gaze like one of those half-seen figures haunting the darkness in lonely places which compel our furtive glances though we would prefer to turn our heads and hurry past. At the foot of the hill stood a tall *pailou* or triple archway of lacquered wood roofed with coloured tiles, but now its rainbow colours had been swallowed by the darkness; it loomed blackly against a flight of white stone steps from which an intricate network of steep pathways led by devious routes upwards to the *chorten*'s base. Disdaining the steps, I chanced to follow a route that took me among pinnacles and fantastic caverns artfully fashioned from rocks carried there centuries ago from distant provinces to imitate the grotesque rock-formations famed by poets from China's southern regions.

On reaching the top of the hill, I walked slowly round the *chorten*'s base, trying to make out familiar objects now blurred and shadowy beneath the soft starlight. Adjoining the *chorten* to the south and facing out over the vast black contours of the Forbidden City stood a small temple with outer walls composed of thousands of porcelain tiles, each bearing a figure of the Buddha in bas relief; but these details were disappointingly lost in the darkness, for the moon which was to illumine our banquet had not yet risen; so I walked round to a small tea-house on the north side where, on hot afternoons, the Empress Tzû Hsi and her ladies had been wont to sit gazing over the water while eunuchs plied their jewelled peacock fans. The lake, stretching from the shore of the island almost to the northern boundary of the park, now gleamed oily black except at the margin where golden pools of light reflected the lamps along the water's edge. At the farther end I could see a bright blur of illumination coming from the Five Dragon Pavilion. These marvellously graceful buildings jutted into the lake at a point where, in the old days, the lacquered barges used to nose up to a flight of steps to disgorge their precious load of chattering ladies attended by obsequious eunuchs dressed only a little less gorgeously than themselves. While I was picturing the scene, an unknown voice said quietly:

'In her day there was no electricity. The attendants carried lanterns of scarlet gauze.'

I swung round startled. I had been so sure I was alone; the soft, almost feminine voice, emerging unexpectedly from the darkness and seeming like a continuation of my thoughts, was disturbing.

'I beg your pardon?'

A shadowy figure, his face barely visible above a dark robe which blended indistinguishably with the night, was standing so close to me that I might have touched his hand. Perceiving he had startled me, he apologized and added:

'I saw you gazing across at the pavilions by the landing-stage. They are beautiful, are they not? But that yellowish light is out of place and garish—like so many things these days.'

'Do you mean to say you were here *then?*'

He laughed, or rather tittered, musically, his voice so feminine that, could I have believed it possible in Peking to encounter a woman walking alone in a solitary place at night, I should certainly have taken him for one. (The Manchu-style gowns of men and women were, even when seen in daylight, not greatly dissimilar.)

'Yes, indeed I was here then. You are a foreigner, but you speak Chinese well. Doubtless you have heard of the *T'ai Chien?*'

'The imperial eunuchs? Of course. But they vanished long ago.'

'Long as a young man sees things; short enough to one well into the autumn of his life. I was already middle-aged when the Revolution dispersed us. Now I am sixty.'

'Were you with *them* long? In the Imperial Household, I mean?'

'Not long. I was castrated in the seventh year of Kuang Hsü [1882], so I had only twenty-nine years in the Forbidden City. How quickly the time passed!'

'Castrated by your own choice?'

'Why not? It seemed a little thing to give up one pleasure for so many. My parents were poor, yet by suffering that small change I could be sure of an easy life in surroundings of beauty and magnificence; I could aspire to intimate companionship with lovely women unmarred by their fear or distrust of me. I could even hope for power and wealth of my own. With good fortune and diligence, I might grow more rich and powerful than some of the greatest officials in the empire. How could I foresee the Revolution? That was indeed a misfortune. I have sacrificed my virility and my hope of begetting children for a dream which, passing fleetingly, stopped short and can never return.'

'And so now you come here sometimes in the darkness to recapture an echo of your dream? But how do you live?'

'I manage well. I am a guide—not one of those so-called guides who live by inventing history for foreigners and by making commissions on things they purchase. I have not yet fallen to that. Discriminating Chinese gentlemen arriving from the provinces prefer to obtain their guides through the Palace Eunuchs' Mutual Prosperity Association. Often they have heard my name from their friends and are kind enough to ask specially for my services. I charge highly, for I am able to tell them many things they could scarcely learn from other sources. You must have heard of the Grand Eunuch Li Lien-Ying? Of course! Well, I was one of his men and among those placed in charge of the Lord of Ten Thousand Years during all the time he lived in confinement after that occasion when he tried to circumvent the Old Buddha [the Dowager Empress].'

After chatting with him longer, I asked if he and his fellow eunuchs were happy in their old age.

'Happy? How could that be? We have no wives, no sons to bear us grandsons and sacrifice at our tombs. We manage to live. We are not often hungry. We dare not ask for happiness.'

It was time for me to leave the island and hurry round to the other end of the lake where Professor Lee and his friends were expecting me. I parted from my sad companion, having found nothing encouraging to say to someone so irrevocably linked to a vanished epoch. The melancholy thoughts accompanying me on my walk along the ill-lighted east shore of the lake were dispersed by the rising moon, which gave added light to the cheerful scene awaiting me in front of the restaurant. Some lanterns and a round table had been set out near the water's edge, where the other nine members of the party were already seated over saucers of melon-seeds and bowls of tea. As soon as Professor Lee had introduced me to the two or three people I had not met before, the tea was cleared away and the first course of the dinner carried to the table. My left-hand neighbour was someone I had already got to like very much—a tall plump man in his middle fifties who, as a practitioner of traditional Chinese medical arts, was more or less obliged to dress formally in a round black skull-cap and a gown of fine silk. This Chang Taifu (Dr Chang), though he had never been abroad, spoke excellent English, having learnt it from his brother, a former *chargé d'affaires* at the Chinese Legation in London; however, for the sake of the rest of the company, we spoke that night in Chinese. His opening remark was:

'The cook here is a relic of the past. In Manchu times he worked in the palace kitchens which had to supply the Emperor's table with not less than a hundred dishes at every meal, a number commensurate with the imperial dignity rather than with the Lord of Ten Thousand Years' appetite. It is said that his meals included specialities from all the provinces of China, as well as certain others which only the palace cooks knew how to prepare. Tonight we shall have to content ourselves with a less elaborate meal—shark's-fin soup, steamed quail-eggs, spiced garlic chicken, mushrooms stuffed with minced prawn, ordinary plebeian food of that sort. Our friend the Professor was probably too busy to come here beforehand, so we'll have to take what comes. Don't expect too much.'

'Ah, but wait!' cried the Professor, laughing at this disparagement of a meal he had doubtless planned and ordered several days in advance. 'P'u Hsienshêng will be able to taste one speciality to be found nowhere else. That's why I asked Lao Pao to be sure to remind him to come. I shall not say what it is. It sounds so ordinary that the name would make him laugh. It is something to be tasted first and discussed after.'

The banquet progressed in the immemorial way of Chinese dinners. There were eight main courses and four supplementary dishes, served at the end with the soup. At first everyone was inclined to be formal; the guests had to be urged to their wine by the host; when he gave the word, we respectfully used both hands to raise wine-cups small enough to be held between a thumb and finger, draining them at a gulp and making half-hearted protests when they were refilled. When a new course was placed on the table, we waited politely until the host had indicated the dish with the tips of his chopsticks and begged us to eat. But, by the time the fourth or fifth course arrived, such restraint had become superfluous and out of tune with the mellow, carefree mood induced by the wine. Guests had begun leaping to their feet and crying: 'So-and-so, I drink to you. Drain cu-u-u-ups!' Everyone was now eating with comfortable abandon. Manchu-style collars were un-buttoned, robes discarded and the sleeves of silken under-jackets rolled up to the elbows as the noise of talk and laughter mounted. Jests, banter and droll stories alternated with lively comments on the tastes, textures and preparation of the dishes; while serious topics (other than food) were avoided for fear we grow inattentive to the main matter. A civilized man does not talk of politics or religion when somebody sets before him a work of art!

After the eighth course, the usual four lesser courses and a soup appeared, but no rice. Rice is the traditional means of enabling the guests to fill whatever space remains in their stomachs when the eight (or sixteen or twenty-four) main courses have vanished; so I was astonished to see the waiter set two large platters of *shaoping* in its place. These sesamum pastries were normally seen only at breakfast; I had never thought to find them served at a banquet! I looked up in surprise. Everyone's eyes were fixed upon me. Then I realized that these were no ordinary *shaoping*, that my comments were awaited as eagerly as those of a valued customer to whom a dealer is displaying newly discovered Gaugin. Biting into one of the pastries, I found inside a piping-hot meat stuffing so ravishingly spiced that I exclaimed:

'Marvellous! It is not difficult to believe these are the creations of an imperial chef!'

Laughingly, the others devoured the two piles of *shaoping* as though the large courses preceding them had been airy trifles.

'Good,' said Professor Lee, smiling. 'I told you that amidst this poor fare would be one thing almost worthy of your notice. The composition of this stuffing was a palace secret. Even now the old cook here refuses to give it away. He has decided to let it die with him. The world, he says, is sinking into barbarity. Soon no one will be left who appreciates the arts.'

'Let us hope,' answered Pao, 'that he will one day change his mind and sell the recipe to a successor at a fabulous price. Why don't we send for him and drink to the old maestro's longevity?'

As was customary, after tea and sliced oranges had been served, the party quickly broke up. While the other guests went their several ways, Dr Chang, Professor Lee and Pao easily persuaded me to accompany them by rickshaw to the lanes of flowers and willows beyond the Ch'ien Mên. Pao, who was still reticent on the subject of Kuei-Hsiang, had often since our evening at the drum-show tried to make me join him on an expedition of this sort, but I had always felt too shy. The distinction between courtesans and plain whores was something I had yet to discover; my knowledge of brothels, derived wholly from books and hearsay, made me visualize them as intensely sordid places where I might easily find myself in an embarrassing predicament—too timid to run away and too disgusted to penetrate beyond the parlour. However, when it appeared that intelligent and respectable people like the Professor and Dr Chang were to be of the party, I began to realize that Ch'ien Mên Wai could not be altogether sordid.

From the busy streets about Ch'ien Mên with their theatres, bath-houses and still-open cake and fruit shops, we passed through dark and silent lanes until presently we found ourselves entering another lively area thronged with people, noisy and gay. The lanes were as narrow as before, but well lighted and cheerful with mingled sounds of talk, laughter and song, the music of fiddles, the ding-dong of rickshaw bells and the cries of people selling cooked food. Noise was flowing all about us. In the heart of this district the rickshaws set us down before a doorway lit with coloured lights and overhung with a lacquer board inscribed: 'The House of Springtime Congratulations'.

Trying to hide my shyness behind an appearance of nonchalance, I followed the others into a large hall, where a male functionary known as the Big Teapot handed us over to the care of a matron—not a sinister-looking hag, but a respectable woman with a glossy black bun, stiff white jacket and black silk trousers; only she was so much like a hospital amah as to have a prophylactic effect on my soaring spirits. Signing to us to follow her upstairs, she led us into a comfortable bed-sitting-room, clean and well furnished, but needing a lot of imagination to recognize it as 'a place of sin'. Tea was served and the matron withdrew.

The two older men, as was their right, seated themselves upon a large bed occupying the place of a couch of honour, leaving Pao and me to sit on hard stools close to a blackwood majong table. There followed such a long wait that I had almost fallen asleep when an outburst of giggling made me open my eyes in time to see three breathtakingly pretty girls come running into the room. With their bobbed hair, carefully ironed silk jackets and modest bearing, they were so far from my conception of alluring courtesans that, had they been more shy, I could have taken them for a professor's daughters. The first girl ran straight across to Pao and, dipping him a graceful, half-ironic bow, cried:

'Pao Laoyeh! You are back! How nice to see you! But why do you not introduce us to your friends? You remember Silver Aureole and Jade Flute, otherwise Number Three and Number Eight, don't you?'

To avoid indiscretion, Pao solemnly introduced us as Father Wang, Second and Third Fathers Wang, respectively; and the girls, pretending to take these names seriously, treated us to the same sort of mocking bows.

'Listen,' said Pao in English. 'The talkative one is Golden Clasp— my girl and therefore our hostess. Ever since I picked her out on my first visit we have, so to speak, belonged to each other. I can't make love to other girls in this house and she can't make love to my friends. When I come here, she behaves to them as if she were my wife.'

'And those other two? They are charming, but how does Golden Clasp know they will suit any of us?'

'She doesn't. They just happen to be unoccupied, so she has brought them in to help entertain. If you like one you may choose her; if not, I can ask Ma [the matron] to call the others in. Even those who have guests now will come in for a minute or two. Up to midnight, only door-curtains guard our privacy, so a popular girl can entertain in two or three rooms at the same time, running in to chat now with one patron, now with another.'

By this time, the three girls had seated themselves between the table and the bed and were chattering with great animation. Often they laughed uproariously, so when Pao gave his attention to them I felt left out of things. I never seemed to catch the point of their jokes and watched in moody silence when the matron reappeared with a plate of fruit and another of sliced water-chestnuts—the number of plates intimating that, so far, we had enjoyed two *yuan* worth of gaiety.

'You are oddly silent!' exclaimed Dr Chang in Chinese.

'Yes, I'm rather stupid. Perhaps I dined *too* well. I can hardly understand what you are talking about.'

My confession produced a cascade of laughter, for which Jade Flute hastened to apologize.

'Excuse us, Third Father Wang. We are stupid girls who have never had the pleasure of meeting foreign dev—er—someone from your distinguished country. You will have to teach us how to amuse you.'

'You see,' added the Professor. 'It's all Dr Chang's fault. He tried out a few political quips on them and is now being beaten at his own game. The girls in this house know how to talk entertainingly. You have to rack your brains to find any reasonably ordinary subject that will stump them. But this is the way for you to learn Chinese; you must treat it as a lesson. Then you'll enjoy yourself.'

Jade Flute, feeling that this was asking a bit much of me, ostentatiously moved her stool away from him and brought it close to my own. After displaying the usual pretence of interest as to my age, parentage, marital status, profession, income, tastes and so on, she went on to make me blush by paying a delicious compliment:

'Third Father Wang, you hardly seem to be a foreigner. You are a real *Chungkuo T'ung.*'

'Why, thank you. That's the nicest thing you could have said.'

*Chungkuo T'ung* is a phrase used of a foreigner who has learnt to talk, act, feel and think like a Chinese. For all their politeness and self-depreciatory remarks, the Chinese never doubted they were humanity's finest flower; so to be called a *Chungkuo T'ung* was a high honour. It implied that, despite my misfortune in being born a barbarian, I had cleverly managed to acquire the traits of a civilized human being! Now I saw that Jade Flute, remembering how they had laughed at my stupidity, had been patiently building up an opportunity to repair the damage. All her preliminary remarks and questions had been aimed at giving substance to a compliment which would have been meaningless if I had not first been given a chance to talk about myself.

Touched by this thoughtful attention and appreciating her skill, I began feeling warmly towards that pretty, clever girl. A medium-size, well-knit, firm-fleshed girl of about seventeen, she had bobbed hair with a fringe over her forehead and eyes that shone with merriment. She was dressed in a short jacket and wide trousers of plain white silk which so added to her innocent and childishly modest appearance that it was scarcely possible to think of her as a courtesan. A sudden wave of tenderness made me wonder for a few seconds about the bleak circumstances which must have led her to such a house; but, just as sympathy began floating through my mind, she giggled happily and cried:

'Third Father Wang, you are dreaming. I believe you have a wife, someone very beautiful and far away.'

Such unaffected laughter put an end to that brief upsurge of chivalrous feeling. It seemed ludicrous to see as the victim of dark tragedy someone so obviously enjoying herself, so healthy and so gay. Whatever misfortunes had driven her to the willow-lanes, Jade Flute at any rate knew the art of living in the present as well as if she had heard Yang Taoshih's advice about actions without fore- or after-thought. My pulling a long, sympathetic face, so far from helping her, would spoil her pleasure in keeping me amused and happy.

Just then Dr Chang remarked that it was almost midnight and time for him to go home. He yawned and, buttoning the collar of his jacket, reached for the long gown he had placed on the bolster behind him. Professor Lee, giving Crystal Spring an absent-minded pat on the bottom, rose to accompany him; yet the girls seemed neither surprised nor hurt. This careless rejection of their favours elicited nothing worse than smiling protests that it was still early, so why go home?

Why indeed? In some alarm I asked the doctor:

'Do you often come to admire the flowers and then go home without picking one?'

'Certainly,' he answered, speaking in Chinese out of courtesy to the girls, and smiling. 'As people get older, their appreciation of girls grows, but at the same time they become less acquisitive. I am sure Lao Lee agrees with me. You young people look to pretty girls for only one sort of satisfaction. We older ones know better, but that is not to say we *never* pick the flowers.'

'How is it in your honourable country?' asked Silver Aureole, though I do not think she really cared.

'In England we have prostitutes, but they do not learn to be amusing, I should think. We are able to spend so many hours a day talking and talking to women—the wives, sisters and daughters of our friends, if not our own. We see so much of them that we are driven to take refuge in men's clubs which exist chiefly for that purpose. Our women even go with us to restaurant dinner-parties! Can you believe it? We don't pay them to talk and look pretty, though I dare say we spend a good deal on them one way and another.'

'How clever your honourable countrywomen must be!' sighed Jade Flute. 'Here in Peking, girls like us have to receive special training, otherwise we would not know *how* to talk.'

'That's true,' put in the Professor. 'We older people had our marriages arranged for us; our wives know all about being good wives, mothers and housekeepers, but seldom how to be companions. Of course conditions are changing fast with all these new schools for girls, and there always were exceptional women like Lao Chang's late wife, or those educated privately at home along with their brothers. Even so, I hope flower-houses will not disappear altogether. Occasionally you will find flower-girls who have more than such ordinary accomplishments as being able to sing or play the lute, to flirt with some subtlety, to talk tenderly, sympathetically or wittily according to your mood: there are some with really exceptional talents. I shall never forget a girl called Small Bluebird who could compose impromptu poems with a facility nearly equal to Lao Chang's, and cap literary allusions like a Hanlin scholar. Why, people even came to her in confidence for advice about political or business matters. She was almost as remarkable as the girl who once saved Peking from being looted by the Western allies by captivating the German general so that he did not know if he was standing on his head or his feet. Bluebird was too rare a jewel to remain long in a place like this. She is now the concubine of General So-and-So who was restrained with difficulty from making her his official T'ait'ai!'

Silver Aureole was beginning to look bored and Golden Clasp was too busy whispering and giggling into Pao's ear to care what we were saying, but Jade Flute listened with a thoughtful air: I saw that she was not only charming but intelligent.

'Another thing can be said for these places,' went on Professor Lee. 'There is nothing crude about them. Your relationship with any of these charming children is a love affair in miniature. First you come here and they talk to you. Then you come again and carry things a little further. When the conclusion is reached, it is something worth while. In France and Italy they have houses of a sort, but I never could get used to romping with a stranger. If you are wise, you will come here again and let Jade Flute teach you these things.'

She smiled with pleasure at the implied compliment; but, with Dr Chang and the Professor on the point of leaving, it looked as though I was expected to accompany them. Just as I made to rise, Jade Flute and her friend, sensing my reluctance, laughingly caught me by the arms and held me to my stool. The touch of Flute's hands worked like magic. Intoxicating feelings of tenderness and desire melted my lingering shyness; I felt that at all costs I must stay until the morning, and was upset when Professor Lee asked reprovingly in English:

'Aren't you coming, John?'

Even Dr Chang was perplexed; and, seeing me still reluctant to push the girls away, said tactfully:

'Lao Pao is getting sleepy. We should leave him to enjoy a good night's rest.'

'Not at all,' exclaimed Pao, breaking off his whispered conversation with Golden Clasp. 'John, please stay a little while. I've got something to tell you.'

I felt like a prisoner reprieved at the very last moment.

All three girls went out on to the landing to see our friends off, leaving me alone with him. My mouth was so dry from excitement that I could hardly speak. It was a bitter, bitter disappointment when Golden Clasp came back alone and firmly shut the door.

'Where's Jade Flute?' I asked anxiously.

Struggling between laughter and surprise, the girl answered: 'It's after midnight, Third Father Wang. She has gone to bed. You had better come to visit her tomorrow.'

I could see that she was impatient for me to be gone and that she thought me stupid for being taken in by the other girls' courteous pretence of forcing me to stay. I ought to have realized from what had been said before that etiquette required such girls to be wooed for some time before they could be won, and that Jade Flute would not dare intrude upon a 'sister' at such a late hour; only I was in no state to think calmly. A few minutes earlier, I had been gloriously certain of tasting bliss; I was suddenly so hungry for Flute that it seemed to me I had fallen absolutely in love—in the most tender, romantic and so-to-speak chivalrous way imaginable. Indeed, looking back on that moment, I still feel the word chivalrous to be not inappropriate, because I would gladly have borne my desire chastely through the night if, by promising that, I could have gained a few more hours of her company. Being deprived of the sight of her seemed more than I could bear; and the unspeakable thought that she might even then be in the arms of a hideous, unloving and unlovable rival caused me agony and inward fury—it was really like a knife cutting at my bowels. If Jade Flute, wherever she was, could have guessed my thoughts, she must either have been touched or else found them ridiculous and incomprehensible.

'My God, Pao! Why didn't that girl come back? I thought she *wanted* me to stay.'

He looked at me guiltily, but without understanding.

'John, I'm really sorry. I do remember promising you the sport of mandarin ducks. I had meant to take you to a place where you could have enjoyed yourself, but then Lao Chang and Lao Lee would have felt out of place or refused to go. With Lao Lee as our host, it was rather awkward. Here, there's not a thing you can do. Even money has no power over tradition in a place like this. But, look here, it's not so very late. We could go somewhere else now, if you——'

'No, no, no!' I exclaimed fiercely. 'Not that!'

Forced to make the best of my predicament, I found that in one way I was fortunate. Love had attacked me in such a romantic form that presently I felt calmed rather than appalled at the thought of having to woo Jade Flute by degrees. In those days, at least, a very young and romantic Englishman did not immediately envisage love in terms of its consummation. His mistress—princess or prostitute—was for him a sacred person who must not be profaned even by thoughts that made no distinction between 'love' and naked desire. There may have been self-deception in this, but not hypocrisy.

Resolutely determined not to let Pao see me as a fool, I forced myself to think of other things and presently remembered to ask him what it was he wanted to talk to me about. As it concerned something private, he continued talking in English, which must have been irksome to Golden Clasp, but she took it well. Pouting with only pretended anger, she went to sit beside him on the bed, where he had made himself comfortable by leaning back against the bolster. From time to time, she took care to fan him with a large round fan made of scented leaves. A tall and on the whole placid girl dressed demurely in plum-coloured jacket and trousers, she looked exactly the kind of person with whom a man could amuse himself without emotional involvement. This may have been her chief attraction for Pao, whose affections were, as I now discovered, still fixed on Kuei-Hsiang. At last he had decided to talk about her.

'I've often felt sorry for the way I rushed off after the drum-show that night. I ought to have apologized long ago, but I was trying, ineffectually, to put Kuei-Hsiang out of my head. It can't be done.'

'What did happen when you went over to speak to her that night?'

He sighed, stretching out his arm to caress Golden Clasp, as though to make up for his still talking English.

'Kuei-Hsiang asked me in a low voice to leave the room quickly and not come back. When I threatened to make a scene, she explained that a Japanese colonel had opened negotiations to pay an unheard-of price for her and that she was to share his house with the full status of concubine. If he soon got tired of her, she would let me know; in the meanwhile, so she said, she was very satisfied with the arrangement and would I please make things easy for her by staying right away. I was furious, as you can imagine. I should certainly have abused her as a common whore preferring money to decency, but her pretence of being mercenary was too unconvincing. When she saw my expression she nearly broke down in front of everybody. What would have happened then, I don't know. I *had* to leave, because that old woman kept hissing in my ear that she was going to have me thrown out by the waiters. When I came back towards our table, I saw the reason for it. That Japanese colonel was sitting there watching everything. If I hadn't left at once I should have struck him.'

'I still don't understand. The old woman, yes. But Kuei-Hsiang herself? How could the Japanese have traced her if you'd both run off to Shanghai? He's not a magician. What made her so absurdly afraid of him? I suppose it was fear, as you are sure she is not really mercenary.'

'You don't know the Japanese. You can't imagine the impression made on our people by the stories brought from the north-east. Didn't you read in the paper last week about the corpses of four hundred Chinese workmen floating down the Huai river from the place where they had just completed some fortifications for the Japanese? You must have done. This Colonel Saito is especially dangerous because he works for the Intelligence. I suspect that Kuei-Hsiang is terrified that if she ran away he would discover the whereabouts of her village and have her brothers carried off to forced labour or her parents killed. Anything.'

'Impossible. We are not in Japanese-occupied territory here; neither is her village, is it?'

'Quite so. But will that be true much longer? Manchuria has gone. Half of Inner Mongolia has gone, and a slice of this Hopei Province of ours, too. They can take Peking any day they want—next year, next month, tomorrow! Even now General Sung's administration here is pretty much under Japanese control, isn't it? I doubt if Saito would bother to hunt down Kuei-Hsiang's family if she ran away. But Japanese pride is an ugly, unpredictable thing. If he happened to take it that a Chinese, a girl, a mere prostitute, had affronted his dignity, he would be capable of having her whole family exterminated.'

'Good Lord! What are you going to do?'

'Do? This for now.' He tightened his grip on Golden Clasp, who obediently laid down her fan and snuggled close to him. 'What else *can* I do? Kuei-Hsiang has my address. She happens to be semi-literate. One day I may hear from her. Or I may not. Living like a monk won't help me forget her.'

When, reluctantly, I got to my feet and said good night, Golden Clasp handed me over to a servant with instructions to call a rickshaw for me. On my way downstairs I noticed that most of the room doors were shut, the curtains no longer visible; but on the ground floor the door of a big room stood open and, the curtain happening to blow away from it as I passed, I glimpsed a dozen or so girls and matrons seated at a large round table enjoying a midnight snack. I thought I recognized the back of Jade Flute's head and was inexpressibly rejoiced that, during the rest of the night, I need not lie awake visualizing her being possessed by the hideous old man my imagination had conjured up as my rival. I might even be able to sleep well, knowing that on the following afternoon I should spend hours and hours with her, no matter how many dishes of fruit piled up on the table. Love with a capital L had seized me—or so I thought.

# 4

# Manchus, Lute and Vampire-fox

IN THE west city, close by the ruins of those gigantic elephant stables built to house the tribute of the kings of Burma to the Dragon Throne, lived an American who had become almost as much a genuine Pekingese institution as the stables themselves. Professor William Luton had during over thiry years in China put down roots deep into the soil; he had been teaching at one of Peking's most famous universities for so long that whatever sort of government might chance to seize power—republican, monarchist or communist —its more intellectual leaders could hardly fail to include some of his former students. I had often enjoyed anecdotes about his taste for exotic flowers and fierce animals, but had never chanced to meet him until, upon a Sunday morning soon after the beginning of my affair with Jade Flute, one of my private students suggested our paying him a visit.

This was a young Manchu called Chu Tê-Ku who used to come to my house, occasionally accompanied by his younger brother, for coaching in English. His immediate ancestors had been noblemen with a considerable palace in the north city; but the family, dispossessed during the 1911 Revolution, was now living in straitened circumstances for which there seemed no remedy. The curse of belonging to a ruined aristocracy lay heavily upon them—the elders especially. Their charm could no longer compensate for idleness, extravagance and ignorance of almost everything unconnected with the pursuit of pleasure. As Chu, himself, once said when apologizing for one of his characteristic failures to do any homework:

'I wonder if you can know how hard it is for us?'

When asked to explain this remark, he switched over from English to Chinese and embarked upon a long disquisition of which the gist is as follows:

71

'Towards the end of the dynasty, although the Imperial Family retained supreme power tightly in their hands, they had come to leave the carrying out of policy to ministers and functionaries of Chinese rather than Manchu race—astute, hardworking officials most unlike ourselves. We Manchus, especially the noble families, continued drawing generous pensions for which we did not have to work at all. Imagine! My talented grandfather gave all his energies to cultivating the arts of agreeable living. My father grew up in an atmosphere where the only accomplishments expected of him were expert horsemanship, skill in archery—this at a time when our enemies had iron battleships—a cultivated taste in dress, manners and deportment and a connoisseur-ship of such seductive trifles as chrysanthemums or goldfish or the jade thumb-rings used in archery. To these he added a zest for every sort of pleasure! Apart from the Emperor and those members of the Imperial Family closest to him, we Manchus, besides being incapable of doing anything to earn our pensions, also lacked the literary skills upon which the Chinese set so much store. My father's Chinese friends had studied history, the arts of government and other useful branches of knowledge; they knew the Confucian classics by heart and were able to compose abstruse 'eight-legged' essays on literary subjects; some of them would get up every day at dawn and practise calligraphy for a couple of hours before breakfast. On the other hand, in matters requiring less strenuous endeavour, we had become more Chinese than the Chinese themselves, so that today we seldom even think of ourselves as a race apart. As far back as fifty or eighty years ago hardly any of us could speak Manchu, much less write it. We've spoken Chinese amongst ourselves since before my grandfather's day, and now we young ones receive exactly the same education as everybody else, yet when some of us manage to do well in the university examinations we surprise ourselves. Idleness, dear teacher, is in our bones. That's how it is. I try to work hard—sometimes. It's impossible to keep it up for long.'

Chu's appearance in itself suggested such a background. Though short of cash, he used to arrive for his lessons in a freshly ironed gown of silk or fine cotton with a three-inch collar, as elegant as it was un-comfortable, and with sleeves and skirts so long that only controlled, leisurely movements were possible to him. Tall, willowy, with marvellously slender fingers and a soft pale skin, he was most obviously a stranger to bustle and toil. On the Sunday morning when he suggested a visit to Professor Luton, we were sitting in a sunny patch of my courtyard close to the two old plum-trees. Though the day was chilly, he still carried an ornamental fan, useful for adding grace to the restrained gestures with which he illustrated his conversation. On one side of it an artist friend had executed, with a nice economy of brush-strokes, the likeness of a phoenix gazing at a blood-red sun. Chu was, I suppose, effeminate, but not in the 'sissy' manner which excites distaste; on the contrary, it was a pleasure to watch him, particularly when he grew animated about some trifle which had taken his quixotic fancy.

Replying to his suggestion, I said: 'Yes, I have always wanted to meet Professor Luton. Do you know him well?'

'Certainly. I am attending his course on European Literature for second-year students. He is trying to make us appreciate Proust. We are most of us so fond of him that we forgive him things which would otherwise cause a riot.'

'For instance?'

'Last week, in class, he cursed the whole Chinese race. He said we lived only for our bellies, that we have combed earth and sky and sea for everything remotely edible, and that we should long ago have become cannibals if human flesh happened to be more delicious than pork! Some of my classmates were so angry that they walked out of the lecture-room.'

'And then?'

'When he realized how we felt, he apologized very pleasantly and soon won our sympathy. He told us he had twice taken a lot of trouble to grow some rare flowers from seeds specially ordered in America. Each time, as soon as the buds opened, one of his neighbours (so he says) sent a child over the wall to pull off all the heads. He believes they were taken away to be cooked.'

'Cooked!'

'Possibly they were. Plenty of flowers make delicious eating. You must have tasted fish or chicken dishes sprinkled with lightly fried chrysanthemum petals. And look!'

He pointed with his fan to a small bush of jasmine growing in the north-east corner of the courtyard just outside my bedroom.

'You often drink jasmine tea, I know. But buying the flowers and tea-leaves already mixed cannot compare with blending them yourself. It is better to choose one of the red teas from Fukien, one of those kinds picked before the summer rains have coarsened the leaves. Don't put jasmine in the canister with the tea, but throw a freshly plucked handful into the pot. And be sure to use buds. The fully opened flower has no taste.'

When we left to visit the victim of horticultural outrage, my suggestion that we go by tram brought a perceptible shadow of dismay to Chu's face, but good manners forbade argument. As my student (though a year or two older than myself), he was bound to fall in with my wishes unless they were too unreasonable. On the other hand, his relative poverty had by no means taught him to adapt himself to a frugal way of life. Tram fares were cheap, but now that horses had gone out of fashion, a gentleman should travel by taxi or, failing that, in the privacy of a rickshaw.

At the near end of the tram, I made to sit down next to four youths dressed like university students, but Chu after one glance at them led me to the far end where we had to stand.

'Why not sit down near those students?' I asked.

'Students! I dare say that's what they call themselves on their passports, if they are not too contemptuous of our laws to bother with such things. Perhaps they do study our city's defences or the weaknesses of important Chinese individuals. They look too smug for plain drug-pedlars. *Pei!*'

Japanese! I recalled Pao's defencelessness against his Japanese rival. I sensed the hatred which had momentarily brought something like ugliness to Chu's generally placid face. Like him, I preferred to stand.

From a tram-stop in the west city, ten minutes' walk brought us to the lane near the elephant stables where Professor Luton lived among his flowers and animals. Like my own lane, it was a typical Peking *hu-t'ung* with high windowless walls, broken at intervals by ornamental roofs overhanging copper-hinged gates of chipped and fading lacquer. Our ring was answered by a gatekeeper stooped with age who, recognizing Chu, left us to find our own way along the stone-flagged path leading to the house. The main building, which surprisingly had no courtyard and faced east instead of south, must at one time have formed part of a larger complex of buildings. Western-style flower-beds and lawns contrasting with formal arrangements of glazed pots containing flowers or ornamental shrubs bore witness to the owner's West-East tastes. To me the overall effect was charming, but to Chu's

Peking-formed mind the lack of symmetrical arrangement looked untidy.

A white-gowned servant, moving noiselessly upon black felt shoes, kept us standing on the steps while he went back into the house to summon his master. The gossip I had heard about Professor Luton had prepared me for some degree of eccentricity; but I was far from ready for what I saw next. A heavily built, bearded American came stalking out, a finger to his lips, making ostentatious rather than effective efforts to tiptoe silently, and carrying in his left hand a freshly severed dog's tail, raw and bloody at the end. It seemed to me that the recent loss of his cherished flowers had driven him completely mad. Chu, who had known him for a long time, showed no change of expression, even when the Professor gestured excitedly to prevent him from introducing me and rebuked him with a burst of elaborate shushing noises.

'Hush! Come in. Come in. But *very* quietly, please. For God's sake don't talk. I've got Wu Kuan-T'ien here. He's in the middle of his performance.'

At these words, everything except the severed tail became clearer to me. All Peking knew of Wu Kuan-T'ien as the greatest living master of the seven-stringed lute—an instrument beloved of the ancients and now so rarely played that I knew its appearance only from pictures. All the same, I still had doubts as to the Professor's sanity; quite as odd as the absurd tail inexplicably dangling from his hand was the fact that, on entering the house, we were greeted by silence. There was not the faintest sound of music; nobody and nothing stirred. Luton, pausing to lay aside his disgusting burden, led us across the room, still on tiptoe and with a finger glued to his lips. It was not until we had passed through another doorway into a much smaller room that I really began to understand.

The little room was occupied by several people sitting in attitudes of absorbed attention. In the centre a tall, thin old man with a wispy moustache sat bent over a lute lying on a low pearwood table in front of him. I must have been half-way through the door before I realized that he was engaged in plucking from it the sweetest sounds imaginable, for the silken strings gave forth notes softer than the buzzing of a single bee!

His audience consisted of six or seven scholarly-looking old gentlemen dressed in gowns of dark-coloured silk suitable to autumn—

deep shades of blue, grey and bronze. Paying no attention to our entry, they sat upright or leaning slightly forward, legs held modestly together under their gowns and hands generally at rest upon their laps. I could have taken them for Taoist immortals rather than human beings. To Pekingese gentlemen of their generation, restless movement and over-casual postures had been made impossible by habits instilled into them from earliest youth. Young people and foreigners might scratch their noses, finger their chins or cross their legs in public; but to these old scholars such behaviour indicated failure to achieve that inner harmony which had ever been the goal of their studies and meditations.

Chu and I sat down gingerly on the end of a small divan already occupied by a cherubic old man whose smooth, beardless face contrasted oddly with that of the figure occupying the centre of a painted wall-scroll hanging just above the divan—it depicted the well-known and attractively ugly Zen patriarch Boddhidharma ferrying himself across a river balanced on a single stalk of corn. Suppressing a smile, I gave my whole attention to the music and was presently entranced. Beneath the maestro's hands, the seven silken strings throbbed and vibrated, producing clusters of infinitely soft notes, now swift, now slow. While his left hand darted up and down the length of the horizontal lute with quick bird-like movements, the inch-long fingernails of his right hand ceaselessly caressed the strings as though five plectrums were being agitated simultaneously. Impossible to describe that unearthly music! It was woven of sighs and murmurs, the tinkle of jade ornaments, the wind in the pine-trees, the whispering flight of pigeons. It was ancient and remote, like ghostly music echoing faintly through the silence of a haunted grove, yet not so much melancholy as sweetly solemn with now and then a hint of gentle gaiety.

When, rather abruptly, the melody ended, Wu Kuan-T'ien rose to his feet and, bowing smilingly in our direction, apologized for not greeting us before. The others also stood up while Luton, after softly enquiring my name from Chu, introduced us to each in turn. He was a man transformed—a man now as calm, affable, dignified and ceremonious as his Chinese guests. Yet his well-meant imitation of the Chinese manner was not without a discernible element of the grotesque. A manner admirably suited to pale, delicately formed men in silken gowns is less becoming in a large, red-faced, bearded Westerner, especially as, lacking a gown, he cannot perform suitably low bows

without an O-shaped space appearing between his trousered legs!
I began to fear that my own efforts to comport myself as a Chinese
must produce a similar effect, that of a heavy-weight boxer miming
a ballet-dancer! (Many years later, I was reminded of this on meeting
a uniformed Harold Acton at an Armed Services function in war-time
London. His greeting to a 'fellow Pekingese'—a low Chinese bow,
hands clasped on breast—went oddly with his smart R.A.F. officer's
uniform. All the same, I felt an instant sympathy with someone who,
like myself, had remained through the years deeply under Peking's
spell.)

Wu Kuan-T'ien, before resuming his lute, courteously interpreted
to us the imagery of his music. The piece just heard had been inspired
several hundred years before by a flock of herons seen rising from the
banks of a frozen river and flying across the snow-bound fields—
themselves snow-white against the sky's blue arch.

> 'The winter sun slants redly on the ice.
> With whirr of wings the startled herons rise.
> Like clouds their shadows graze the frozen fields—
> The earth, it seems, wings snow-flakes to the skies.'

The maestro's next piece portrayed the melancholy of a warrior
riding home after serving twenty years in the barren wastes beyond the
Great Wall. At first delighted by the green of the young corn, the blue
smoke rising from cottages undisturbed by war and by the familiar
sounds made by chattering village-girls washing clothes in a stream,
he is later distressed to find how few of his boyhood friends are left
to welcome him home.

> 'Back through the pass, now twice ten years are gone;
> Back to my home to nurse old age in peace;
> Well I recall this greenly springing corn,
> Smoke from the hearths and laughter from the stream.
> Tying my horse to a tree where no trees grew,
> Bending my steps to a house that stands no more,
> Smiling at youths who gaze back in amaze,
> I'm welcomed by a grey-beard who knows my name!'

When this piece had reached its poignant conclusion, Mr Wu and
all the other old gentlemen went off to attend a celebration in a Taoist

monastery famous for its carp. I gathered that what I had just heard had been in some sort a rehearsal for a performance to be held there after the midday feast. Left alone with Chu while Luton was escorting them to the front gate, I suddenly remembered to ask for news of his younger brother, who had not attended any of our lessons since about two months before, when about to sit for his senior middle school passing-out examination.

'When is Tê-Lin coming to see me? I suppose he passed all right?'

'No, he was unlucky.'

'Really? That's too bad. Still, it's no reason for staying away from me, is it?'

'And then, as a matter of fact, he died.'

I was so unprepared for this shock and Chu's tone was so unfeeling, so utterly casual, that at first grief was swallowed up in anger. It was incredible that he should convey the news of his own brother's death so belatedly and with the callousness of someone talking about a deceased jackdaw. How could I have been deceived by the shallow charm of this wretched youth into thinking him a sensitive and affectionate person?

After an awkward pause, I said slowly: 'Tê-Lin dead? Good God! Impossible! How could it be?'

'Well, my father scolded him for failing his examination; so, that night, he swallowed raw opium—suicide, you see.'

*And then Chu giggled!*

Horrified, incapable of speaking, I glared at him in appalled silence. Just then Luton came striding back into the room, chattering excitedly about Wu Kuan-T'ien's performance. While Chu made polite responses, I sat there like a creature boorish and half-witted. How could I attend to their talk with the sound of that heartless giggle ringing in my ears? Tê-Lin had been a friendly, attractive boy, only a few years younger than myself—and now he was dead! Yet I, who had met him not above a dozen times, was more deeply moved by his loss than his own brother!

I am sure that if Chu had succeeded in carrying off his attitude of inhuman callousness until it was time for us to go, I should have told him I never wished to see him again; but a second shock was to follow. In the middle of something knowledgeable he was saying to Luton about Chinese music, his voice faltered and he began to sob. Leaning back in his chair, he fought ineffectually against a whole succession of sobs, his body jerking with their force. Luton, recovering quickly, showed great presence of mind in seizing him by the arm and half leading, half dragging him into another room. For ten minutes I was left to myself with time to reflect upon my conduct in being angry with Chu instead of showing sympathy and concern. Presently Luton returned—alone.

'Chu asks me to make you his apologies. He's ashamed of having spoilt your first visit here and says he cannot face you now. I have put him in a rickshaw and sent the poor boy home.'

'Yes, yes. Of course that's best. But I'm overwhelmed. I don't know how long ago that awful thing happened, yet never by a word or a sign did Chu . . . And, would you believe it, just now while he was breaking the news to me, he actually laughed! God, he spoke as if the boy's death were nothing to him. And then that laughter!'

'Did that surprise you so much? Lots of people here would behave in that way under similar circumstances. You'll get used to it. He must have argued that you are not, as yet, an intimate friend, so he ought not to burden you with his personal grief. His giggling is less surprising than his not having told you earlier. You've noticed, haven't you, that some sort of laugh or smile is the normal Chinese response to misfortune; it goes with shock, fear, embarrassment and sometimes with anger. Surely when you scold one of your students, you don't take his grin for insubordination? The more your words shame or hurt him, the more the kid grins, doesn't he?'

After thinking back for a while, I told him that the people I had met in South China had never carried this trait to such lengths as Chu. 'And if that was the cause, why his sudden switch to tears?' I added.

'You didn't find that strange, did you?' he asked in a tone that suggested I was being needlessly obtuse. 'These guys are after all just as human as we are—all too human, I guess. If they *seem* otherwise, it's because propriety is so important to them. All their actions are governed by it—up to when they reach breaking point. Beyond that —well, the youngsters especially have no more control than you or I. Less, maybe, because their emotions have been bottled up until something bursts inside them. When that happens, the Book of Rites is forgotten and the *Tajen*, the would-be superior man, finds himself as much at the mercy of his feelings as any other guy. Come now, you mustn't let me treat you to a lecture. Could you, in spite of everything, summon up an appetite for lunch?'

His dining-room, lighted by windows intricately latticed to form the pattern known as 'cracked ice', showed clear evidence of his taste in things Chinese. The furniture was built of darkly gleaming wood with simple functional lines; its extraordinary beauty left me in no doubt that it was genuine Ming. The only pictures were a set of black and white landscapes depicting the four seasons; I should have recognized the brush-strokes as the work of some antique master even if the silken mountings had not been yellowed with age. On the other hand the food, though served on fine porcelain plates with an apple-green glaze, was so uncompromisingly Western that Luton felt it necessary to apologize.

'I just love Chinese food, but not every day. It's too rich for a New England stomach. You'll have to make do with ox-tail soup and grilled fish. Do you mind?'

Ox-tail soup? An obscene grey object, driven from memory by the shock of Tê-Lin's death, suddenly returned to mind. It had most certainly not been an *ox*-tail! I decided to swallow down my soup before daring to question him. When I did refer to the tail, he gave me a peculiarly penetrating look, as though trying to assess how I should be likely to take his answer.

'It looks like an Alsatian's tail. My number one boy handed it to me when he called me out of the music-room to tell me of your arrival. I guess I'd better save the rest of the story till you've seen something for yourself, otherwise you'll think I'm crazy.'

From a slight constraint in his manner, I sensed he was sorry I had seen the wretched thing. Although it was chilly, we had coffee on a terrace set about with pots of pink and white oleanders, sitting in the sun away from the hibiscus-shadowed trellis. After coffee, Luton jumped to his feet exclaiming: 'Care to see my menagerie?'

In a corner of the garden, secluded by a thick-set row of flourishing camellia-trees, we came to another terrace surrounded on three sides by cages and barred enclosures. It was like a zoo. Of small and smallish animals he had about thirty comprising perhaps ten or a dozen varieties, together with a much larger number of birds including peacocks. I particularly remember some evil-looking civet cats glaring at us banefully as they paced up and down their cage, and a pair of hideous grey monkeys chattering with glee and stretching their paws through the bars of their cage to welcome their master. To our left was an enclosure that towered over the rest, its heavy iron bars covered with

Courtyard scenes within
the Forbidden City

A marble-balustraded canal winding through the Forbidden City

A small pavilion in the Pei Hai Park

fine wire netting. It contained three grey-furred animals which I took to be undersized and unfriendly Alsatians of impure stock.

'Why must those dogs live in a cage?' I asked. 'Are they dangerous?'

'Dangerous, sure; but hardly dogs. Haven't you seen wolves before? No? Well these fine fellows were captured somewhere in the Manchurian forests; they are fierce enough to welcome a chance to bite your throat out. Though they know me and my number one boy so well, we never go in to feed them without taking a whip. And now you shall hear what happened this morning. Just before the music started and a little while before you came, Lao Liu, my boy, came in to feed them as usual. The gate is always padlocked, by the way, and he opened it with a key which had been in my pocket ever since I fed them myself last night. Well, while he was still in the cage, after distributing a basket of raw meat, he went over to that trough there to turn on the water tap. Just in front of it, he saw lying on the ground a tail —a freshly bitten-off tail with blood staining the earth close to the severed end. His first reaction was to stare at each of my three wolves, looking for injuries; but, as you see, there is nothing wrong with them and their tails are all in the right place.'

'How very odd! I suppose a poor dog rubbing itself against the outside of the bars or making efforts to be friendly with the wolves incautiously pushed its tail inside. All the same, I don't see how a tail of that size could——'

'Exactly. That's the whole point. The mesh is much too fine. And look at it; it's in perfect condition. Not a hole or a gap anywhere. I wanted you to see that for yourself.'

'Could the wolves have dug up the tail of some dead animal from under the ground?'

'A long-dead animal with a tail still able to bleed?'

'No, I see. So then?'

'How should I know? Nothing I can think of makes any sense. I guess you don't altogether believe me, do you?'

'Of course I believe you. Doesn't Lao Liu have some explanation to offer?'

'As a matter of fact, he was able to explain it at once, but what he said sounds so crazy that you'll find it easier to believe the goddamned thing grew there of itself!'

'I'd like to know what he said, though.'

Luton laughed uncomfortably. A pause followed, as though he still could not make up his mind whether to tell me. When he did speak, it was with apparent irrelevance.

'At the bottom of my garden is a fox-tower. Most mornings some of my more ignorant neighbours persuade my gatekeeper to let them in to burn incense there.'

'Really? You mean it is a shrine dedicated to a *huliching?*'

'Thank God, no. A *huliching* is a sinister and deadly sort of fox-spirit. I wouldn't want to live here with one of those. No, this one is just a *huhsien* who was (or is) a male fox credited with the power of turning himself into the form of an old man—harmless enough, but he's fond of creating insoluble mysteries and of perpetrating those stupid practical jokes all *huhsien* seem to enjoy.'

'You believe this?' I said, hiding my astonishment.

Again he laughed in some embarrassment.

'Maybe "believe" is too strong a word. Shall we say I don't entirely disbelieve?'

'I see what you mean. I suppose, when you have spent years and years in a city where even the papers report such things as factually as an outbreak of measles, you do begin to wonder. Did you see in the paper last week that column about a burglar who climbed a tree in full view of the policemen chasing him and then, turning into a small brown fox, disappeared among the leaves? They were afraid to shoot, for fear it would come and haunt them.'

'Sure, that's just what I mean.'

'But how does Lao Liu connect the *huhsien* with your wolves and how could even a *huhsien* get that tail into the cage?'

'It is enough for Lao Liu that this was one of the *huhsien*'s silly, incomprehensible jokes. He doesn't attempt to reason about it. *Huhsien* are not credited with doing things for any particular reason, but people do believe they are magicians who can do physically impossible things—getting that tail into the cage, for example.'

I had to be content with that. As far as I know, no more acceptable explanation of the tail incident was ever found. The story is in any case a good example of the absurdly pointless behaviour attributed to that sort of fox-spirit. Luton was kind enough to take me straight from his private zoo to the fox-tower at the other end of the garden. A low grey-brick building with an upper storey to which there was no entrance and a lower storey too confined to allow more than one of us to enter at a time, it contained nothing of interest. There was just a dusty niche containing the *huhsien*'s spirit-tablet and a chipped china incense-burner filled with ash, in which the red stubs of burnt-down incense-sticks stood upright.

Afterwards, as Bill pressed me to stay longer, we spent the rest of that increasingly chilly afternoon in his study, our talk proceeding naturally from the genial *huhsien* to the grisly *huliching*. Concerning the former, even I had a fresh story to contribute. As I have said, the *kungyü* where I had stayed before finding a house of my own was a converted mansion divided up into rooms and sets of rooms run on the lines of service flats. To get to my own part of that sprawling nest of courtyards, I had to pass a smallish room in the north-east corner of the main courtyard, at a place where a shady elm-tree rose from a neglected rockery with stones about the height of a man and a miniature cave. In this room lived an old woman who used to totter about on feet crippled in youth to make them attractively small. During most of the day, she could be seen sitting in her doorway, smoking a tobacco-pipe so long that, when she had it in her mouth, her hand could by no means reach the tiny bowl; to light it, she had to call Ting, an ugly little country girl who served her without wages in return for food and lodging. Occasionally, when I returned to the *kungyü* late at night, I would notice that the light in her room was still on and hear the old lady talking to someone in a loud, grumbling voice, her words distinctly audible through the thinly papered windows. At first I used to assume that she was talking to Ting or that she had visitors, but one night I heard her say in a tone of annoyance:

'Please, Mr Fox-Spirit, stop playing the fool with me. Give back my pipe at once.'

Half laughing, half astonished, I stopped to listen for a reply. First there was silence. Then came Ting's piping treble, remarking unconcernedly: 'There, madam. The pipe's back now. What a troublesome fellow he is!'

'Silence! You rabbit's child. How dare you talk about Mr Fox-Spirit like that! Last night when I took my shoes off to ease my corns, he hid one of them somewhere for so long that I nearly died with longing to go across to the urinal. He's never really spiteful like that unless you've been disrespectful to him.'

'Yes, madam.'

After that, silence fell again and I walked on to my own courtyard.

In the morning, while one of the *kungyü* servants was dusting my room, I questioned him about the matter.

'Oh yes, Laoyeh,' he answered promptly. 'There's a *huhsien* there all right. That's why Chang T'ait'ai gets the room so cheaply. Some tenants are afraid to stay there, although they've no call to be. But he is a bit tiresome, the old joker. The last people to rent that room, a married couple with a six-month baby, only stayed three days after paying for a whole month in advance. They could hardly turn their eyes away without the baby's being lifted off the bed and put down somewhere else. Still, it was always done gently. No harm in it at all.'

'Heavens! How incredible! What does this *huhsien* look like?'

'How should I know, Laoyeh? He's not seen; he's not heard. It's just that things go flying about the room. That's how we know he's at home.'

To Bill Luton, my story must have seemed as commonplace as an account of some neighbour child's pranks. He capped it with several more astonishing ones followed by a ghastly tale concerning a remorseless, deadly *huliching*.

'About ten years ago,' he began, 'I was living out in the country close to Tsinghua University. One summer, a student living in one of the hostels there died rather suddenly. According to the university authorities, this poor guy, P'an, had been suffering from a bad case of T.B., but had successfully concealed it from them until a few days before his death. The men sharing his hostel, while confirming this, hinted pretty broadly that the illness had been aggravated by the guy's uncontrolled indulgence with a lovely but mysterious prostitute. This was only part of the truth as they saw it, but you must have noticed how careful students are these days to avoid being thought superstitious. Thorough-going sceptics, most of them—or so they like you to think. In spite of this, a third and more sinister account of the kid's death soon began to circulate. I guess it was pretty widely believed, though no one liked to admit it. People said that young P'an had had a sizzling affair with a girl who made out she was the daughter of a farmer living in the neighbouring village. They often used to meet after dusk in one of those deserted one-room temples which speckle the countryside on both sides of the road leading to the Summer Palace. You must often have seen them—no bigger than farmers' cottages, but with dark-red walls. Anyway, she made love to this guy, P'an, with an ardour that sent him right off his head. As a sickly guy, he had been guarding what remained of his health by eating special foods, sleeping long hours and things like that. Yet, with this girl, he behaved like a healthy young peasant.

'Then, so the story runs, came an evening when he reached the temple a long while before the agreed time. While waiting for her, he sat somewhere in the gloom of the shrine-room gazing across the fields, which, at that time of the year, always look pretty good in the after-glow of sunset. Though it was still light enough to see everything outside, it had already grown dark within the temple itself when he heard what sounded like the scuffling of a large rat. Looking down, he was just in time to see a very small golden fox struggle over the high stone lintel of the doorway. It was such a pretty creature that he held his breath for fear of frightening it away; but it soon scurried into the thick darkness on the far side of the altar. The next thing he heard scared the pants off him. It was the voice of his girl humming a tune under her breath. Though he had been watching the only door all the time and was quite positive she hadn't come in, there she was some-where on the other side of the altar!

'He had heard enough stories about *huliching* to tumble to a pretty god-awful conclusion, so he got shakily to his feet, meaning to make a run for it. Too late, of course. She saw him in time, ran towards him and threw her arms round his neck.

'After that? You know what they say about a *huliching*. She is irresistible. A guy who has once tasted her embrace is beyond saving. I doubt if P'an tried very hard to run away. You may know too well that a *huliching*'s ardour conceals a vampire greed for your energy; that she will suck your life from you without pity. You may realize death will come within a matter of weeks or days, but you can neither save yourself nor bring yourself to ask help from others. Every day you think: "Tonight I'll go to her for the last time and, tomorrow, take the first train to Nanking—anywhere that's a hell of a distance away." But you never go. It's always tomorrow and tomorrow, until, sucked dry of the last drop of energy, you stagger or are carried home to die.'

I shivered. Bill Luton, in relating this gruesome story, had passed from smiling matter-of-factness to a grisly solemnity. No longer a raconteur striving for effect, he had become a man powerfully moved by his own words. I was glad when, of his own accord, he decided that one such story was enough and turned to pleasanter things. When, after tea, he was strolling with me to the gate, I glanced uneasily at the fox-tower, of which the squat upper storey emerged from a clump of white-flowered shrubs called *Yehlaihsiang*. Their heavy perfume arises only towards nightfall, so I must have imagined the funereal scent of lilies which seemed to be emanating from them then. Bill, noticing how the tower drew my eyes, remarked reassuringly:

'The guy living there, if he exists, likes to tease people—nothing more than that.'

From the end of his lane, I took a rickshaw straight to the House of Springtime Congratulations, for I naturally preferred visiting Jade Flute at an hour when she would not be called upon to entertain two or three patrons at a time, leaving a substitute to talk to me while she was laughing with somebody in one of the other rooms. My visit that evening was my fifth. All of them had been pure joy, except that I found it hard to behave intelligently, that is to say without disclosing too much of the fever-state of my feelings; a part of me which remained sane warned me that, if she guessed how close I was to idolatrous worship of her, she would either take fright or else feel something like contempt for her mad foreigner. Now that I had nearly qualified for full intimacy, the matron avoided popping in and out after bringing the tea and fruit, as had been her annoying wont during my earlier visits.

Jade Flute, herself, received me laughing with pleasure and at once drew me on to the bed, where we took up half-sitting positions with our backs against the high bolster, and gave ourselves over to the same sort of minor intimacies which precede the consummation of love among respectable people in the West, though she took care to ensure my observance of a tiresome restraint. If I exceeded certain well-defined limits, she would slip away from me and attend to the teapot or hand me a slice of orange.

'Third Father Wang, you look troubled. Is anything the matter?'

'Not really. This afternoon I heard a grim story about a vampire-fox which may have affected my spirits.'

I said this to avoid having to tell her how near to madness this constant restraint was driving me, but she took it as a joke.

'Ha-ha-ha-ha! So that's it! Come now, confess you are terrified of me. You believe I am a *huliching* and you are longing to tear yourself away. Poor Third Father Wang, you are doomed. Be sure I'll never let you go. You may resign yourself to a beautiful death. Life is short for those who love a vampire-fox, but *oh*, so exciting!'

I could not help laughing. As she spoke, she parodied a vampire luring its victim so amusingly that, in my delight, I tried to seize hold of her. Eluding me with a graceful leap, she stood up laughing and went across to the table to pour me another bowl of tea so that my hands should be better occupied.

'You should know, Third Father Wang, that it is a sin to embrace before sunset. The sun will be offended and withdraw its light from the world.'

'The sun has set!' I cried.

'Not set; still setting.'

'Then I shall come tomorrow at midnight. How's that?'

Her back was towards me as she poured the tea, but she turned her head and gave me a sidelong glance of consent which set my heart racing. To tease me, she replied:

'I am afraid Ma [the matron] will not agree. We are not permitted to entertain foreign dev— your honourable countrymen alone and after midnight, you know.'

'You said yourself I am a *Chungkuo T'ung*.'

'Yes, Father. Do you think Ma knows what that is?'

'Anyway, I shall come.'

'Thank you, Third Father Wang. I shall tell Ma to expect you.'

On the following night there was, of course, no difficulty at all. After waiting an age between the departure of the last of her guests and the completion of her midnight snack, followed by all those mysterious rituals which every woman insists on performing before going to bed even though her mate is ready to swoon with longing, I at last had her for my own. Adoring her as the one and only lovable girl in the world, I passed with her what still remains the happiest night of my life. Jade Flute cannot possibly have realized that the pleasure she had dispensed so often and to so many men was, for me, something perfect, something unique and (of its kind) never to be equalled throughout my life. Even now I have no fear of the mockery these words must excite: however sordid the reality of those surroundings and circumstances, they were transformed for me as by multi-coloured fires. The depth and sincerity of my own feelings, joined with Jade Flute's generosity in giving me infinitely more than the perfunctory services I had paid for, drove all mere parody of love and beauty from our bed.

.     .     .     .     .

As Chu had stayed away from his lessons with me several times in succession, I went with some misgiving to call at his house for news of him. The family had long ago exchanged their ancestral palace for a shabby, tumble-down place in the north city, consisting of eight small and dismal rooms opening upon a single courtyard. Here seventeen people lived in a mixture of squalor and magnificence, their poverty matched by their aristocratic aversion to routine activities. The paper windows were torn, the courtyard full of rotting leaves, the gutters choked with rubbish. On the other hand, the potted flowers looked tenderly cared for, the insufficient meals often included expensive seasonal delicacies, and the crudely fashioned, unpolished wooden furniture taken over with the house stood leg to leg with lacquered cabinets inlaid with ivory and semi-precious stones.

Their one retainer, grown old and wrinkled in the family's service, having opened the gate with a sweeping bow, preceded me across the courtyard walking slowly with a ritual pretence of tremendous haste. He announced me to his master in impressive high-pitched singsong tones as though I were one of the Imperial Tutors or Privy Councillors who had called upon the family in the days when he was still a serving-boy.

Chu's father received me with nicely graded courtesy. As a 'friend from a distant quarter' and as his son's tutor, I had a right to cere-monious and solicitous regard; but, as a youth much less than half his age and more especially as a barbarian presumed ignorant of the more intricate niceties of social intercourse, I need not be pressed more than once or twice to seat myself farther into the room than my host. Needless to say, when tea was served, we both employed two hands to raise the bowls to our lips and I took care to sip in unison with him. A lengthy exchange of compliments and polite conversation took place before I ventured to enquire why Tê-Ku had not been to see me since that day at Bill Luton's.

'My fourth son has gone away for a few weeks to stay with his Third Aunt near the Jade Springs. He has been a little unwell lately. Naturally, he should have called upon you to take leave, but he left somewhat hurriedly. Permit me to offer his excuses to his teacher.'

Though certainly aware that I knew of the tragedy which had occasioned Tê-Ku's illness and retirement to the country, he permitted no grief to mar the blandness of his features or the even tones of his voice. Still less did he introduce a topic requiring expressions of grief from a guest with whom he was not intimately acquainted. If his youngest son had been closer to me, he might have acted differently; but Tê-Lin had only sat in occasionally during his elder brother's lessons and had not even in a formal sense become my pupil. There seemed no reason to burden me with the family sorrow. I did wonder if perhaps he were waiting for me to offer condolences; I think I should have done so had I been less unsure of how to begin, especially as the cause of death had been suicide partly attributable to the old man's having lost his temper with the boy. With so much difference between Chinese and Western concepts of propriety, when in doubt, I usually waited in silence for a lead.

Old Mr Chu pressed me to stay for lunch, but as this would have involved keeping the rest of the family waiting while we two ate together, and as I did not want my bowl to be loaded with the very best of whatever food they had, I found some excuse for declining. I had already stood up to take leave when I noticed that the parrot cage hanging as usual over Mr Chu's desk was empty. Recalling his fondness for an ancient and almost featherless bird, I enquired where it had gone. Mr Chu heaved a sigh.

'Poor Ying-Ko is dead. He succumbed to opium-deprivation.'

'Excuse me, Chu Hsienshêng, *what* did you say was the cause of death?'

'Ah, you are surprised, P'u Hsienshêng, and no wonder. You see, Ying-Ko had shared my study—here and in our former home—for forty years. Last month, upon the advice of my doctors, I passed a few weeks in hospital to be cured of my addiction to opium. Up to then, I had smoked in here twice a day for rather more than fifteen years. In a small room like this, the smoke-clouds are inclined to hang near the ceiling for hours on end and the deceased bird could not avoid inhaling them. No doubt he enjoyed the experience immensely. It was the same with the mice behind those bookcases. A few days after I entered the hospital, they died off, one after another, but nobody guessed the reason. When Ying-Ko also fell sick, I allowed two weeks to pass before thinking to order my servant to puff a little smoke into its face morning and evening. By then it was too late. Aiyah! I feel lonely without my bird!'

In this matter, I suppose he saw no reason to conceal his feelings. A guest's pleasure would scarcely be spoiled by the death of another man's bird. However, it did occur to me while I was riding home in a rickshaw that his words and the tragic sigh accompanying them had conceivably referred obliquely to the death of Tê-Lin, his son.

Something much more memorable was to happen to me at the end of that day. Towards midnight, I paid what may have been my fourth or fifth post-nuptial visit to Jade Flute. Upon the night of our coming together I had experienced a bliss seen even at the time as being of too high an order ever to be completely recapturable; but nothing had happened since to make me suspect that I loved her with less than 'all my heart'. Yet, upon this night, the golden dream was so perceptibly tarnished as to shock me into perceiving that it might presently fade altogether; that Jade Flute, from being queen of goddesses, might again appear to me as an ordinary girl, always to be thought of with affection but less certainly always to be adored. The suspicion broke upon me with the force of a frightful heresy, something to be driven instantly and for ever from my mind, but which, despite fierce opposition, lurked still upon its rim, impossible to destroy. With shame, I grew to feel that my love never had been an altruistic and all-consuming passion, justifying its existence under sordid circumstances by its own high nobility.

Lying awake by her side, I found myself appalled. However powerfully I resisted it, the knowledge that my love had already begun to spiral down towards its own extinction was now rooted in my mind. Though I could not foresee the speed with which this would happen, I was already faced with a dim realization that ignorance, inexperience and childish romanticism had combined to lure me into passing off a long-suppressed yearning of the loins as a true yearning of the heart, thus mistaking swiftly withering autumn leaves for the purest gold! Perhaps the shame of that self-deception would be with me yet, if I had not one day come to know that a true yearning of the heart is something no mortal woman can ever wholly satisfy!

# 5

# A Taoist Sage, a Hermaphrodite and a Dissolute Singing-Master

THE first winter snow was falling in soft heavy flakes and lay within the lanes already ankle-deep. The sheen of yellow, green and blue upon the roofs of palaces and temples had been obscured by a layer of pure white crystal. The pines and elms bore a glistening burden gathered since the night. Much of the city lay wrapped in profound silence, for the soft shoes of the furred and blue-quilted figures hastening back to the warmth of their stoves fell soundlessly upon the snow. More than ever, Peking seemed a city where ghosts might walk with men.

A scarf across my face, my raised fur collar caressing the full ear-flaps of my hat, I made my way through a gate in the east wall of the city and hastened past a fleet of tightly curtained hooded carts to the yawning gateway of the Tung Yüeh Temple. Since Pao had chanced to bring his Taoist kinsman to my house, I had spent several afternoons drinking tea with Yang Taoshih in his cell and being initiated by his conversation into a view of life scarcely changed since Lao-tsü rode beyond the Pass almost two and a half millennia ago. Now on this wintry afternoon I found him seated near a charcoal brazier, patiently instructing a child acolyte in the mystery of breathing the all-pervading Life-Force into his 'veins'. The child, whose ruddy cheeks, smooth almond-coloured skin and brilliant eyes made him beautiful enough for the progeny of a Taoist Immortal, was more docile and attentive than intelligent. His master did me special honour by dispensing with formality and waving me to sit near the brazier while he continued his efforts to drag an unpromising pupil into realms transcending life and death.

'Don't be so rigid, little rabbit. Keep your back straight; sit as

91

though your spinal column were a straight line reaching to the top of your head, but *don't strain*! You were not conceived by the wedlock of iron bars! Sit naturally. Be alert, but relaxed. *Aiyah*, that's better. Now breathe.'

I watched the boy inhale slowly through his nostrils until his lungs were almost full and then check the movement by imperceptibly slowing the intake of air till it ceased. He managed to hold his breath for what seemed to me a creditably long time and then, at a nod from the Taoist, he let it go.

'No, no, no! Not like that. You are not a fire-carriage-head [railway-engine]. Let the air come out slowly, as slowly as it went in. And breathe out silently.'

However often the exercise was repeated, the poor child could never prevent his breath escaping with a hiss. Soon even his normal breathing became laboured and his cheeks redder than their natural colour; so the Taoist dismissed him, saying:

'That is enough for today, you little devil. You may not achieve immortality, but you can always find a rich man to employ you—as a human bellows!'

When the boy left us, he was almost crying with vexation and remembered only just in time not to run out of the room without turning to bow to his teacher. Waiting until the door had shut behind him, Yang Taoshih broke into a grin.

'What a pupil! Charming, willing, but hopeless! No, don't get up; I'm just getting the kettle-tripod. There, now we can make tea. You shall taste the white-leafed tea of Yunnan. Well, *pengyu* [friend], how are things with you? Will you take rice with us? Ah, I forgot. You like to eat late and sleep late. Here, we dine at six, go to bed early and rise at three-thirty. But don't disturb yourself; there is plenty of time before dinner.'

While he was putting me at my ease, I glanced about me at the familiar but ever-delightful cell. To reach it from the main gate, I had passed literally through hell. The great court of the temple was surrounded by thirty or forty adjacent doorless rooms containing life-size representations of the masters and denizens of the various hells—cruelly calm and self-possessed judges, ferocious lictors with hideous animal or goblin faces, miserable victims shivering before the judgement seats or being led away by demon-tormentors to be frozen, grilled, fried in oil, sliced, disembowelled, dismembered, impaled, sawn in half, ground to dust, pressed on spikes, or tantalized with foods and liquids that turned to fire at the touch of their lips—each punishment logically related to the nature of the misdeeds listed on the placards tied to their backs. Such sights must have struck terror into the hearts of believers, to others they were either laughable or disgusting. But, here in this room, everything contributed to my understanding of the concept of life which sees every object as precious, in that all things are pervaded by the ineffable and infinitely mysterious *Tao*. With growing pleasure, my eyes took in the antique bronze brazier and the pumpkin-shaped kettle standing above it on a spindle-legged tripod; the white tea-bowls of eggshell-thin porcelain placed on a table of dark-red lacquer so cracked with age that it was patterned like an untaut fishing-net; the tracery of the lattice windows with tiny panes formed of translucent mother-of-pearl; the brick *k'ang* (sleeping platform) blanketed beneath a thick Central Asian carpet patterned with dark-blue flowers and foliage against a creamy-white background; and the time-mellowed wall-scrolls depicting sages lost in contemplation of nature's mysteries, or gambolling with bizarrely coloured mythological beasts—half recognizable as old friends inhabiting the borderlands of my own consciousness.

While drinking my third bowl of tea, I said: 'Tell me, Yang Taoshih; I have often wished to ask why the greatest of Peking's Taoist temples has to be disfigured by that macabre spectacle of hell. Yours is a sublime doctrine; where is the need for such—may I call it "crudity"?'

He smiled roguishly, eyes puckered and lips curved on the brink of laughter.

'Human nature, P'u Hsienshêng. People like it that way. Tell them they are holy and beautiful, that every one of them is a living embodiment of the sacred *Tao*, and they will think you are a stupid fellow, or smell your breath to see if you are drunk. But tell them they are worse than devils or hungry ghosts and only fit for hell, then they will respect your powers of perception and ask you privately to reveal the special tastes of hell's judges so they will know how to bribe them. Your honourable countrymen are, if you will permit my saying so, no better than our own people. In my youth, I went for a year to a Christian school where, besides learning world history and algebra, I was taught that we are miserable sinners conceived and born in sin! What a travesty of truth! Our teachers—an Englishwoman and a young girl who insisted she came from *So-ko-lan* [Scotland] and not England—were entirely ignorant of man's divine nature! With people like that everywhere, what to do? You must make a peasant believe he is at death's door before you can persuade him to call a doctor.'

'So real Taoists don't believe in hell at all?'

'There are Taoists and Taoists. I myself do believe in hell. Hell is each moment of this life until you recognize your own divinity— until you've learnt to stop grasping and thirsting and longing for this or that and trying to rid yourself of something else, like monkeys squabbling over empty nutshells or vengefully biting their own tails.'

With a pair of long iron chopsticks, he added more charcoal to the brazier. Then I asked my second question.

'I was fortunate enough just now to watch you setting an acolyte on the road to immortality; but in my ignorance I saw him as a small boy trying so hard to hold back his breath that he ended up breathless and sorry for himself. In my humble country, too, children are taught deep breathing, but only with a view to expanding their lungs for health's sake. You, I understand, look upon breath control as the royal road to transcending life itself. I find that puzzling. Also I'm puzzled by something you said at our second or third meeting about breathing with the *veins*! Would you care to explain something of this to me?'

He did not answer at once, for I had placed him in the impossible position of one called upon to explain in a few words something that requires the gradual building up of a whole background of fresh concepts and ideas before it can make sense. Presently he remarked mildly that the scope of my question was rather wide and again withdrew into silence. At last he said:

'As you know, P'u Hsienshêng, all things and all beings are permeated by the *Tao*—the Great Ultimate upon which each and all depend for their existence. Nothing is outside or apart from it. Unhappily, for certain reasons, men remain ignorant of their exalted nature. All of this I have explained to you before. In a conventional sense, some things are seen as more solid, more lasting than others; it is harder to comprehend their essential fluidity. Their seeming solids blind us to the true state of spontaneous being expressing itself in an endless and iridescent stream of flux, like rainbows dancing upon the spray of a waterfall. So we have come to believe in *things*, to put our

faith in a selected few of them, to cling to some, to abhor others—
arbitrarily. Now the great *Tao*, as you know, divides into *yin* [negative]
and *yang* [positive]; and these, by infinite combinations and permuta-
tions, produce all the myriads of seemingly separate objects, concepts,
processes and all the rest. Among them, one of the most mysterious,
and certainly the most potent in leading us to awareness of our true
state, is the *ch'i*. Because the word *ch'i* is commonly used also for "air"
and "breath", the vulgar suppose that our breathing exercises are
wholly concerned with the inhalation and exhalation of breath. In
truth, they are not. Owing to the subtle connection between *Ch'i*, the
Life-Force, and *ch'i*, the breath, such exercises lead not merely to the
inner circulation of air by means of the lungs and to important changes
in the rhythm of ordinary breathing, but also to an increased absorption
of *Ch'i*, the Life-Force, which circulates by invisible channels conveniently called veins or nerves and not to be confused with their
grosser counterparts. Concerning these veins, I can tell you no more.
Such knowledge is given only to those who have prepared themselves
for instruction by a systematic ordering of their lives which you, if
you will excuse my saying so, have not begun.'

His remarks about *Ch'i*, the Life-Force, did not seem at all fantastic
to me, for I recalled that in so many languages the words for 'spirit',
'spirited', 'inspiration' and so forth are similarly related to those
meaning 'air' or 'breath'. It may be that the ancients in various parts
of the world had an intuitive knowledge of the connection between the
air we breathe physically and the mysterious spirit underlying concrete
forms. So instead of asking him embarrassing questions he was not
prepared to answer, I next enquired about the results of Taoist
breathing exercises.

'As to that,' he answered willingly enough, 'I can offer you a
choice of several traditions. The more popular one teaches that we
achieve immortality in this body and mount to the realms portrayed
on these wall-scrolls—a paradise of mountain peaks, convoluted
rocks, waterfalls, bamboo-groves, pine-forests, clouds and rainbows,
where dragons, phoenixes and griffins shall be our playmates and
laughing nymphs will fan the charcoal beneath our tea-kettles and
pewter wine-pots. There, if we are so minded, we can play chess with
the lives of mortals for stakes, or seek a further degree of immortality
by compounding the elixir of life according to the recipe guarded from
men by Tsang O, Goddess of the Moon. It may be you have heard

that when our Taoist poet, Li T'ai-Po, leapt into the T'ungting Lake to embrace the autumn moon's reflection he was not drowned as some have thought, but carried to heaven, with pennants waving and banners streaming, by a team of immortal dolphins.'

'Yes, indeed. There is a biography of him which describes him as undergoing a purifying transformation of the flesh and mounting skywards with the dolphins to delight the Immortals with his poems and wine-inspired drollery. But do you believe in this kind of immortality?'

'I am inclined to think we must first die. A human body is tiresome. I shall be glad to be rid of mine.'

'And then?'

'If, by opening up our subtle veins to the influence of the *Ch'i* and by successful concentration upon that secret gateway to knowledge lying close behind the forehead, we fan our vital spirit till it glows; then, after living here in perfect health for anything between a hundred and a hundred and fifty years, we shall survive death in a special sense hardly to be comprehended and impossible to put into words.'

'How old are you?' I asked with seeming irrelevance.

'Forty-eight by your count, forty-nine by ours.'

'I enquired because something you said reminded me of a Taoist called Milky Way dwelling in a sea-girt hermitage not far from Hong Kong. He displayed the athletic powers of a youth of twenty, his appearance was that of a man less than forty, but I know for a fact that he was approaching his seventieth year. Since meeting him, I have never dared try to guess a Taoist adept's age from his appearance. For all I know, you might be thirty or a hundred and thirty.'

It was close on six o'clock and time to go. I recoiled from the thought of exchanging the drowsy warmth of Yang Taoshih's cell for the biting cold outside, but I had sent a note to the White Russian who had once offered to sell me Crim wine, telling him I would call round at half past six and take away a dozen bottles, to be used at a party I was to give the following evening. Though I had not seen him again since he had accosted me in the park, I had chanced to find his card in the pocket of my jacket. Half an hour's ride in a rickshaw ineffectually quilted against the cold brought me to his gateway, shivering uncontrollably, my teeth chattering and my fingers frozen stiff.

An old Russian woman who answered the bell led me across an

The porcelain temple upon a hill
in the Pei Hai Park

A ceremonial archway
in the Pei Hai Park

One of Peking's countless pairs of stone lions in the Pei Hai Park

unkempt, snow-blotched courtyard into a stuffy and over-decorated sitting-room where she left me to wait for her master. In the centre of the room was an iron stove from which a curly iron pipe carried some of the heat into the room beyond: a superfluity of carpets, curtains and hangings added to the fug. In spite of the tropical temperature, I had, after removing my overcoat, to beat my hands against my sides to restore the full use of my fingers. Walking impatiently about the room, I glanced without much interest at the dozens of enlarged photographs displayed between the hangings. At first I found them too drearily monotonous to be worthy of much attention, but presently my curiosity was aroused by something unexpected which all of them had in common. My first impression that they formed a dull collection of half-length portraits of engaged or recently married couples had been wrong; for, though all of them depicted couples standing cheek to cheek or demonstrating mutual affection in some similarly conventional way, the woman adored by these different men was in every case the same; and it seemed impossible for any young woman to have been engaged or married several dozen times! Of the men, some were Europeans, others Chinese who mostly wore military uniforms with badges of high rank. The girl was a dark-headed Russian beauty with eyes expressive of unlimited ardour and a smile which revealed exceptionally small, perfectly formed teeth.

It was her teeth which first drew my attention to the resemblance between this unknown girl and the man I had come to see; and when at last he came running into the room, arms outstretched in welcome, I saw that the likeness was absolutely striking. Clad in a voluminous dressing-gown of violent purple, his chin freshly shaved and his long hair thrown back from his forehead, he caused me a moment's embarrassment because I half thought he was a girl who had mistaken me for an expected lover. But it was Alexander Mikhailovitch all right, inexplicably delighted to see me.

'Your note has told me that your dear name is John,' he said, pressing me on to a chintz-covered sofa and plumping himself down close beside me. 'So I shall like to call you Ivan until we are loving friends, then Vania or Vanushka. Me you will call Shura, as everybody does. Alexander Mikhailovitch? Who is he? No one know. Shura? All Peking know Shura.'

Overwhelmed by his effusiveness, I drew as far away as I dared from the half-embrace in which he held me, but lacked the courage to lift his podgy arm from my shoulder where it had settled as soon as my neck was out of reach.

'Yes,' I said, hurrying to stress the reason for my visit. 'Did my note reach you in time for you to have the wine ready?'

'Surely, surely. You may take six dozen, twelve dozen if you have such desire, and at costing price only. My east room is chocking-blocking with them. But first we shall talk, you and I. I have been awaiting so long. He will come, I say to myself, not tomorrow maybe, but in a week or two weeks. Shura, be patient to wait, I said. And when you have not come, I tell myself that oh-my-god he has lost my name-card, that I am *idiot* not to ask where he live! Now today, dear friend, you are really come. We must drink in celebration. Crème de menthe is good, yes?'

I found myself in a quandary. I wanted urgently to leave that stuffy, boudoir-like room, to hide myself from that absurdly affection-ate creature, especially as he seemed likely to capture me in full embrace at any moment; but it would have been too heartless to wither his ridiculous pleasure in my visit so abruptly. His demonstrative behaviour made the hairs on my arms stand on end, but it was too obviously the result of genuine feeling to be just revolting. His naked candour at least deserved a better reward than a churlish refusal to stay in the room with him. While not at all homosexually inclined, I have never belonged to the punch-'em-on-the-nose school of normality. However, I dare not delay making my own feelings clear to him. Moving still farther towards the end of the sofa, I said:

'I suppose the pretty girl in those photos is your sister? How charming she looks.'

'Vania, why are you absurd? You have seen that it is me, Shura.'

'I see. Well, would you mind telling me if—er—she is a man or you are a woman?'

'Ivan, you are so difficult. You speak like there are two Shuras. Man? Woman? I am both!'

'That is not a very clever answer.'

'But it is simply true. I shall prove it to you—medically!'

He jumped to his feet as though to perform a 'medical' demon-stration there and then. I had half risen in protest when I realized he was busying himself over a tray where a liqueur bottle and glasses stood ready. By the time he had handed me a third of a tumbler of crème de menthe, I had decided what must be said and begun to gabble out the words, avoiding his eyes for fear of the pain I might see there.

'Look, Shura. I don't really care what you are—man or woman. Please understand that when I came here for the wine I had no idea you had been anxiously expecting me to come round and—er . . . By all means let's have a drink together. Only please be a good chap and understand that——'

A subdued voice from Shura, now busily engaged in pouring himself a second drink, interrupted me.

'I know, Vania, I know. Please not to say. Always it is the same nowadays, but nearly always. Ah, if you see me before when——enough! We shall drink to a pure friendship, yes? What Englishmen, not knowing Plato much, so funnily call platonic, yes?'

Shura was very good. Contrary to my expectation, I never suffered the smallest embarrassment from him again, neither on that evening nor during any of our subsequent encounters. He must have discovered that people he liked would vanish from his life if he persisted in treating them like flies wooed by the spider. Months later I learnt his unfortunate history, partly from his own lips and partly from Bill Luton.

Shura had been born a girl and had grown past puberty apparently quite normal. During her twelfth year her father, a Tsarist official, had been killed in the Russian Revolution, so Shura had fled her home in Tomsk and joined a party of refugees whose wanderings brought them at last to Peking. From the age of fifteen she had, like so many of her countrywomen, been compelled to earn her living as a cabaret dance-hostess; and, being exceptionally beautiful, had for several years enjoyed phenomenal success. Among her patrons—mostly Chinese officers and a few Russians who at that time still had money to spend—was a young Chinese general who actually offered to marry her. She had by then grown fond of Chinese people and willingly accepted his proposal; but, before and after her engagement, she became alarmed by the appearance of inexplicable physical changes in herself. Unhappily, these changes became so impossible to conceal that the amazed general hurriedly got himself transferred to another city; and they continued almost to the point of transforming her into a man—but not quite. According to Bill Luton, who had a reputation for uncanny knowledge of other people's secrets, Shura's exceptionally virile growth of facial hair and his well-developed feminine bust (now modestly restrained by a special garment) were not the most striking of her (now his) contradictory sex-attributes. Poor Shura, after months of grief and shame, managed to put on a cheerful expression and returned to the night-club as male cashier.

Before I left him that night, several rounds of sickly liqueur gave me the courage to enquire why he had seemed so sure that my purchase of his wine had been only a secondary object of my visit. His answer rings truer to me today than it did then.

'Vania, when your eyes see someone lovingly, if that person even give you nice smile, you easily will think you are loved the same.'

If only I had realized it, something of that sort had recently happened to me. Jade Flute's combination of good nature and professional skill had not been alone responsible for my reading into her smile feelings reciprocating my own. I had been too blind to see either of us as we really were; and when at last I half sensed the truth from the smiling dispassion with which she encountered the signs of my diminishing affection, I was inclined to blame her for having, as I thought, led me on.

At eight o'clock I felt I could leave without hurting Shura's feelings. I asked him to have the wine loaded into one rickshaw and another ordered for myself. Fluttering the sleeves of his purple dressing-gown, he protested that it was absurdly early to leave, but I managed to get away by promising to visit him at the Kavkaz Club one evening in the not too distant future.

'There, Vania, you shall see me making tête-à-tête with the cash machine,' he added bitterly. 'But for you I shall give it a cool shoulder when you come.'

.         .         .         .         .

When the snow had been falling long enough to lie thick and hard upon the ground, Dr Chang (for a reason connected with the snow which I did not understand until the feast began) sent me a large red invitation card, bidding me to dinner a couple of days later at a restaurant bearing a famous name which stood in the heart of the busy quarter beyond the Ch'ien Mên. Beneath the formal Chinese sentences, printed in gold, he had added two more in English, using ordinary blue ink—'I promise you the restaurant will be warm,' and, 'How goes the music of the flute?' Following the Chinese custom, I wrote the word *chih* (know) on the card and returned it to the messenger. It meant that I had noted the contents of the invitation, but it did not commit me to accepting or declining. However, as I was not a much-courted public man so overwhelmed with invitations as to have to circulate from restaurant to restaurant or mansion to mansion taking a course or two at the tables of as many hosts as I could manage, Dr Chang could count on my turning up.

His question about Jade Flute I was too ashamed to answer, though I had nothing worse to fear from him than an understanding smile. In those days I took myself too seriously to be able to think lightly of my own stupidity. Forced to recognize that I had been in love with nothing more than a self-created image in Jade Flute's likeness, and that a quite different but equally attractive girl could have inspired in me the same apparently exclusive passion, I felt so absurdly foolish that I blushed to think of it. My heart had been taken in by an age-old trick played by my body: while joining in the flower-house game of simulating love affairs on a miniature scale, I had forgotten that it was a game! The last bandage had been ripped from my eyes the night before Dr Chang's invitation arrived. Taken to another flower-house by some young university colleagues, I had met a girl with jasmine in her hair and a gamin-smile who, within half an hour, had managed to inspire feelings identical with those formerly aroused by Jade Flute! Too young to recognize their beauty, I regarded myself with savage contempt.

Dr Chang would have seen nothing abnormal in a young man behaving like a bee among the flowers, though he himself, contrary to popular report, had long ago passed beyond that stage of immaturity. It was Pao whose ridicule I chiefly feared, because I had more than once had the temerity to hint to him that my 'constancy' towards Jade Flute made me his superior in such matters! This was all the more ironic in that the boot was clearly on the other foot; his attachment to Kuei-Hsiang never wavered.

Of the dark and rigorously concealed side of a flower-house existence—the tragedies which drove girls into and cast them out of such places—I asked nothing and learnt little until my return to Peking many years later. My experience during those early years argued in favour of flower-houses rather than against them. At any rate they taught me some valuable (though not very well learnt) lessons, and perhaps saved me from making an even bigger fool of myself. Certainly nobody in England had been both honest enough with me and sufficiently free from prudishness to make clear the ease with which fleeting, rainbow-hued desires lead to marriages which are hell for both husband and wife. Had Jade Flute been other than a courtesan, and her company nevertheless accessible to me, I should undoubtedly have married her before discovering the dismal truth. Then the remainder of our lives would have been passed among those squalid makeshifts which follow marital disenchantment. In the West, there are no flower-houses to teach such lessons. There, on the contrary, 'romantic love' is ceaselessly vaunted in novels, films, tooth-paste advertisements and in all other available media. Self-deception is widely encouraged and, when marriage intervenes before the rainbow colours fade, couples find themselves in chains. It has often struck me as ironical that Thomas Hardy, some of whose novels movingly illustrate this theme and give such clear-cut warning to romantic lovers, was in his day accused of corrupting young readers' minds! Our parents and grandparents would have done better if they had made him compulsory reading for everyone on the brink of marriage.

.          .          .          .          .

In Peking it was the pleasant custom for professors and lecturers arriving shortly before their classes to be offered the refreshment of hot towels and glasses of tea. On the bitterly cold noon preceding Dr Chang's dinner-party, the janitor who brought them to me also handed me a note from the Department Head, Professor Lee. It was an invitation to me to join some of the prospective guests in working up a gargantuan appetite by a long walk in the snow! I was requested to meet them in a tea-house in Ch'ien Mên Wai at half past three in the afternoon.

Arriving at the tea-house full of curiosity to discover the meaning of this seemingly uncharacteristic suggestion, I learnt that we were going on an expedition to view the snowscape in the vast precincts of the Altar of Heaven. The Pekingese, glutted with so many ancient or lovely sights, seldom went out sight-seeing in the ordinary sense of the word, nor did they walk much for pleasure, but they loved to visit places where some seasonal effect of nature vied with or enhanced the beauty of the builder's art. Thus, the boats on the wilder lakes lying outside the palace gardens were in demand only when the first green of early spring touched the naked willow-branches bordering their margins; and in summer scholars travelled from fifty or a hundred miles around to write poems to the peonies flaunting their glory in the usually deserted courts of the Forbidden City. Expeditions were made to the temples peering from crannies in the Western Hills only when autumn had turned the woods about them to scarlet, bronze and gold, or when spring renewed the foliage destroyed by winter; and in the coldest weather old men braved the cruel wind to enjoy the pure-white metamorphosis of buildings and gardens lying within the city walls.

Of all Peking's enchanting sights, the beauty of the Altar of Heaven is the hardest to describe. Its sublime austerity is mocked by words. It is what it is—the most fitting architectural expression of man's highest aspirations in all the world. With Professor Lee and three of his friends, I passed through the outer gate into a forest-fringed enclosure so enormous and so mantled by silence that the great city lying all about us seemed to have vanished. No fresh snow had fallen for several days; the walls of the enclosure appeared to bound almost the whole arc of a dazzling turquoise sky. Shoes crunching the crisp snow, we emerged from the rim of trees into the great flat space surrounding the Temple of Heaven and the Altar which, lying at a distance from each other, were connected by a marble causeway. We had to visit the Temple first, just as courtiers take delight in gazing at a pretty maid of honour before and not after the Fairy Princess arrives. It is unique in that it consists of just one building—a circular hall, its dimensions dwarfed by a heavy triple-tiered roof of azure blue, which stands upon a marble platform mounted by a broad flight of balustraded steps. On that winter's afternoon, the whole of the upper tier of tiles and the outer rims of the other tiers lay hidden beneath shining carpets of snow, but the sheltered parts of the latter showed a sufficient expanse of gleaming porcelain to provide a breath-taking contrast of blue and white reflecting that of sky and snow-bound earth. I was eager to go inside and refresh my memory of the gorgeous coloured and gilded patterns ornamenting beams, pillars, walls and ceiling within; but my companions, who for once were less inclined to dawdle than I, insisted that unless we kept moving briskly the cold would injure us. So we followed the slippery ice-covered causeway running southwards towards the Altar, which formed a straight line except where it skirted a building in many ways similar to the Temple behind us, but smaller.

'Look!' said a thin-faced old man enveloped in a round fur hat, woollen scarf and gown lined with grey fox-fur. 'The Son of Heaven used to change into sacrificial robes here before approaching the Altar to make his annual report and petition to Heaven. I remember the scene so well. Thrice, in my capacity of Secretary to the Board of Rites, I was present when the Emperor Kuang Hsü performed the sacrifice.'

He fell silent, deeply moved by the sad changes which had swept the dynasty away; but his words had called up a vision. I could so clearly imagine eunuchs and officials in splendid robes thronging about me. They walked in the train of Heaven's Son as, purified by his long fast, he majestically approached the Altar to conduct his solemn communication with Heaven on behalf of all people in the world. For he alone among human beings was Heaven's true Son; he alone had the right to petition the Highest Divinity as a son petitions his father. Reflecting on the sublimity of this scene, I accompanied the others through an archway in a low circular wall and came face to face with the Altar itself, wholly unprepared for the shock I was to receive! With its three concentric circular platforms of glistening marble slabs arranged around the central slab in multiples of nine, unwalled, unroofed and thus directly open to the face of Heaven, the Altar had always seemed to me the noblest monument ever built by man. Could the Taj Mahal itself have been seen against this peerless unblemished whiteness, this unsurpassed simplicity of form, it would have seemed fussy and even tawdry! No imaginable effect of sunshine or storm could mar or enhance its perfection. Cloudless skies could not add to its mirror-like tranquillity, nor gold-rimmed black and purple storm-clouds vie with its awesome majesty. But snow! This faery edifice of spotless white rising from a wide expanse of hard, smooth snow, and framed by the tracery of snow-laden branches in the surrounding forest, seemed lost—pure whiteness lost in white purity!

I turned towards my friends, expecting their faces to reflect my disappointment. Instead, they were like men entranced. Motionless, oblivious now of the cold, they gazed in silence until at last the spell was broken by excited exclamations.

When the old man in the fox-fur gown looked round to discover my reaction, I was forced to say:

'Yao Hsienshêng, I do not understand. Why are you all so moved? I love the Altar as you do; but today it is lost, swallowed in a white brilliance equal to its own.'

'That,' he answered, 'is what we came to admire.'

'But——'

'Do you not see? Artists struggle all their lives to capture the infinite in works either great or small. At other seasons, the Altar reflects the infinite to perfection, except that it cannot suggest the concept of infinite space. Now, void rising from void, it has become a true mirror of the universe's real form. How our friend Yang Taoshih would enjoy it!'

Two of the others nodded their agreement, but Professor Lee kept silent. Knowing he had no special sympathy with such Taoistic conceptions, I asked him if he shared his friends' delight.

'Of course,' was his unexpected answer. 'It is superb. Last time I came here, the marble was solid. Now it has liquefied and overflows the park.'

With an orange sun lying close to the horizon, the black cold of a North China winter's evening gathered strength to pierce the thickest furs and a rising wind drove us back towards the outer gate. As the restaurant selected by Dr Chang was also in Ch'ien Mên Wai and scarcely a quarter of an hour's journey by rickshaw, although the dinner had been set for six o'clock, we arrived even before our host. There were to be eight of us in all, a number too small for a conventional restaurant party. The usual custom was for the host to order a 'table of food', consisting of eight or sixteen main courses and a few subsidiary dishes, for the ten or at most twelve people who could be accommodated at a round table of conventional size. For larger parties, several 'tables of food' would be ordered; but, as each would cost the same whether all the places were filled or not, it was unusual to invite fewer guests than could be accommodated. However, the dinner that night was to be of a special kind requiring no tables at all, except for the preliminary tea-drinking.

Dr Chang arrived about half an hour after us, very surprised to find us already waiting for him. As soon as the last of his other guests had had time to drink a bowl or two of tea, he ushered us not into a dining-room, as I had naturally expected, but into a courtyard where a mound of glowing pine-log embers threw a ruddy glow across the snow. The fire was surmounted by a finely meshed iron grill in the form of a dome and surrounded by a wooden platform furnished with bowls, chopsticks and various utensils. The guests were expected to stand around it, right foot supported by a low bench, left foot remaining on the ground. In reply to my enquiry as to the reason for this novel way of standing, the others could only tell me that it was part of the restaurant's tradition for this kind of feast. Under these circumstances, there was none of the usual ceremonious argument as to who was unworthy to sit where, so the meal began at once. Each of us helped himself with specially long chopsticks to a mouthful of thinly sliced beef, twirled it in a bowl of black soya sauce covered with a floating mass of raw, shredded spring onions, and held it to the grill. So thin were the slices that in a second or two the heat of the red embers had done the meat to a turn. It was eaten with hot unleavened bread supplied from the kitchens and followed, mouthful by mouthful, with thimblefuls of peculiarly potent *paikan*. The flavour of the grilled beef, which owed its exceptional quality to the fragrance of the pine-smoke, was more delicious than anything of the kind I had tasted; the blissful warmth radiating from that magic circle of crimson light seemed doubly luxurious when our eyes fell upon the foot-deep, tight-packed snow lying all about us; and our laughter rang out gaily as the *paikan* produced its beneficent effect.

I remember scarcely anything of what we talked and laughed about during that feast; even the subjects of Dr Chang's impromptu four-lined poems escape my memory. Though the surprising quantities of meat we consumed neutralized the alcohol so that no one passed beyond the happy stage, we were probably all a little drunk. Just one small passage of the conversation has remained with me. At the beginning of the feast, I noticed that most of the interstices of the grill were choked with the charred remains of earlier banquets. Addressing a podgy, jolly-looking man on my left, who was said to be the Singing-Master from Peking's most famous opera house, I said:

'Do you not think, Hsienshêng, that this grill should have been cleaned before the feast?'

'*Cleaned?*' He stared at me with open-mouthed pretence of horror until, recollecting I was a foreigner, he recovered his politeness and answered: 'This grill has not suffered a cleaning for three hundred years. I presume the attendants dust it gently every day, but were they to remove the droppings inside these spaces, this succulent beef kebab would taste no better than roasted beef cooked at home. Do not permit yourself to be alarmed, Hsienshêng. I have heard that your honourable countrymen fear germs more than the rage of malevolent demons, but consider the heat of this fire! Even demons would be cooked through in a moment. Allow me to pledge you a toast.'

Pausing while we downed our *paikan* simultaneously according to the manner of Chinese toasts, he added:

'We Chinese have always been fond of refining whatever we borrow from neighbouring peoples into something perfectly suited to our tastes. This feast, you will agree, provides us with an interesting example. The nomads beyond the Great Wall cook their primitive *K'ao Jou* [kebab] on swords or skewers held over a smoky dung fire in some windy desert. We have transformed it into this! It must be eaten amid fallen snow, that the fire may appear more red and more joy be taken in its warmth; only pine-logs impart the fragrance we desire; and to this fragrance we add the subtle flavour only obtainable from a grill preserved from rigorous cleaning throughout three centuries! Are you not reminded of those porous teapots of Fukien earthenware? It would be a crime to go beyond rinsing them lightly, for the flavour of the tea absorbed each time they are used increases their value day by day. It is said that, after constant use for twenty years, they can convert plain boiling water into a full-bodied tea. Exaggeration? I shall remember to buy a pot and, after twenty years, invite you to my poor hut to test its virtue.'

As the party broke up before nine, some of the guests wished to put their mellow state of intoxication to good use by seeking further pleasure. I was inclined to accompany Dr Chang and the Professor who were going to pass the rest of the evening in a flower-house where a long-standing flame of Dr Chang had been asked to rehearse for them some folk-music from the south. I was anxious to meet this girl, who was said to sing beautifully and to play the *chên* (metal-stringed lute) with a skill inherited from her southern ancestors. However, the podgy Singing-Master, Mr Hu, had decided otherwise.

'Chang Taifu, you must permit me to have the pleasure of entertaining this English gentleman tonight. We have become excellent friends already, so it is certain we were intimately connected in a former life. P'u Hsienshêng tells me he is fond of exploring new delights, and it is possible that my poor hut can offer him some trifling amusement in return for the pleasure his company will afford me.'

'And what is that?' enquired Professor Lee suspiciously, before the doctor could answer. 'Why are we not invited? You are surely not going to introduce him to one of your actresses, hoping to surprise him when the lovely seventeen-year-old maiden removes her make-up and discloses the features of a man in his fifties? That has been done to foreigners before and P'u Hsienshêng is too much of a Pekingese to be taken in so easily.'

'I must confess, Hsienshêng,' replied the Singing-Master equably, as though unruffled by my friend's coldness, 'that the idea had not occurred to me. It has possibilities, especially if the victim is given time to succumb to an attachment before he learns the truth. To P'u Hsienshêng, my old friend from a previous incarnation, I intend no such discourtesy. Who knows but that he was my father or my mother? Tonight I propose only a little music and conversation in surroundings which may be novel to him. I live, as perhaps you know, above the theatre.'

Though the Professor made no further objection, I noticed that while we were putting on our coats both he and Dr Chang took the Singing-Master a little to one side, where they seemed to be speaking to him rather severely. Watching in surprise, I saw the jolly fat man, face still wreathed in smiles, bob his head up and down as though in perfect agreement with them. Something he told them brought smiles to their faces, too, and all seemed well. Their farewell bows expressed the proper degree of mutual esteem.

Two rickshaw-pullers padding side by side over snow too crisp to be a hindrance drew us swiftly to a theatre not far from the restaurant. Warm from the *paikan* and wrapped in furs, we gave the cold no time to seep into our bones. Instead of taking me through the main entrance, with its profusion of coloured electric bulbs, the Singing-Master led me round to a smaller doorway giving on to the theatre from behind. Inside the two-storey building, we were jostled by actors in full costume bustling excitedly to and from the stage. This atmosphere, far from being novel to me, reminded me of my visits back-stage in several London theatres. Theatre people have in common something stronger than any racial tie. Climbing a steep flight of stairs and walking to the end of a corridor, we passed through a doorway thickly curtained against the cold, and entered a room where calm prevailed. Even so, its general untidiness and the colourful odds and ends with which it was littered were as eloquent of the theatre as the muffled wail of fiddles and crash of gongs reaching us through intervening floor and walls.

Invited to sit down, I perched myself ceremoniously upon the extreme edge of a blackwood divan, as wide as it was long, my feet and knees pressed politely together and my body half turned towards Mr Hu, who was taking his seat beside me. Immediately he exclaimed:

'Old friend from a previous life, why stand on ceremony? Are you not feeling the weight of that fine dinner? Be at ease. Lie back. Rest yourself. You'll find no gentle scholars here.'

We reclined sideways against some hard square pillows, so that we faced each other across a miniature table placed in the centre of the great divan. Just then two girls came hurrying in. They were so pretty and so neat that I should have risen to greet them as members of the family if their single plaits and short jackets had not proclaimed them attendants of some sort. Bobbing their heads, they chanted in unison: 'Laoyeh, you have returned,' after which they busied themselves bringing tea and sweetmeats to the little table. Then, while one of them remained in attendance, the other was sent to find someone called Little Wang.

'This girl's not bad, is she?' said Mr Hu, patting the remaining maid lightly on the bottom as she bent to pour his tea.

'Laoyeh,' protested the girl, smiling broadly. 'What will this gentleman think?'

'P'u Hsienshêng is free to think what he likes,' he chuckled. 'Besides, who asked you to speak, you little she demon? Why are there only two of you tonight? Where are the other two idle-bones? When I bring home a distinguished guest, you should all be here to attend to his needs. Call them at once.'

'Excuse me, Laoyeh. You kept Third Sister and Fourth Sister up during the whole of last night. Today, you were in and out all the time. You must allow them *some* time to sleep, otherwise they——'

'Silence, you devil-girl. Here comes Little Wang. We wish to hear no more from you.'

The girl pouted and glanced jealously towards the door which had just opened to admit a handsome youth of fourteen or fifteen carrying a fiddle of the kind called *hu ch'in*. In his brand-new gown of quilted blue cloth, he looked softly handsome enough to pass for a girl. Apparently knowing what was expected of him, he sat down upon a stool without waiting for instructions and, fiddling vigorously, burst into song. I knew just enough of Peking opera music to realize he was displaying extraordinary virtuosity, but not enough to enjoy the performance. His powerful falsetto and the thin screech of the *hu ch'in* were too foreign to my ear; they made me regret I was missing the easily enjoyable folksongs to which my friends were probably listening at that moment. However, the Singing-Master seemed pleased with Little Wang; besides rapping his fingers on the table in time to the music, he now and then went so far as to shout encouragement; so I, incapable of jerking fingers or knee in time with such a complicated rhythm, took care to shout an enthusiastic '*Hao!*' whenever my host gave the lead. The song reached its climax so long after I had begun praying for the end that I was willing to risk any degree of discourtesy rather than be compelled to sit through another. Only God knew how many Little Wangs, Little Ch'êns and Little Ch'angs might be brought in to display their talents. In reply to the Singing-Master's look of enquiry, I said frankly:

'Hu Hsienshêng, I feel greatly honoured that the star pupil of a renowned Singing-Master has sung especially for me. I am deeply grateful to both of you for the performance. But my Western ears are so untrained that such artistry is wasted on me.'

Little Wang's face at once broke into a shy, understanding grin. Seeing him not at all offended, the girl standing behind him smiled sourly. She looked good-natured, but her face for some reason had registered malicious pleasure while I was speaking the words she hoped would spoil his triumph. Obviously she hated seeing him serene and untroubled. My confession also perturbed Mr Hu, but this I think was only because he had to cast about in his mind for some other means of entertaining a difficult guest. Having hindered me from joining Dr Chang, he was obliged to find some means of making my visit worth while. Suddenly, with eyes puckered and plump face creased into a grin, he barked two short orders.

'Little rabbit Wang may go. Precious Orchid, you may bring those things in now.' Then, as they hurried to obey, he turned to me and added: 'Do you care at all for opium? Have you ever smoked it?'

'Never,' I answered. 'I once knew of a parrot that died of opium deprivation, and I have a friend in Canton who cured himself after twenty years of addiction solely by practising some Buddhist methods of mind-control. I believe that amounted, in the eyes of the doctors, to something not far short of a miracle, but somebody there told me only an addict could fully appreciate how utterly miraculous it was.'

Again the Singing-Master's face fell. Unwilling to disappoint him a second time, and in fact quite eager for this new experience, I hastened to say:

'Of course, if you happen to have some opium, I shall be delighted to try it.'

I had guessed the nature of Precious Orchid's errand correctly. She returned with an oblong tray containing a small oil-lamp protected by a peculiarly shaped glass chimney and a thick pipe about two feet long. The latter was made of wood with an ivory mouth-piece at one end and a porcelain bowl projecting from the stem about six inches from the other. There were also some mysterious implements whose purpose was not yet clear to me.

'Do you often smoke, Hu Hsienshêng?' I enquired.

He was now stretched out at full length with only his head supported by the bolster. Breaking off a segment of what looked like a stick of black toffee, he impaled it upon a sort of knitting-needle as he answered:

'Not often enough to risk becoming addicted. It is good, though, to smoke a pipe after a heavy dinner. It lightens the stomach.'

With practised movements, he held the point of the needle to the flame, causing the opium to sizzle merrily. When it was cooked, he formed it into a pill by rolling it against a square of ivory fixed to a silver stem, and pressed this pill upon a pea-sized hole in the centre of the covered-in pipe-bowl. Finally, holding the pipe with both hands so that the opium came close to the flame of the lamp, he inhaled the smoke with a prolonged hissing noise until his lungs were full. Expelling it slowly so that it rose in the air like a cloud, he remarked:

'P'u Hsienshêng, you must be patient. When you have watched me several times, so that you know exactly how to hold the pipe and how to inhale, you shall try some yourself.'

Privately I wondered if this were not an excuse to smoke his fill before offering the pipe to me. If so, it was possible that he was an addict in spite of his denial. But all I said was:

'Are you sure no harm will come to me?'

'Harm? None whatever. You will feel relaxed, yet mentally alert. It may keep you from sleeping tonight, but you will enjoy a happy sort of wakefulness.'

'That is something I did not expect. In the West we always associate opium with dreams and sleep. Tell me, are you not afraid you may become addicted?'

'Certainly not.'

'How can you be so sure?'

'Because I have known all my life that opium makes a good friend when strictly under control and a dangerous enemy when control is relaxed. Taken occasionally, it soothes the body, enlivens the mind and gives birth to charmingly poetic fancies, or else to heightened ability in dealing with practical matters. That depends upon your mood. To the wise, opium is a friend, to others a curse. People take to smoking it too often for so many reasons. Used in one way, it temporarily increases male virility, which makes it attractive to old men with young concubines. Used in other ways, it is a cure for pain, boredom or any of man's ten thousand ills. For someone who is not careful, there comes a time when he feels ill without it; thenceforward he is chained to his opium-couch morning and evening for the rest of his life. A slow deterioration of health sets in, due to over-heating of the brain, weakening of the essential life-force, chronic constipation and lack of appetite—all of which lead to undernourishment. Poverty-stricken addicts let their children go without schooling, or their wives without the necessaries of life, rather than endure the intolerable pains of deprivation. I have seen opium calm the fierce spirits of evil men and ruin the lives of good ones. Actors, you know, find that it improves their voices and gives them energy when needed most. So most of our stage-people, singers and actors, acquire the habit in youth. If their voices are good enough to bring them applause and affluence, it does them some present good and no *immediate* harm. If they are failures, addiction drains them of money as thoroughly as a thousand leeches crawling simultaneously upon a man's body would drain it of blood.'

He smiled complacently at this horrid picture, as though to imply that for us it had only academic interest, yet he had inadvertently given me the impression of a man speaking from personal experience, and I noticed that he smoked fully ten pipes before remembering to offer one to me.

'By the way, Hu Hsienshêng, would it be indiscreet to ask you what my friends said when they took you aside just before we left the restaurant?'

This time, his smile was one of would-be good-humoured tolerance tinged with annoyance, and he glanced meaningly towards Precious Orchid who, to his relief, had unceremoniously seated herself on a stool in the corner and gone to sleep with her head against the wall. As the other girl had not returned and there was nobody else to overhear him, I thought for a moment that he was going to tell me exactly what they had said: but, skirting the subject vaguely, he answered:

'Actors and singers have much to put up with in our society. We have been looked down on since the world began. Scholars like our friends, Lao Chang and Lao Lee, though they court us for our talents and invite the more famous of us to some of their feasts, are tiresomely suspicious of our morals.'

'Suspicious of your *morals*! That is a big surprise. Why, both those gentlemen are at this very moment being entertained by a flower-house singing-girl. They surely do not worry themselves about your morals, Hu Hsienshêng.'

'Old Father Heaven! Enjoying prostitutes is not immoral! How could it be? What are they for?'

'No? In the West——'

He interrupted me impatiently, saying: 'Would it surprise you to know that a humble, self-educated Singing-Master who has never spent a day in one of those modern Westernized schools or universities has some small acquaintance with your Ancient Greeks? The stage has been my life, you see, and Sophocles and the others read well in Chinese translation. You are kind enough not to be surprised? Good. I sometimes think we Pekingese are close kin to those Ancient Greeks. We like to tread a middle path. We see no harm in enjoying —anything. Evil lies only in excess.'

'Quite so. But surely Lao Chang and Lao Lee, as you call them, would thoroughly approve that sentiment. After all, they too are true Pekingese, by birth or by long residence in this city.'

'Certainly they would approve that sentiment. But then, you see, they cannot imagine a Singing-Master who is not guilty of all kinds of excesses.'

'That is very unreasonable,' I answered courteously. But Mr Hu's mood had changed; he greeted my words with roars of laughter and shouted:

'Ha-ha-ha! Do you not understand why I am so annoyed with them? They are absolutely right! Never have I heard of a singing-master who, in his actions, abhorred excess! Ask Precious Orchid here. Ask any of her so-called sisters. Ask . . . but never mind that. How could anyone belonging to this theatre-world of ours and having money in plenty not be guilty of excess? Those Pekingese who follow the middle path and know the meaning of "enough", do not include actors and singing-masters. Now put this mouthpiece to your lips and inhale deeply, while I hold the bowl over the flame for you.'

I did so. The smoke was mild and tasted smoother than the mellowest tobacco. Its immediate effect was nil; but after my third and last pipe my sense of physical well-being was perceptibly heightened; also I grew very talkative. My thoughts, without being interrupted by visions or dreams, did to some extent become like coloured pictures projected upon the cinema-screen formed by my closed eyelids. My host's ten pipefuls, to which he was now adding several more, produced no visible effect upon him at all. (His natural talkativeness in any case left no room for increase.) Had he been less chubby and healthy-looking, I should have had no doubts as to his being an addict. As it was, I kept an open mind.

According to my watch, I stayed with him for over three hours in all, chatting with increasing animation and drinking bowl after bowl of tea in a vain effort to rid myself of an abnormal thirst; but something had happened to my time sense so that, when I left, it seemed only a short while since I had been listening to Little Wang's performance.

As he had foretold, on reaching home and going to bed, I lay awake all night, feeling neither a desire to sleep nor any need of book or friend to help me pass the hours till breakfast time. My sensations by no means amounted to bliss; they were pleasurable, but only in the rather negative sense that I was physically at ease and generally content to let my mind drift upon the currents of idle thought. I felt sure I need not fear any craving to taste the drug again, but nor would I say no if the opportunity presented itself.

# 6

# White Russian Interlude

WHEN spring began its hesitant advance and Peking's courtyards were inundated with the pink and white foam of
early fruit-blossom, I went to pass a morning drinking tea
with an old gentleman who played at selling curios. I say 'played at',
because he much preferred fingering them, gazing at them or discuss-
ing them with an appreciative guest, to parting with them however
stiff the price. His apprentices, still clad in their winter gowns of
blue quilted cotton, knew me well enough to usher me straight
through to the room behind the shop; for the shop itself was but a
vestibule to Aladdin's cave, a place for selling trifles with which old
Hsü himself could not be bothered. All business of any consequence
and the handling of all his real treasures took place in the comfortable,
well-lighted room behind.

On my way through to the inner doorway I received a confused
impression of colours winking from the gloom. Lying upon shelves
and tables in what seemed like higgledy-piggledy confusion were
bolts of tribute silk, lacquered nicknacks from the south, bowls and
vases with the brilliant colours and elaborate ornamentation of the
late Manchu period, jade snuff-bottles and jade jewelry in heavy gold
settings, figurines of soapstone, crystal and rose quartz, carved
ivories and plates of pure-white porcelain both mounted upon blackwood stands, cabinets inlaid with mother-of-pearl and semi-precious
stones, as well as incense-burners and sacrificial goblets of dark
bronze. All these things I saw as confused patches of colour, divining
their shapes and kinds from what I remembered from my former
visits.

Old Hsü received me with hospitable expressions of delight.
Though I knew little of the finer points of jades, porcelains or any of
his other wares, I had, ever since Bill Luton had first introduced me

there, shown an enthusiastic desire to learn which had gradually won the old dealer's heart. It was our custom to preserve the fiction that I might conceivably want to buy something; this avoided my having to remonstrate with him when he busied himself for hours bringing out a random choice of objects from his cupboards. Each was carefully unwrapped, displayed upon its own and as carefully put away before his hands felt for the next. All his finer pieces were protected by specially made boxes with blue cloth facings and padded silken linings; the cavity in the padding of each exactly fitted the object it contained.

'Here,' said old Hsü, sliding out the ivory clasps of the fourth or fifth box taken down that day—an unusually small one—'is a trifle perhaps worthy of your attention. As it is somewhat of a rare piece, the price may be more than Hsienshêng cares to spend, but you will not object to glancing at it?'

Nearly every piece was introduced with a formula to that effect, no doubt to avoid the implication that he knew as well as I did there was no single thing in his back room which I could afford to buy. The object he presently drew forth from its silken nest was a dark mud-brown stone about two inches long carved to resemble a turtle. The colour struck me as unattractive and I saw no great merit in the figure apart from the carving.

'Well, Hsienshêng?'

'You'll think me very stupid, but I must confess myself too ignorant to form an opinion, Hsü Hsienshêng.'

'You know what it is, of course.'

'A turtle.'

'That, certainly. It is also a very early Han jade, discoloured by resting almost two thousand years in its owner's grave. Its special virtue, apart from the protection it affords the wearer, lies in our knowing its authentic history. It was carved for that Prince Ch'u whose collection of jades so excited the cupidity of his royal uncle that he had to flee with them to a neighbouring state, whence, having married the ruler's daughter, he subsequently returned as conqueror of his uncle's territory.'

'The story is an interesting one, but why should knowing it greatly enhance the value of the jade? Presumably few people have heard of that Prince Ch'u.'

'In our profession, P'u Hsienshêng, we judge the value of an object by several criteria—substance, workmanship, symbolism, age, rarity and its power to suggest a beauty beyond that which is revealed to the eye. Apart from all these, a reliable pedigree naturally augments its owner's pride in it. We are a people with a profound veneration for the past. It is good to gaze upon and handle something which makes the figures described in our historical annals live again for us.'

He showed me several similarly ancient jades, discoursing more than half the morning upon their histories and merits. When the unexpected arrival of a wealthy Swiss connoisseur put an end to my visit, I took the opportunity while passing through the shop to buy a pair of blue china griffins costing eight *yuan*. I did not especially want them, but they were about the first objects to catch my eye; and, as in the past old Hsü had always shown me to the outer door himself, this was the first time I had had an opportunity to spend a little money there.

Near the end of that lane, I found myself unexpectedly face to face with Shura, who was followed by a boy carrying a large rolled-up rug he must have bought somewhere nearby. I guessed its colours were atrociously bright.

'Vania! How nice! But I have right to be angry with you, yes? Why you have not gone to see me at the Kavkaz?'

I made my excuses, but nothing would satisfy him until I had definitely set the date of my visit for the following Saturday.

'You promise? Not just maybe?'

'I promise,' I answered, and managed to convince him that I meant it.

.    .    .    .    .

The Kavkaz had once been the centre of émigré night-life, but as few of the Russians in Peking had remained prosperous, its Russian atmosphere depended upon seven or eight Russian dance-hostesses and the friends who dropped in to drink tea or cheap local beer with them, while gazing wistfully at the more affluent customers able to afford spirits or wines by the bottle. No longer young, and with a tendency to bulge in the wrong places, most of these Russian hostesses found it hard to compete with the slim, elegant Chinese girls the owner of the club had insisted on adding to their ranks. On the appointed evening I arrived there at about ten. Shura, who was sitting at the cash register near the door, jumped up to welcome me.

'So, Vania, you have come and I am happy. Just now I have a little thing to do, so you please find one table and await me. Tonight, our beautiful Katia, who went from us last year, is come back just to make you enjoy. For this you will make Shura a big thank-you.'

Alarmed, I walked over to a table not too near the two-man band, glancing at the Russian women near the piano and hastily shying away from their burning glances. The Chinese hostesses, who formed a little group by themselves, were too well assured of popularity to bestow attention on an indifferently dressed newcomer. I sat down and ordered a bottle of Shura's Crim wine which seemed about the cheapest thing on the menu. Then I remained staring at the tablecloth dumbly awaiting my fate. The best I could hope for was that whichever of those blowzy Russian women came over and introduced herself as Katia would not expect too much of me.

A shadow falling on my table from behind compelled me to look up. The next moment I was on my feet and prepared to 'make' Shura an even bigger thank-you than he expected. Before I could speak, a lovely voice enquired in English:

'You are Alexander Mikhailovitch's friend, monsieur?'

'Yes. And you are Katia. How nice of you to join me. Won't you sit down? The wine is just coming, but we shall need another glass. Boy!'

'A glass of brandy for me, monsieur. And, first, shall we not introduce ourselves? I am Ekaterina Petrovna, daughter of Count Peter Ivanov Chaeff, formerly staff colonel in General Denikin's army.'

I mumbled my own name and helped her into a chair. Formality so unsuited to the place and circumstances of our meeting struck me as slightly absurd, but I liked everything else about Katia. Tall, slim, beautifully proportioned, she was dressed tastefully in a simple evening gown of primrose yellow; her jet-black hair curled upwards from her shoulders in the fashionable 'Cleopatra style'; her eyes, black and fascinating, were set off by her pale, smooth skin. I judged her to be about twenty-five. Unfortunately Shura was very long in coming. I have always been a shy person and, at that time, I had had no experience whatever of making myself amusing to girls who expected some deference to their social rank. Katia's formality made it impossible to behave spontaneously with her. As she refused to dance and I could think of little to say, the conversation soon languished; and, though I tried to make up for my boorishness with glances of admiration, these were not well received. She was no doubt too used to them to be so easily flattered. Worse still, her code of refined behaviour seemed to entail no obligation to conceal her boredom; indeed, she drank so fast and so copiously that, by the time Shura came to my relief, her ladylike manners had fallen from her like a cloak.

'Shura, darling. You promised me your friend would be handsome, charming, amusing and very rich—everything a girl desires. But what do I find? He cannot be rich, for he offered me wine and forced me to demand brandy. Handsome? M'yes, in a boyish way, but his head is too big for his body. Charming? Only if silence in a night-club has its charms. Amusing? Shura, I don't even want to laugh *at* him!'

Apparently more saddened than surprised by her behaviour, Shura emitted a long sigh followed by some chiding sentences in Russian. Then he turned to me and said:

'You will please forgive Katia. I said to her not to drink before she come here. She has not listened and is already very much drunk.'

'*Drunk!*' screamed Katia in a voice that drew all eyes to our table. 'You dare to say I'm drunk! Alexander Mikhailovitch, you lie! *Mais vraiment*, you lie! Except the vodka at dinner and some beer at Olga's, I have drunk nothing this evening but the few glasses of brandy I had to force Monsieur to buy for me. I shall not stay here to be insulted. You must learn to look after your boy-friends by yourself.'

She got to her feet with what was meant to be a spring and, looking at me contemptuously, exclaimed:

'*Adieu, monsieur*. The pleasure of meeting you is not to be repeated, I think. You seem well born, but you have much to learn. First, never offer a lady wine without giving her a choice of something better. For the rest, Shura should know well to teach you how ladies like to be amused. Me he insults upon the instant of our meeting. *Kavkaz n'est pas encore chic*. It has become vulgar. *Jamais* shall I return to it. *Jamais, jamais!* Shura, dear, I spit upon you.'

Delivered of this absurd speech, of which every word could be heard from the neighbouring tables, she walked unsteadily from the room and from my life. As she had promised, I was never to have the pleasure of meeting her again—*jamais, jamais*. Her insulting behaviour, her vulgar display of atrociously pronounced and fragmentary French, made it quite doubtful if she were a daughter of the Russian nobility; all the same, she was a lovely girl and I should have been delighted to re-encounter her in her soberer moments.

'Shura, is Ekaterina Petrovna really the daughter of a titled colonel?' I asked.

'You are bad to ask this question, Vania. We Russians have lost too much. You must permit that we keep or invent some pride, yes? Katia is a very, very wonderful good girl with a big warm Russian heart, but she drink too much. For this the boss, Alexei Alexeivitch, tell her not to work here no more, though customers had come to her like bees.'

Shura knew how to lay himself out to be good company. My visit to the Kavkaz, undertaken without enthusiasm and nearly spoiled by Katia, became a pleasure after all. Though the accordion music was mediocre and I did nothing but drink and talk to Shura, I was glad to be there. However, the only memorable event of the evening after Katia's departure was the arrival after midnight of a Father Vassily, also known as the Ruski Lama. Up to that time, I had paid only slight attention to the people around me—Americans and assorted Europeans wearing ordinary day-clothes, with a sprinkling of young, Westernized Chinese dressed in the same sort of jackets and thick pullovers. Many came in just for a drink or two and then left. The club was seldom more than half full and the atmosphere not especially gay. The few men who danced so often chose the pretty Chinese girls as partners that I found myself willing them to take on the Russian women before they became permanently stuck to their chairs. I was afraid some of them might be in need of money for their next meal, but my compassion fell short of compelling me to dance with one. It was Shura's flow of anecdotes about the comedies and tragedies of émigré life which kept me there so late, despite my having to put up with his frequent absences when the cash register claimed his attention.

Shortly after midnight my eye was caught by a party of shabbily dressed Russians sitting over their beer in company with two of the oldest and least attractive dance-hostesses, neither of whom could have been less than forty. Previously, they had seemed bored and depressed, but now their talk was loud and happy. They had been joined by a tall man dressed in the long black garments of a Russian priest, but his hair, instead of falling on his shoulders in the usual way, had been so closely shaven that at first I thought he was naturally bald. Apart from this odd circumstance, his expression of authority, the way he held himself, the deferential behaviour of the others and the austere glass of water standing in front of him among the beer-bottles, all combined to make him a truly remarkable figure in a place like the Kavkaz.

Much intrigued, I asked Shura if he knew this extraordinary person. 'That, Vania dear, is Father Vassily. In Russia he was priest. Then he has gone away a long time in Mongolia for something and taken strange knowledge from the Lamas. Now he tell that the life of spirit is not found in churches, and our Russian priests call him Antichrist. But he is good, Vania. He heal sickness and make miracles. Also he knows well to make our sad Russian hearts happy.'

'Where does he live now? In Peking?'

'He says he is bird with nowhere for putting his head. He goes and comes—Peking, Harbin, Mukden. Just now he stays in Yung Ho Kung, the Lama Temple in the north city. The Mongols call him Ruski Lama and have so much respect to him. You wish to know him?'

'Yes,' I said eagerly. 'Indeed I should be very sorry not to meet him.'

The description of Father Vassily had put me in mind of Bemaiev —that colourful figure who, though less famous than his fantastic contemporary, Rasputin, had nevertheless won a name for himself in St Petersburg as a Russian (of Buriat extraction) who possessed the key to the secrets and powers guarded by the High Lamas of Mongolia and Tibet.

'I shall arrange for you, Vania; but not now. You speak no Russian. Now he is making those people happy, we leave him for them. Later we shall go, you and I, to the Lama Temple to talk with him.'

I was beginning to feel the effect of the several bottles of sweetish wine we had drunk between us; and, as the Kavkaz was filling up at last so that Shura had less and less time to spend away from the cash register, he consented to my going home. The visit to Father Vassily was fixed for the following Sunday, when he might be persuaded to invite me to the 'love-feast' he was holding that night.

The next morning, on getting up later than my usual hour, I was pleasantly surprised to find Tê-Ku waiting in my study.

'My goodness, you've been away a long time,' I said. 'I hope you are quite fit again.'

'Yes. I had what is called a nervous breakdown and have been staying quietly in the country with my aunt. Now I'm ready for more lessons, if you forgive my leaving Peking without your permission.'

I told him not to worry about that and insisted on his sharing my breakfast, which disappointed him because it included none of the hoped-for 'English delicacies'.

'By the way, Chu, I'm feeling a bit down after a late night at a Russian night-club. I was thinking a boiling-hot bath and a massage might put me right. Care to join me?'

He accepted with pleasure, a visit to a bath-house (especially in winter) being one of those enjoyments few Pekingese, rich or poor, can resist. Besides, it was always more fun to go with someone for company. Not far from my lane was a large bath-house of the middle sort, neither dirty on the one hand nor expensive on the other. The two Chinese characters *Tsao T'ang* written large, black against green, on the wooden screen in front of the doorway advertised its existence with eye-compelling force. A serving-boy standing inside the gateway led us past crab-apple trees on the point of blossoming to a building where the hot steamy atmosphere made us pull off our overcoats and wish we had on less warm underclothing. Taking it for granted that we should prefer a private room, he guided us along a corridor with doorways spaced at short intervals on either side. One of these was ajar and the boy, lifting aside a thin curtain, bowed us into a small room only just big enough to allow space for a couch to each side of the narrow gangway leading through an inner doorway to an even smaller compartment containing two enamelled baths.

'Chu, this will be rather dull. Do you mind very much if we go to one of the public rooms? Chinese bathing pools are more fun for me than the kind of bath I've been used to all my life.'

Though he was a youth opposed on principal to anything smacking of second class, he agreed so readily that I gave him a sharp look to see whether he was just falling in with my wishes or really welcomed the suggestion. His expression of undisguised relief made me want to laugh. I suppose he had suddenly felt embarrassed at the thought of disrobing before a foreigner in a private room—yet not so private that less than three people would come in to minister to each of us in accordance with the complicated ritual of the *Tsao T'ang*.

Noticeably contemptuous of our plebeian taste, the attendant handed us over to another boy, who conducted us into a public room.

Here, fifty or sixty people could have been accommodated in the two tiers of bunks around the walls and a block of similar bunks in the centre, each of which was draped in clean white towelling and provided with a small pillow. About thirty of them were occupied by recumbent, towel-girt figures who had reached various stages of the 'treatment'. Some were being rigourously massaged or had surrendered their toes to the sharp nail-chisels and skin-paring instruments of the foot-boys; others were lying blissfully relaxed with pots of tea and plates of small-eats close to hand, or had surrendered to the warmth of the steamy atmosphere and fallen asleep. The number of attendants visible was at least half as many as the number of patrons. No doubt more of them could be summoned from other rooms if necessary.

After undressing and handing over our clothes to be hung on high pegs out of reach of pickpockets, Chu and I, girt in large towels, walked through to the first of the bathing-rooms beyond. This was a chamber with a tiled floor surrounded by some thirty wall-taps, where we had to soap ourselves from head to foot and rinse off the dirty water before entering one of the pools in the adjoining chamber. Had we made use of a private bathroom, even this washing process would have been performed for us by attendants.

When we were as clean as we could make ourselves, we left our towels and passed on to a low-roofed hall containing three pools, each the size of a medium swimming-pool in England. Chu chose the farthest and hottest of these, as he was used to scalding himself in very hot water. Even though I entered the middle or so-called temperate pool, I had to lower myself in gently because, by my standards, the water was almost too hot to bear. My face grew scarlet and presently drew the attention of a dozen or so people bathing in the same pool; they began staring at me and two of them, who were still young boys, ventured some loud-voiced jests.

'Look, Kuan Kung has joined us,' said one, comparing me to the Chinese God of War—a fierce-looking warrior with cheeks as red as glowing coals.

'No, the gentleman is from America,' replied the other, laughing. 'He's a Red Indian. Didn't you know?'

Unable to invent a suitable repartee, I joined in the general laughter. Though no rudeness had been intended, the older bathers were relieved that the strange-looking foreigner, whom they had not expected to understand Chinese, took the jest so well. Suddenly gusts of laughter shook us all, uniting a dozen strangers into a gay company of friends. This sort of easy intimacy was one of the reasons why I preferred bathing in the public rooms. Our pool was served by four attendants. When any of them was free, a bather would summon him; whereupon the attendant would slide a life-size 'crucifix' into the pool and spread-eagle his patron upon it, half in and half out of the water. Next, tying a wet towel tightly round his right hand and forearm, he would give him a vigorous massage lasting about ten minutes. When my turn came, the masseur succeeded in producing rolls of filth from my recently soaped body; the hard towel rubbed these black, worm-like rolls from pores opened wide during my immersion in the hot water.

I suppose I ought to have felt sickened by the thought of all the dirt rubbed into that pool from the skins of others since its last weekly cleaning and change of water, but a modern European cannot hope to enjoy Asia if he insists too much on his accustomed artificial standards of cleanliness. Personally, I had no difficulty in adapting myself; too much in love with Peking to allow such details to interfere with my enjoyment of her many and varied charms, I comforted myself with the thought that the Pekingese were anyway cleaner than most Englishmen of, say, my grandfather's day; and I could be reasonably sure that the fastidious gallants of an earlier period, such as Sir Philip Sidney or Sir Walter Raleigh, not to speak of Queen Elizabeth I herself, stank of things much worse than Peking's ubiquitous but antiseptic smell of garlic. However, comparisons of this sort were needless; life was so good then that I accepted all of it with both hands, never thinking of rejecting such precious ointment for the sake of an odd fly or two.

After my turn upon the 'crucifix', still tingling from the massage, I returned to my bunk in the outer room, where Chu soon rejoined me. In the interval we allowed ourselves for tea-drinking before submitting to the next round of massage, Chu nearly took my breath away by saying calmly:

'You will be happy to know my father has found you a wife.'

'Well! *Thank* you! Thank you very much! I hope she's beautiful, talented, amusing, reasonably docile and, above all, an excellent cook.'

'Probably she's most of those things. I haven't seen her.'

'Then how on earth . . .'

'It's my father's idea, not mine. And yet in some ways she might suit you well. And you are about the only possible husband for her.'

'Chu! What *are* you talking about?'

Just then two hefty men approached us and, smiling like torturers seizing upon their victims, subjected us to a form of massage which left us no breath for speech. For half an hour I grunted and groaned, finding it impossible to emulate Chu's stoic silence. Iron fingers kneeded my flesh, heavy fists pummelled me—arms, legs, back and belly—as though processing a lump of dough into one of Peking's fifty-two varieties of farina. Worst of all, those iron fingers unerringly sought and found certain nerves to which they gave salutary but agonizing tweaks. At times I wanted to yell to the grinning Shantung giant to desist, but was restrained by pride and by the thought of the delicious aftermath these horrors were designed to produce. At last we were left to the peaceful ministrations of foot-boys, who inspired no fear so long as the victim kept his eyes turned away from the sharp chisels plied about toe-nails and toughened skin with a seeming carelessness that concealed the exactness of their skill. Meanwhile, it was possible to talk again.

'Chu, please tell me more about my lovely wife. Begin at the beginning, keep the middle for the middle and end with the end. The matter affects me rather closely, you see. I don't want to be muddled.'

'Do you read the Tientsin papers? Of course not; why should you! But my father does. Last night he came across an item which set him thinking; that's why he sent me round today. It distresses him that you should have come to live so far from home without a wife to look after you. The first time I spoke of you to him and told him you were not married, he said: "A man well over twenty, earning his own living, and still no wife? It's against nature! How can your teacher with a house and servants of his own be even tolerably comfortable with no wife to look after them for him?" Since then, he has often referred to your bachelor state. And now he is happy to have found the solution.'

Chu broke off at this point to call a passing tea-boy and order a plate of dumplings stuffed with a conserve of young black beans pounded with sugar.

'Or do you prefer sugared lotus-seed stuffing?' he asked me.

'Any kind of stuffing you like. For heaven's sake, go on with my marriage-story. I'm fascinated by your father's concern. I didn't know he bothered to remember my existence except during one of my rare calls.'

My student looked hurt, but this was not on account of what I had said about his father.

'Why do you say that any stuffing will do? The steamed dumplings here are delicious. They deserve a little thought. Black bean conserve is better suited to the season; but, in this hot room, sugared lotus-seed will remind us of summer. Which is it to be?'

'Oh, let it be the sugared lotus-seed stuffing. Now will you please go on with your story.'

'The item in the Tientsin newspaper had been inserted by the sponsors of a well-bred young girl forced by unique circumstances to advertise for a husband.'

'Then I'm very sure she won't suit me. Any girl who has to advertise for a husband must have something wrong with her. I can't feel much gratitude to your father for wishing her on to me.'

'Please wait till you've heard the rest. The girl is a European, probably a Russian by birth, blonde and blue-eyed. Abandoned by her real parents while still a baby, she was taken in by a well-to-do Chinese couple who, knowing nothing of her parentage, have brought her up as their own daughter. They seem to be old-fashioned people and live, I think, in a large joint-family household somewhere in South Manchuria. Except for her appearance, she's exactly like a Chinese girl; she can cook, sew, embroider and even write essays. She has never been to school, but the family tutor taught her the sort of classical works that old people think good for women, those emphasizing decorum, modesty, duties to parents, brothers, parents-in-law, husbands—that kind of thing. In every way but one she is exactly the kind of daughter-in-law that conservative families would welcome with joy—*but*, conservative parents do not allow their sons to marry Europeans! That goes without saying. To them, this girl is still a European, though she knows nothing of English, Russian or any other foreign language and her mind probably works in a way that is entirely Chinese. My father has decided that, if enquiries show that everything claimed for her is true, then she is the ideal wife for you and you the perfect husband for her. You are a European like herself, fluent in Chinese and accustomed to our Chinese ways.'

'It's wonderfully thoughtful of your father. You will have to explain to him that a Chinese girl, one of my own choosing, would suit me much better.'

'Oh no! I should not dare. My father is dead against mixed marriages. That's his whole point. An English girl might be a burden to you, by being unwilling to live all her life in Peking or by forcing you to live like those Legation Quarter people; a Chinese girl of good family is out of the question; and for my teacher to marry a girl not of good family would seem to him unworthy of you, or likely to bring you undesirable connections. So you see . . .'

Wiping my lips after the last of the dumplings, I replied:

'Look, Chu. Your father seems serious about this, but surely *you* don't agree with him?'

He laughed uncertainly.

'Yes, my father is serious. To me the idea seems droll. I told him you would never agree—and yet? Is there any harm in taking a trip to Tientsin, where she is staying with her sponsors, just to admire the scenery?'

'You mean go and look the poor girl over?'

'Why not?'

'I'll think about it,' I said insincerely, for the idea seemed to me preposterous. After that, I lay back on the bunk and gave myself up to the drowsy contentment which is the culminating pleasure of a visit to the bath-house. Bathing for the sake of cleanliness could be done at home, whereas the *Tsao T'ang* ritual produced a delicious relaxation and feeling of well-being equal to and more wholesome than what I had experienced after smoking opium. For a while I speculated about the girl whose chance of finding an acceptable husband seemed so slender. With her background, she was probably quite unfitted for any sort of job, and her foster-parents would surely stand in the way of any casual meetings with young men, however anxious they were to avoid a 'daughter' of theirs having to remain a spinster. Poor girl! Unless she were astonishingly pretty, there seemed no hope for her to escape spinsterhood, which in those days was considered a terrible fate for any woman.

Her story reminded me of the far worse fate of another Russian girl, whose present condition was not at all unique. One evening Pao had been accosted on his way to a dinner-party at my house by a hard-faced Chinese who abruptly offered him what he called 'a foreign-devil girl and near-virgin of seventeen'. Characteristically, Pao had agreed to visit this prodigy there and then. Arriving at my place when dinner had reached its last course but one, he took his place at table and launched into her story. She was a young Russian girl called Tania, probably even less than seventeen years old. A month before she had spent all the money she possessed to pay for the long railway journey from

Harbin to Peking, because her fiancé's silence had made her afraid he was going to break off the engagement. She was very much in love with him and had come to throw herself on his mercy. On arriving at the cheap Russian boarding-house where he lived, she had been curtly told by the landlady that the young man was dead—'and a good thing, too, filling up my second-best room and never troubling himself to pay the rent!' Stunned by grief and having nowhere else to go, she had implored the landlady to take her in until she could find work; but the woman, who may have been having a hard time making ends meet, had gruffly turned her away. So there was Tania in a strange city without either friends or as much as the price of a meal. Plenty of people in Peking would have pitied and been glad to help her; but, by bad luck, she had poured her story into the ears of the first Russian she happened to meet, and soon found herself living as a prostitute in a disreputable Chinese hotel. Her 'protector' and a Chinese accomplice only fed her properly when she had entertained a customer and handed the money over to them.

One of my guests twitted Pao with having become her customer, which seemed to me the only explanation of his having been left alone with her long enough to hear her story; but Pao laughingly denied it. Then another guest, who was an Englishman and a new-comer to Peking, had asked indignantly why he did not go at once to inform the police. 'No use,' said Pao. 'Those people could easily persuade the police that Tania really owes them money. In that case, their way of getting it back would not be accounted a crime.'

Lying in the bath-house recalling the misfortune of Tania might have led me to reflect grimly upon the fate of Russian émigrés in general. Instead, I fell asleep. Sympathy for individuals known to me by hearsay never affects me as sharply as sympathy for a friend or an acquaintance, for in the latter case there may be something I can do and, besides, their sufferings are visualized more vividly.

An hour later, Chu and I both woke up at about the same time. Outside, our drowsiness was dissipated by the cold air, giving place to exhilaration.

'I feel on top of the world!' I exclaimed.

'And I feel like a man who has gone to his host's place *on foot*!'

'Whatever do you mean, Chu?'

'It's a way of asking myself to lunch. I'm as hungry as a man who has been forced to walk a whole mile!'

The Temple of Heaven

Approach to the Altar of Heaven

'Oh, Chu!' I said, laughing. 'You talk like a man who has never walked.'

'I never have,' he answered, 'except now and then to please you.'

     .          .          .          .          .

On Sunday, before our visit to Father Vassily at the Lama Temple, Shura gave me lunch in a Chinese-owned restaurant serving Russian food which he described as cheap and good. It certainly was. During the meal our conversation again ran on the difficulties faced by White Russians settling in Chinese cities already over-populated and offering them little chance of well-paid employment. Nor were economic difficulties the only ones. Between the two races there was a difference of character and outlook hard to bridge. (Today, under their respective Communist régimes, the younger generations in both countries are being moulded along similar lines, but the sons and daughters of Old China and Old Russia were temperamentally about as wide apart as human beings can be.) It was inevitable that the thousands of White Russians living in the larger cities of North China had to suffer special disabilities. Poverty, the status of 'poor whites', constant misunderstandings and, in many cases, mutual contempt severely hindered their relations with the Chinese upon which their efforts to prosper depended. Shura illustrated these things by stories told with wonderful good humour. Though he must often have felt sick at heart, he preferred laughing at absurdities to dwelling upon tragedies.

'Vania, I must tell you something else that is so funny. You will see how the Chinese are thinking of us. One day my dearest American friend, Jimmy, go to a Chinese girl-house in Mukden, where they never see Europeans except Russians. When he go in the girls did not make him a good welcome. They let him sit alone and talked like he is not there. Then the madam come to ask: "*Kuei kuo shih na-i kuo?* [What is your honourable country?]" and he told he is an American. So the girls who were listening run up then and make the big fuss of him. And, Vania, do you know what they say? They say: "*Hao chi-la* [Splendid]! He is not a Big-Nose; he is Foreign Devil." Ha, Vania why you don't laugh?'

'I'm not sure that I got the point.'

'Up in Mukden, they call Russians Big-Nose; but other Europeans they call Foreign Devil like here in Peking. You know what Jimmy say to Shura? He say: "Those Chinese girls go to bed with a devil more quickly than they speak good morning to you poor, bloody Russians!" Ha-ha-ha. Jimmy is always funny like that.'

Towards the end of lunch, I asked if there were not any Russians who had carved out satisfactory lives for themselves in China. Shura thought they numbered very much under twenty per cent and perhaps under ten. They were mostly traders doing business with Inner Mongolia and Central Asia, from which furs, skins and other products arrived by truck or camel caravan; or else they were engineers and administrative staff employed on the Chinese railways in the northeast. Surprisingly few Russians had married Chinese wives or possessed really close Chinese friends and, though most of them spoke Chinese fluently, few could speak it well.

'And how does Father Vassily fit into all this?'

'Father Vassily is saint. His home is everywhere. But God sent him for Russians and Mongols, not Chinese.'

From the restaurant in the Tung An Market our rickshaws took us along the straight road leading to a northern gate of the city, the same road that Pao and I had crossed on our way to the Confucian Temple. Since I had glimpsed the mighty Lama Temple called Yung Ho Kung that evening, I had never been back; so when Shura led me through it towards the residential buildings behind, I was staggered by its vastness. We passed great courtyards and enormous halls with roofs and pillars that had once been as splendid as those of the Forbidden City, but were now fallen into a tragic state of neglect. The lacquer hung in shreds from the wood; roof-tiles had been cracked or pushed aside by sturdy tufts of weed and grass; the wood-carving embellishing doors and windows, denuded by long neglect, lay naked to onslaughts of sun and rain. Had their pillars and beams been less sturdy, several of the smaller and less important buildings would have been in a state of collapse. At that hour of the afternoon, few monks were about and those we saw looked as shabby as the buildings in their care. Gone was the grandeur of former days when the emperors had given lavish subsidies for the upkeep of this birthplace of the glorious Emperor K'ang Hsi and official dwelling-place of the great Buddhist prelates from Lhasa. No doubt important Tibetan dignitaries still came and went, but China's republican government, as devoid of spiritual aspirations as of martial ardour, was below interesting itself in such matters. Nominally Confucian-cum-Methodist, its leaders had had religion decried in the school textbooks as anti-progressive superstition, while temples of no matter what religious or historical significance were allowed to fall into ruin.

As I followed Shura through the broad, mouldering courts, glimpsing now and then the gleam of votive-lamps reflected upon gold within the still splendidly appointed interiors of the principal shrines, I recalled some of those passages in which Chinese poets living in similarly troubled times had lamented the departed glory of palaces abandoned to solitude and ruin. Revisiting scenes where music and shouts of revelry had resounded, they had heard only the moan of pigeons, the sighing of branches and the pathetic tinkle of wind-bells hanging from the eaves. It was easy to appreciate their feelings, there in the silent courts of the Yung Ho Kung, for on that day a colourless sky increased their atmosphere of desolation; I felt it might not be long before their inhabitants crept away leaving them undisturbed to become the homes of scorpions and bats.

Presently the scene changed. Towards the rear of that vast compound, we found the residential quarters as busy as a thriving village. Here were hundreds of small houses bordering slit-like lanes thronged with colourful if shabby Mongols, both monks and laymen. A few of the houses, somewhat larger than the rest, were ornamented with decorative carving and preserved an air of lingering prosperity, but those I saw could scarcely have been the residences of important church dignitaries from Lhasa and Urga, whose private courtyards probably formed yet another section of that bewildering maze. Shura, with the air of a man on familiar ground, led me briskly through the crowded lanes to the gateway of a building secluded by its own scrap of courtyard. Within were four identical doorways, one of which opened on to the cell-like room where Father Vassily awaited us.

As the Father looked up from his writing-table, I obtained my first clear view of his face; it was at once impressive and disappointing. At the Kavkaz, I had thought his expression of authority derived from nobility of character supported by an inner calm—now I was less sure. The affability and dignity of his greeting was not free from a hint of arrogance; nor did his features reflect the calm dispassion and true gentleness of a saint. Nevertheless, with his tall cassocked figure, his closely shaven head, bloodless skin and magnificently compelling eyes, he was an arresting sight; I could understand the awe and devotion accorded to him by his Russian disciples despite his unorthodox blending of Christianity and Buddhism. I noticed that, whereas Shura made the sign of the cross (possibly in deference to a small ikon hanging in a far corner of the room), Father Vassily greeted us hands palm to palm, as though he had divined I am a Buddhist! Even Shura did not know that.

The Father began by asking me a lot of questions about myself in surprisingly good English, the very first of which showed clearly that he was acquainted with my conversion to Buddhism. Shura in his rôle of devoted disciple listened in silence, hanging upon his words and never venturing a remark unless addressed. Meanwhile, a knot of Mongols had gathered in the open doorway, attracted by the novelty of beholding three foreign devils conversing in an uncouth language; but when a jolly fellow, well dressed and wearing his fur hat at a rakish angle, like a layman of some consequence, ventured a step inside the doorway, a sharp unfriendly look from Father Vassily sent him cringing back to slink away like a scolded puppy. I felt a moment of anger. Mongols are a proud, gay, carefree people afraid of nothing in *this* world; the incident suggested that the Father was more feared than loved here in this temple where they had made him welcome. These Mongols were presumably in a position to rid themselves easily of an unwanted stranger within their gates; surely nothing but fear of his *supernatural* powers could stand in their way.

Presently Father Vassily began to talk about himself, while showing some reticence concerning his past. When I enquired why he had, as it seemed, thought fit to add some Buddhist doctrines to those of the Russian Orthodox Church, he replied that the very form of my question showed I was too ignorant to understand the reasons. Somehow he managed to deliver this snub without offending me. I believe I felt a kind of pleasure in being snubbed by him; and, for the second time that afternoon, I glimpsed something of the strength of his power over his disciples. Yet, whereas Shura sat head in hand gazing at the Father as Peter or John might have gazed at Jesus, my own admiration contained seeds of suspicion and dislike. It was revealing that the Father's reticence about the genuinely spiritual benefits obtained during his long residence in a remote Lamaist monastery on the shores of Lake Kokonor did not extend to the merely occult. He enjoyed hinting at the miraculous powers conferred upon him by his Lama, whom he called the Amdo Hutukhutu. The gist of that part of his conversation was:

'The Mongol Lamas have received from India through Tibet the whole of the Ancient Wisdom preserved intact. The wisest among them know the secrets of life and death, of how an initiate may stretch forth his hand and grasp the ultimate sources of power upon which the magic forms and colours of this universe depend. Thus he may juggle with them *like toys* and work good or ill for his fellow creatures.'

Then he noticed my expression and added unctuously: 'It is thus that I, Father Vassily, have it in my power to staunch the heart-wounds of our poor Russian brethren here. Shura, isn't it so?'

'Yes, Vania, yes,' answered my friend with a tiny shiver of ecstasy. 'Father Vassily is very, very wonderful for making the sicks well and the sads happy.'

Neither Shura nor Father Vassily (unless by occult means) knew that, soon after my arrival in China, I had received an initiation from a high Tibetan Lama who had spent some weeks instructing a small group of laymen to which I then belonged. I had meant to discuss this very fully with Father Vassily, but now I decided to hold my tongue. My comparative ignorance of the high matters involved in my initiation did not hide from me that the Father's talk of grasping the sources of power and *juggling* (!) with them—though no necessarily without some truth—was a terrible perversion of Buddhist Doctrine. My own Lama had sought power solely as a means of liberating himself and others from the bondage of corporeal existence; he had taught us we must throw off the shackles of lust, passion and ignorance in order to make a total conquest of our illusory egos, thus robbing them of their power to lead us again and again back to the womb; we must free ourselves for ever from the frustrations of ego-centred life and ego-centred preparations for death. Father Vassily, I thought, enjoyed juggling with some small fragments of the universe because he craved the egoistic excitement of being able to tame men as though they were animals. My harsh judgement of him was based not only upon his words, but upon the unconscious play of his facial expressions. Unlike Shura and his friends, I was determined to resist falling under his spell; yet, unless I wished this to happen, I must avoid being often in his company. I knew he had already sensed my rising antagonism, for he was smiling at me as Goliath must have smiled as the youthful David.

Before I left Shura alone with the Father to discuss his spiritual affairs, I was obliged to accept an invitation to a love-feast to be held that same evening at an address which the latter wrote out for me in handwriting so exquisite that it might have been a painstaking transcription of a sacred text instead of the hastily scribbled note it was. I am sure Father Vassily had not really wished to invite me; but, for the first time since entering his presence, Shura had taken the initiative and the Father could not very well refuse, unless he were prepared to let me walk out of his life still disliking him, which his vanity would not permit. Moreover, as if determined I should not underrate him, he managed, even after I had stood up to go, to bring me almost to my knees—not in adoration, but because my shaking legs would hardly support me.

The room had been murky even at the time of our arrival in mid-afternoon, for the weather held promise of more snow; the open door and paper-covered windows did not admit much light from a sky sun-less and moisture-sodden. The feeble flame burning in the ikon-lamp high up in the farthest corner of the room had been a single point of brightness in the gloom behind Father Vassily's chair. There was no stove and Shura and I had been glad of our coats. From the first, Father Vassily had been sitting with his back towards the ikon and with the two of us facing him across his writing-table, so the silver hanging-lamp had been within our range of vision all the time. The flame, lack-ing some required attention, had gradually diminished to a mere speck of white-fringed blue until, flickering and flaring once or twice, it had suddenly gone out. Perhaps our staying so long had prevented the Father from replenishing the oil at the proper time.

Just as I rose to say goodbye, it occurred to me to wonder whether the ikon were Christian or Buddhist or even a figure specially wrought to suit Father Vassily's eclectic beliefs; so, bending forward slightly, I tried to make out its form, but was unable to distinguish it from the surrounding shadow. The Father, who had also risen and walked a pace towards me, noticed my glance and smiled. Suddenly his deep voice intoned a few sonorous words which made Shura blanch and cross himself; and something happened to compel me to think for a moment that the lamp *had taken fire of itself*! The effect was so shocking that I had to brace myself by putting both hands on a chair-back and to stand in that ignominious position staring open-mouthed at the ikon. Suddenly it dawned on me that the faint illumination did not come from the lamp at all. No flame was visible, and the quality of the light falling upon a small bronze female figure was harsher, colder than the glow of an oil-fed flame! Father Vassily, as I presently noticed, had also fixed his eyes upon the ikon and was intoning incomprehensible words under his breath. When he turned back to face me, the light vanished abruptly, eliciting from the terrified Shura a long-drawn and ecstatic 'A-a-a-ah!'

'As you see, it is the Mother,' said the Father softly—but whether he meant the Virgin or the White Tara of the Mongols I did not know. I left the room in confusion, forgetting to say goodbye to Shura and replying to Father Vassily's injunction not to forget the love-feast with a timid 'Yes'. During the whole of my walk alone through the narrow streets of the monks' quarters into the first of the great courtyards beyond, I felt too dazed to think properly or to find my way without making many mistakes; but, when I had somewhat got over my fright, two ideas emerged from a background of chaotic thoughts—first, I did *not* like Father Vassily; second, the unnerving manifestation of white light in the midst of the gloom had not been a mere conjuring trick, it had emanated from the force of Father Vassily's own mind!

I dined that evening in the stuffy atmosphere of the British Legation. The compound of the English Palace with its Chinese-style hall of ceremony, its low white houses and broad English lawns formed a spacious setting unsymbolic (except for the surrounding walls) of the legation officials' narrow, cut-off lives. As a young, unimportant member of the British community belonging to that tiresome succession of poor devils more or less gone native, I had no doubt been invited less from motives of courtesy than to fill an unexpected gap. In any case, my host was not put out when I rose to leave immediately after the coffee. I had to make my excuse a vague one, because depriving myself of wholesome British company for the sake of a love-feast with two such odd companions as Father Vassily and Shura might well have caused offence to the distinguished Britons present, besides confirming their opinion that non-consular European students of Chinese either were or soon would become lunatics.

A rickshaw set me down at a dilapidated gate opening from an obscure lane running through one of the poorest quarters of the west city. Beyond the unkempt courtyard stood a largish building comprising a single oblong room of five or six *chien*. The people assembled there formed a tableau of which I was vividly reminded when, more than twenty years later in the Himalayan town of Kalimpong, I came across one of the more sober accounts of the life of Grigori Efemovitch Rasputin. The illustrations showed the same sort of long table covered with a cheap white cloth untidily spread with samovar, tea-glasses and dishes of such incongruous edibles as cakes and fish; and the same sort of people (except that these were shabbier) sat or lounged round it on high-backed chairs. Most of those present were women, of whom many were middle-aged or elderly. Apart from Shura (whom I accounted as a male) the two other men of whom I have a clear recollection were an imposing, heavily bearded railway official always addressed as Colonel, and Vitushka who was an undernourished, stoat-faced boy with bulging eyes. The latter sat sideways to the table accompanying his hauntingly lovely voice on a Russian guitar. Though the song he was singing was more dirge-like than tuneful, the unbelievable purity of his soft tenor made it a joy to listen. Had the long-dead Grigori Efemovitch been able to come dancing into the room to kiss all the ladies, young and old, he might well have thought himself back in his modest Petersburg home, but for one all-important detail—every glass contained undoctored tea and not a bottle of wine was to be had.

The entrance of Father Vassily, erect and dignified, brought the others scrambling to their feet with cries of joy. The rest of the evening resolved itself into three distinct stages. First came a dull supper-party, during which hardly anyone except Shura made allowance for my ignorance of Russian. Next, a sort of prayer-meeting took place as we sat at table, its tedium presently enlivened by people springing up with ecstatic cries and executing short bursts of lively dancing. Though as yet they had no partners, they leapt about with mounting abandon as though unable to contain their joy, whirling and stamping to non-existent music—or was it the music of their own minds which I alone could not hear? Lastly came the *real* dancing.

At a sign from Father Vassily, Vitushka seized his guitar and poured forth such a torrent of song that the tunes merged into one another like the colours of a rainbow. The same signal sent most of the others rushing headlong towards partners whom, regardless of sex or age, they seized in a loving embrace and twirled about the room— leaping, stamping and shouting like hashish-addicts, but never losing the rhythm of the dance. Indeed, they danced so marvellously well that I could not believe my eyes. Old, ugly, dowdily dressed women and even the portly, bearded colonel had suddenly become young and agile—almost beautiful! Clasping each other in tight embraces or separating a while to whirl and twirl upon their own, the couples danced with a wild joy, kissing cheeks, brows and lips, and throwing back their heads to sing until the whole building echoed the wild splendour of their rich Russian contraltos and shook to the boom of the colonel's bass. Shura, advancing on me with open arms, had laughed aloud at my expression of terror and turned aside to clasp a fat woman whose blowzy form would at any other time have revolted him. He pulled her away from the table into the heart of the dervish throng, where they too became ageless and sexless as gods, and wild as laughing lunatics who have suddenly discovered what this world is all about. Then I looked at Father Vassily.

The priest, still in his place at the head of the table, had risen and was looking with shining eyes upon his God-intoxicated followers. Immediately, some part of my dislike slipped away from me like water from an oilskin cape. No one seeing him thus could doubt the sincerity of his joy in their unproud, unhumble, unrestrained demonstration of pure Christian love.

About the time Vitushka's voice gave out, and long before his fingers faltered to a stop, the first of the dancers to collapse fell to the floor. I seemed to be alone in feeling alarm for her; the others paid no attention except by taking reasonable care not to step on her too often or too hard. As for her partner, who was also a woman, she continued dancing and singing with arms outstretched as though unaware of her loss. The next to hit the floor was the bearded colonel and his young, buxom female partner. Sprawling where they had fallen, they made no effort to move out of the way of dancing feet; I believe they had dived simultaneously into total trance. When another hour had passed, only four of us, including Father Vassily who was now standing by my side, were still on our feet. Shura had long been out of sight and was presumably lying entranced under or over the body of the fat woman somewhere behind the table. Suddenly the sweating Vitushka dropped the guitar from his bleeding fingers, just in time for the last couple to stagger on to a sofa, whereat Father Vassily enquired gently:

'Well?'

'I'm overcome,' I answered truthfully. 'But what happens now and what is the point of all this?'

'Nothing happens now,' he laughed. 'Were you expecting an orgy? They will sleep for a while in Heaven, seeing themselves young and beautiful as angels. Then they will awake to find themselves fat, thin, wrinkled, ugly, some old and others in pain or ill. The world's greyness will close them in, shutting out the light of Heaven, but the peace of

God will remain in their hearts for a day or more, making hard lives easier to bear. I am sad for you, Ivan, that you have not learnt how to abandon yourself. It is because you are still young and often happy. God's peace is something you will learn to value later.'

'Father, you know I am a Buddhist and I thought you were—more or less. What is this talk of the peace of God between us?'

'Tsk, tsk! *Ech*, what a silly thing to say! God's peace is there for all of us, no matter by what name you call it. Years ago I lost belief in a God of our Russian sort; all other gods are strangers; but I believe in God's peace. You have seen how these ugly faces and lolling bosoms were transfigured and made beautiful.'

I stared at the contorted forms encumbering the floor. Ugliness most surely lay upon the sleepers now. Yet could I deny they had been beautiful for just a little while? And Father Vassily, himself? What to think of him? I have since read that people often asked concerning Father Grigori Efemovitch Rasputin: 'Is he saint or devil?' Father Vassily, I think, was both.

# 7

# Peking Duck and Opium Clouds

AT LAST there came a day in early spring that was almost warm.
Fur hats and fur-lined gowns had vanished from the lanes.
Tiny leaves or the green promise of leaves to come lay upon
naked branches not long since draped with icicles. Laggards among the
fruit-trees which had shrunk from blooming amidst the snow were
hurrying forward their blossom. The palace walls blushed redly in the
sunshine and the air was scented with promise. Meanwhile, a once
famous warlord had died too suddenly; it was whispered that Japanese
agents had set him thus precipitately upon the road to the Yellow
Springs (the portals of death).

Early in the morning, before I had finished my breakfast, Pao
arrived and insisted upon my leaving with him at once.

'Today you will see something of a kind you may never see again,
John. General Huang was very rich with the spoils of the provinces he
once controlled; his family are going to stage a funeral grand enough
for Manchu days. Why? Filial piety, fear of haunting by his spirit, love
of ostentation *and*, if certain others get their way, a guarded demonstration of anger with the Japanese—very guarded. I doubt if anyone will
be persuaded to shout slogans at a funeral. The Dwarfs may or may
not be impressed by a tremendous procession and costly rites put on
partly with subscriptions from people who want to demonstrate
Chinese resentment at their killing a general who, though none of us
loved him, did have the grace to spurn the bribes intended to corrupt
his loyalty.'

There was no difficulty about out entering the general's mansion.
No attempt was being made to differentiate between genuine mourners
and strangers carried along by the great stream of people converging
on the marble steps and flowing through the wide-flung gates. The
principal courtyard and some others adjoining it had been temporarily

roofed over with matting to convert their several buildings into a single block. A hundred tables had been set with dishes of food and cauldrons of rice gruel for the funeral breakfast provided for all-comers. The chief mourners in their robes of unbleached sackcloth were not as yet visible; most of the people pressing about us were dressed in dark-coloured gowns surmounted by the short black ceremonial jackets worn upon all formal occasions. Some even wore old-fashioned skull-caps of stiff black satin with a small cloth button in the centre of the crown—white for relatives of the dead, blue for more distant connections and red for those not obliged to mourn. Instead of wreaths, many hundred strips of blue or white silk (the colours of mourning) hung from the walls of the public rooms; they had been embellished with Chinese characters tersely extolling the dead man's alleged virtues. So thickly did these scrolls hang that some were altogether obscured from view. The names and official titles of the donors, which were appliquéd in small characters to the left of the laudatory inscriptions, indicated that they came from friends and patriots in every part of China. With one exception, everything I had seen so far was a large-scale replica of what may be seen at any middle-class Chinese funeral ceremony. The exception was something entirely new to me. At the various gateways stood fantastic figures wearing tall archaic-looking hats and mediaeval Chinese military uniforms; their bizarrely coloured masks equipped with red lolling tongues of gross dimensions and the piercing cries they uttered proclaimed them demons. At first I was at a loss to understand the presence of these half-comic, half-terrifying, yelling creatures amidst that decorous throng, but Pao explained that they were lictors from the court of that dark Judge whom the general's spirit was about to face. By bribing the lictors, it was hoped that a moderating influence would be brought to bear upon the Judge!

'Good lord! Do the general's relatives really believe in such things? The lictors look like characters in a gruesome story from the pen of P'u Sung-Ling.'

'Certainly they don't believe such nonsense. You should know by now that ancient customs die hard in China. Imagine the waste entailed by a funeral on this scale! The money they have spent already and will continue spending for several months to come on the general's obsequies would be ample to endow a fair-sized hospital! No, don't look shocked. I see things one way, you another. I'm afraid you would like us to make our country into a museum of antiquities just for your benefit. Let's go and pay our respects to the general.'

He led me through two crowded courtyards to a third and smaller one containing cyprus-trees which indicated that we were approaching the family's private ancestral temple. The doors had been thrown back to admit as many as cared to come and prostrate themselves before the coffin. In the centre of the hall, supported on trestles, stood the largest coffin I had ever seen, gilded at the ends and covered with thick scarlet lacquer. Pao believed that the heavy wood composing it had been brought all the way from Liuchou in South-East China; for the wood produced there, properly sealed with a special glue, is able to preserve bodies intact for decades if not centuries. Behind the coffin stood an altar furnished with candles, incense and offerings of food; while, still farther back, rose a newly carven spirit-tablet bearing the general's name and titles, as well as a full-length portrait of him dressed in a civilian gown. The floor to either side of the altar had been covered with plain mats woven of fine grass, which were occupied by the deceased's wives and progeny, for those in deep mourning must not sit on chairs. All were dressed in coarse unbleached sackcloth and the women protected from the public gaze by a curtained enclosure of the same material.

As Pao and I were carried forward by the stream of people pressing from behind, we presently found ourselves directly opposite the coffin, so we fell to our knees and bowed our faces once to the ground in salutation of the dead. Simultaneously, the throng of mourners who knelt upon their mats facing us touched their faces to the ground to mark their gratitude. Only the moans and sobs coming from behind the women's curtain provided a stark touch of realism to this ceremony, which by its very elaborateness tended to overlay the poignancy of death. Looking at the faces of the general's sons and grandsons, I could not tell how much genuine grief was decorously concealed by the stiff formality and pageantry preserved from ancient times.

The crowd, which still came pouring into the mansion, was so great that those who had already paid respect to the dead and perhaps eaten a few mouthfuls of the funeral breakfast were obliged to leave, thus making room for those who followed. So Pao and I decided to pass some hours in a tea-house while waiting for the procession to begin. The waiter showed us to an upper room which must have reminded Pao of the place where the drum-troupe performed, for presently he startled me with unexpected news of Kuei-Hsiang. A single glance at his face was enough to convince me that the many girls he had enjoyed since their parting had not substantially diminished his affection for her. Though he did not speak much of his own feelings, his tense expressions and slightly hesitant speech made them obvious.

'Kuei-Hsiang has left Saito. Her letter reached me last month on the Feast of Lanterns. She says her brother came during Saito's office hours and insisted on taking her away. They left by train for somewhere north of here and rejoined the rest of her family in what she calls "a safe place". She says it's impossible for her to come back to Peking but that, if I still want her, she hopes I'll go north to join her.'

'What can it mean?' I asked. 'What safe place can there be in the north, closer even than we are to Japanese-occupied territory?'

He sipped his tea slowly, as though he wanted time to choose his words.

'She gave a Peking address as her poste restante. I couldn't find out anything from the people living there. But putting two and two together, I'm inclined to think her eldest brother has persuaded the whole family to put themselves under the protection of some organization working against the Japanese. Who could bear to let his sister live with one of them? I wish I had had the courage to persuade her to go over to the Communists with me, instead of trying to take her to Shanghai.'

'The *Communists*! Why especially to them?'

'People do, you know. With our provincial government and our city mayor bound hand and foot by Japanese interference, and with our Central Government doing less than nothing to prepare this part of China for the coming invasion, those who want to put up a fight have only the Communists to turn to. I know I'd be a rotten Communist. I've not much sympathy with their methods; but sometimes I think I ought to join them. I'd be with them now if Kuei-Hsiang had given me her address.'

'My poor, dear Pao. What would *you* do with the Communists? From all I hear, they are out-and-out puritans. No flower-girls, lute-players, dance-hostesses, singing-girls or masseuses for you there! If Kuei-Hsiang and you got tired of each other, what on earth would you do?'

Stung by my frankness, he looked at me with an expression almost of hatred.

'You are as bad as my uncle. Why can't you see that a young Chinese man amuses himself with girls and so on just because our rotten, supine Government offers him no chance to do something worth while? Soon we'll be slaves and running-dogs to the Japanese. Do you think music and girls can fill my life then?'

'Pao! You always look like a contented cat in a creamery. I never dreamt you are dissatisfied or unhappy—except for Kuei-Hsiang.'

He laughed angrily and yet half amused in spite of himself.

'There you were wrong. Elegant young men like your bosom friend Chu Tê-Ku can keep happy with just girls, flowers, amusing conversation, music, good food and plenty of dilettante companions like themselves—maybe. I don't know. I'm not Chu. I could never understand why you like people like that so much. They see life as an intricate game to be played humorously, gracefully and always without much involvement. I see it as something too precious to squander. Of course, I do squander every day of it, but that's because I am unlucky enough to be born a Chinese at a time when China is in the hands of men as useless as Chu, but a great deal more ruthless and—I grant you— less superficially attractive. I may look like a contented cat, but I'll show tiger's claws if anyone gives me a chance to use them on the Japanese.'

'Well! I must say I do like Chu. I don't like to hear him mentioned in the same breath with those Nanking officials. But I do see what you mean. In your place, I might—oh, God knows. Anyway, let's not be late for the funeral. If you were as hard as you make yourself out to be, you would not have had the kindness to come round this morning and take me to it. Poor Chu would be most upset if he knew your feelings for him. He admires you tremendously—especially your energy. He says you sometimes walk when you could ride!'

We strolled towards the Tungssû P'ailou, an elaborate ceremonial archway spanning the route of the procession. Already there were crowds of people lining both sides of the road, but we easily squeezed through to a place in the front rank. The Chinese are marvellously indulgent to strangers in such matters. There we stood for about an hour, getting gradually chilled in spite of the milder weather. When at last the procession appeared, it was so long and advanced so ponderously that it took over an hour to pass through the archway. My memories of this mammoth feast of colour are confused. Its components included two hundred young boys in blue and white mourning garments carrying white paper fronds which streamed out above their heads; and several bands of musicians (both European-style and Chinese) spaced at insufficient intervals so that the sad wailing of Chinese flutes and clarionets clashed with the cheerful bray of trombones, fifes and horns. There were relays of professional magicians casting handfuls of paper spirit-money to appease those hardy demons who had withstood the ear-splitting din created by the professional exploders of fire-crackers. Trains of Mongol lamas dressed in red and yellow silks blew thunderously upon their eight-foot horns or thwacked the thin, resonant drums carried before them by hefty alcolytes. Chapters of Chinese monks in robes of black with red or yellow-ochre stoles chanted Buddhist sutras to a tune brought across Himalayan passes and Central Asian deserts by pilgrims returning from India a thousand years before.

Presently the coffin itself made its majestic approach, carried high upon a mighty catafalque borne by fifty or sixty blue-jacketed, blue-turbaned bearers. Close in front of it walked the dead man's family in their pale sackcloth robes, the women still sheltered from view by curtains stretched from eight verticle poles and forming a portable rectangular enclosure. Over a thousand relatives, friends and sympathizers (all of them male) followed behind, some with white mourning bands encircling the left sleeves of their ceremonial jackets. As the middle ranks of this section of the procession drew level with us, Pao pressed my arm and we stepped forward to merge ourselves in that sea of mourners, whom we accompanied for more than a mile. Presently people began dropping out in increasing numbers and at last the coffin was transferred to a white-draped lorry to be carried to a temple near the Western Hills, there to lie perhaps for years awaiting an auspicious date for the final obsequies. Now I could understand why the family had gone to the enormous expense of obtaining a coffin of special Liuchou timber impervious to air.

To those who had been hoping for an anti-Japanese demonstration, the funeral was a disappointment. Not only did the onlookers refrain from shouting slogans or showing other signs of patriotic fervour, but those Japanese living near the route of the procession came out to watch or photograph the pageant with evident enjoyment. However, the general's children had amply demonstrated their filial piety by taking every known precaution to ensure his smooth passage down to the Yellow Springs and his welfare in the world of spirits beyond.

The Altar of Heaven

Astrological instruments in the East City

Besides this, the citizens of Peking had been provided with a spectacle seldom equalled since Heaven's Son was driven from his Throne.

. . . . .

Several days before Ch'ing Ming (the Spring Festival), I received a note from the Singing-Master enclosing two tickets for an operatic performance by the greatest of all living female-impersonators—Mei Lan-Fang. Already approaching fifty, Mei had managed to keep his voice close to the peak of its perfection and he could still play the part of a seventeen-year-old girl with unrivalled grace and mastery. I offered the other ticket to Chu, because Pao was sometimes in a mood to be scornful about traditional arts, whereas my student loved them more than most other things in life. To make certain of arriving at the performance (which I was not certain of being able to appreciate) in a suitably mellow mood, I decided to prepare myself by dining off Peking duck.

The restaurant I chose was one of those renowned for the perfection of its roast duck, but too expensive for me to be able to afford a 'table' of twelve courses sufficient for ten or a dozen guests. Instead, I invited five people whom I warned in advance not to expect an elaborate dinner. In matters of this kind it was always hard to convince Pekingese that you meant what you said, for immemorial custom demanded that a host decry the fare provided, however much his tables groaned beneath mounds of expensive foods. Even rare and subtly flavoured delicacies such as bears' paws, fish-lips or camel's hump, not to speak of common stand-bys like sharksfin soup, sucking pig, fowls stuffed with nests made of swallows' saliva, or plovers' eggs in chicken broth, must be offered with the words '*Mei yiu ts'ai*' (There's nothing to eat)!

My guests were Pao and four of my private students including Chu Tê-K'u, all of whom were slightly older or just younger than myself. When the waiter had shown us into a private room, the other three, being less intimate with me than either Pao or Chu, were inclined to treat me with the rather tiresome deference due to me as their teacher; for they were accustomed to ranking teachers close to their own parents. However, with Chu's help, I managed to convince them that, in this case, true obedience must consist in treating me as one of themselves.

'After all,' I said, 'some of you are slightly older than I am and, if I happen to be your teacher, it's only because English is my native language.'

My argument was finally accepted in principle, but not without smiles of embarrassment; and, though I was host, nothing would induce anyone except Pao to sit 'above' me. While we were still debating this, a youth called Wu Kuo-Ming declared:

'My father will demand from me a detailed account of how we have behaved to you, sir. What will he think of me if I have to confess that I sat above my teacher? Already he is displeased that we have permitted our teacher to play the host to us.'

So that was that. Pao, taking precedence over the rest of us by virtue of his age, sat in the seat of honour facing the door; I occupied the seat on his left which ranked next to his own; Chu sat to his right in the third place of honour, and the other three sat 'below', backs to the door.

Peking duck, *as prepared in Peking*, must be allowed to stand first among the culinary miracles of the world. The dish which goes by that name in Hong Kong, Bangkok and elsewhere is, at best, but a pale reflection of its august prototype; for even a duck maestro imported from Peking is as powerless to display his art in other cities as a concert pianist performing on a tinkling piano in some village hall. The accumulated wisdom and talent of generations of Pekingese duck-breeders, the unique qualities of Peking's water, herbage and climate, as well as various other local factors, are all essential to the rearing of suitable birds. When a party has assembled at table, the maestro emerges from his kitchen and offers for inspection several partly cooked birds impaled on a spit. Their skin gleams like golden-orange lacquer; their dimensions are those of small, plump geese. For a solo performance, that is to say for a Peking duck dinner pure and simple, with the duck courses undiluted by extraneous dishes, the customary procedure is thus. Two, three or four birds, selected by the host with careful assistance from the more expert of his guests, are brought back to the table sizzling from the spit. Their crisp lacquered skins have been sliced so cunningly that each pair of chopsticks can effortlessly detach individual mouthfuls to which no flesh adheres; for the flesh, however delicious in itself, would detract from the supreme perfection of the skin. Each golden segment, after being dipped in a reddish-black sauce and placed with shreds of spring onion upon a wafer of hot bread, forms a morsel incomparable both as to taste and texture. Alas, this

ambrosiac food, so utterly satisfying to the palate, has one drawback—
even the skins of a dozen such birds would form too light a meal to
produce that comfortable state of repletion without which a feast
would be incomplete. So the banqueters, having enjoyed the last
mouthfuls of skin, descend to eating the ducks' lesser parts. The rich
grease collected during the roasting, when combined with a dozen
eggs, forms a satisfactory omelet; the flesh denuded of its skin can be
diced with bamboo shoots and served as duck sauté; the livers and
gizzards can be fried in batter; and, from the bones of ducks which
underwent this metamorphosis the previous day, a soup is prepared to
accompany the rice served towards the end—but these, of course, are
mere echoes of the music which has gone before.

'Well,' I said in Chinese as we downed the last cups of *paikan*
before turning to the soup, 'I know the moment has come when I
should apologize for entertaining you with such poor and scanty fare;
but, as a guest in Peking, it would scarcely become me to speak
disrespectfully of one of your city's noblest arts. So perhaps I may be
allowed to congratulate you on spending your lives within a mile or
two of this delectable restaurant. May I?'

'Certainly,' answered a student called Hsiao. 'We shall allow that.
Yours is the case of a man who has borrowed his friend's chef. After
the feast at which he is host, if he praises the food he offends against
custom; if he decries it he offends the guest whose chef he has borrowed.
There is in old riddle as to what, in this case, the host should say. It has
never been satisfactorily solved.'

'Very true!' cried Wu Kuo-Ming as our laughter subsided. 'You
have reminded me of the misfortune which overtook our first Chinese
minister to Paris towards the end of the Manchu Dynasty. Once he
gave a banquet to some French dignitaries at a famous Paris restaurant,
which the *maître d'hôtel* personally supervised. During the last
course our minister, speaking through his official interpreter, made the
usual apologies for the "scanty and poorly cooked food" he had
provided. I suppose they caused consternation among his guests, but
nothing serious occurred until a few days later. Then he received a
communication from the French Ministry of Foreign Affairs informing
him that only his diplomatic immunity had saved him from prosecution
by the angry restaurateur on a charge of wilful and malicious defama-
tion calculated to destroy the restaurant's reputation!'

While I was still laughing at this absurd but probably authentic anecdote, Pao reminded my other guests that Chu and I were due at Mei Lan-Fang's performance, so the party broke up in a hurry. On our way downstairs, relays of servants took up the cry of the waiter I had tipped, calling:

'Guests leaving. Three *yuan* ti-i-ip! Tha-a-ank you!'

'Do you know', said Chu, giggling from the effect of the *paikan*, 'that if you had forgotten to leave anything, we should have been followed to the street with the cry: "Guests leaving. No-o-o-o ti-i-i-ip!" Old Father Heaven, how embarrassing! It happened once to my father.'

'To your father? I am surprised. He seems a person who would tip generously even if it left him without money for his next meal. He has what we call the grand manner.'

'Exactly. You understand him well. When he's hard up, he'll order something costing only three or four *mao* [thirty or forty cents], like a bowl of prawn and mushroom noodles; and then leave half a *yuan* [dollar] or a whole one for the waiter. That day he left nothing because the fellow had tried to pass off some quite ordinary river fish as Tientsin *li yü* [carp]. Before that he was a good customer there; he's never been back since. He would forgive an outright theft much more readily than a cruel deception of that sort. So would I.'

The distance from the duck restaurant to the theatre was so short that even Chu had no objection to our going on foot. We walked slowly, knowing we should be only a little over two hours late for the performance. To have arrived sooner would have been tedious, as great actors like Mei Lan-Fang seldom condescended to appear on the stage until two thirds of the way through the opera in which they were performing. Their understudies were good enough to satisfy those undiscriminating ticket-holders who, to get their money's worth, sat through six acts from the very beginning. Such people were usually countrymen or visitors from distant provinces. The true Pekingese, princes or rickshaw-pullers, knew the stories and often the words of the operas by heart; so there was no need to waste time on the under-studies. My own reason for choosing to be late was a different one. My ears had not learnt to take kindly to a shrill falsetto accompanied by the screech of fiddles and the crash of cymbals, nor could I catch the sense of the words being sung. After less than three years in China and less than two years in Peking itself, all I could hope to appreciate, besides the acrobatic feats of the warriors and the lavish costumes, was the skill of a middle-aged man in creating the illusion of being a sweetly shy little girl, tender and graceful.

Peking opera, which also contains elements of ballet and drama, has recently appeared in Western capitals too often for a person as unappreciative as myself to venture a detailed description of it. I enjoy many kinds of Chinese music, but remain insensitive to the charms of this particular sort. Whenever I listen to it, I am reminded of its origin in the arid wastes beyond the Great Wall, from where it was imported into China only seven hundred years ago. Such music is as distant from either the silken fluttering of the scholar's lute-strings or the cold purity of rustic flutes heard by moonlight as Stravinsky's works are distant from those of Mozart on the one hand or from plaintive Hebridean folk-music on the other. For all its acquired sophistication, it retains clear traces of its barbaric origin in Mongolia. Especially during my early days in Peking, though I loved the rich colouring of the masks and costumes and thrilled to the terrible combats of warriors wielding their weapons with blood-chilling ferocity, it was only at rare moments that I was carried out of myself to share the delight of the Chinese audience.

By the time Chu and I entered our dress-circle box—a sort of cubicle forming part of the dress-circle itself—Mei Lan-Fang had just emerged. No longer recognizable as the middle-aged man to whom I had recently been introduced by the Singing-Master, he had become a lovely young girl whose every gesture emphasized her femininity. Dressed austerely in robes of black with long white sleeves reaching to the ground, he employed a hundred different means to portray shyness tempered by coy humour, timidity forcing itself to dare, affection struggling with maidenly constraint, playfulness peeping from behind a mask of decorum, or bashfulness concealing languorous glances behind a silken sleeve. I joined enthusiastically in the roars of applause whenever they greeted some tiny gesture by which the heroine 'unconsciously' revealed whatever happened to be passing through 'her' mind. Though I have forgotten which opera it was, I vividly recall its heroine. Mei Lan-Fang's performance was so impressive that even Chu, whose expressions of pleasure were usually smilingly restrained, grew hoarse with shouting applause.

'Tomorrow night I shall bring my father and several of my uncles,' he said, laughing. 'Even they will have to admit that *some* things are as good today as they were when we Manchus ruled.'

As the performance ended nearly half an hour before midnight and it was too early to go to bed, I suggested going round to the back of the theatre to thank the Singing-Master for the tickets. Like people of his kind all the world over, he was a night-bird who would surely not think our visit ill-timed. Chu, who clearly would have preferred me to go alone, yielded to my persuasion without enthusiasm, but the reason for his hesitation was not immediately apparent. The door of the untidy upstairs room occupied by the Singing-Master was opened to us by Precious Orchid, who took care not to let us inside. The sound of suppressed feminine giggles coming from within made me fear for a moment that we had disturbed Mr Hu at a moment when he was imparting some of his art to one or other of Precious Orchid's three 'sisters', but I was wrong. Gazing at Chu with such undisguised pleasure that he actually blushed, she informed us that Hu Laoyeh was to be found at the Tê I Lou Hotel smoking opium in Little Wang's company.

'That's odd,' I said without much conviction. 'The Singing-Master assured me he rarely smokes opium, and yet . . .'

Chu stared at me in amazement.

'Surely you didn't believe him? You say he's fat and jolly-looking, but I think it likely he smokes a whole *liang* [Chinese ounce] every day. Whoever heard of a singing-master who doesn't smoke?'

'Then why . . .'

'Smokers are like that. My father used to be the same. They always pretend, even to themselves if possible, that they are not addicted. A few of them really aren't, but more often they are just trying to convince you or themselves that they are still their own masters. As if anyone outside a cloister or a hermitage is ever master of himself! In my family, we accept the fact that man is a slave to his habits. As my father says, all we should expect from people is reasonable restraint —just enough to make them tolerable as companions. The self-opinionated, tight-lipped Confucian scholars would condemn him for requiring so little of himself and others, but I think Father is more honest, more of a realist, than they are. Of course, in practice he has his standards, too; but he frankly admits they are hard to live up to. By the way, if we are going on to the Tê I Lou to find your Hu Hsienshêng, please remember to introduce me only by my surname and not to give him my address, will you?'

'Why such precautions? Hu Hsienshêng is a charming fellow.'

'I'm sure of that, as you like him. Still, that sort of man has too much to do with female-impersonators. They—never mind. If he should take a fancy to me and find some excuse to call at my house, my father would whip me.'

'So, in your allegedly casteless country, you still despise actors! And barbers, too, just as in ancient times?'

'I don't despise anyone, especially amusing people like actors, but you can't have them running in and out of your house. Entertaining them in restaurants is the proper way.'

'But why?'

'For one thing because they—because my father would be angry.'

The Tê I Lou was a hotel outside the Ch'ien Mên which owed to Japanese protection its immunity from visits by the police. Equipped with baths, telephones, majong tables and several sorts of cuisine, it had become a nest of small opium dens (one to each room) where some people were said to pass the whole of each day between rising at noon and returning home at dawn to sleep. Pao and others had told me that the Japanese were using every sort of criminal means to soften up North China before swallowing it whole. Opium, the little brother of heroin and morphine, merely required a watchful eye. The smoking habit was already so widespread in China that all the Japanese had to do was to give protection to the bigger dens and to ensure that adequate supplies were brought in from Manchuria by Korean roughs with whom the Chinese police interfered at their peril. Far more destructive in their effects were their efforts to popularize heroin addiction. For this purpose they made use of the most curious and crafty means. For example, special prostitutes were trained to require from the youths who slept with them supernormal potency and to teach them how to increase their powers by the use of heroin—a drug which bestows temporary virility, followed by impotence, physical debility and moral apathy! Moreover, in the Japanese Concession in Tientsin were 'book-shops' where a man could receive a morphine injection, pay cash and walk out all within the space of two minutes. These and worse abuses, such as the peddling of drugs to schoolchildren in the form of sweets, were all investigated and reported by Western journalists, but the papers they wrote for seldom printed their findings. The hair-raising but carefully documented report of Timperly, a New Zealand journalist, had, I believe, to be published at his own expense.

Knowing something of these matters, I expected the Tê I Lou to be a sort of chamber of horrors, but I cannot honestly say that the atmosphere we found there that night was vicious. While searching for the Singing-Master, we entered a number of rooms each furnished with padded divans and the six to eight lamps necessary to accommodate about thirty smokers per room each day. At that time of night, they were crowded to capacity with people who, judging from their dress and appearance, came from every sort of social background except the richest; for those able to pay fat bribes to the police naturally found it more convenient to smoke at home. In any case, the proportions of educated and illiterate customers seemed to be about equal. (In a country where illiteracy is widespread, a foreigner soon learns to distinguish the more literate people at a single glance; the difference in facial expression is striking.)

Some of the customers we saw were busy cooking little pellets of opium over their lamps or inhaling clouds of smoke from their heavy pipes. Others sat or lay upon the divans talking to one another with the noticeable animation which opium-smoking produces in almost everyone. Those not ready yet for a smoke were seated at square tables playing majong or bending over delicious snacks brought in by hawkers or ordered from neighbouring restaurants. We saw very few people asleep or sleepy-looking; and only two or three elderly and undernourished men resembled my previous conception of 'dope-fiends'. In fact I was disappointed to discover that, if the sour smell of beer could have been substituted for the sweet and all-pervading odour of opium, the atmosphere would have been very much indeed like that of a London pub on a Saturday night. This was nothing like the sort of hell I had pictured. In order to regain a proper attitude of disapproval, I had to remind myself of some grisly stories I had heard about the sufferings of addicts unexpectedly deprived of the drug.

We found the Singing-Master in a room on the top floor. He was reclining with his back to the door on a double couch, facing Little Wang across his tray of smoking-paraphernalia. Now I did receive a shock. Precious Orchid had implied that Little Wang had gone with the Singing-Master just to keep him company, but we entered the room to find him right in the middle of puffing out a great cloud of smoke. The sight of that long, thick pipe pressed against the red lips of a soft-skinned, pubescent child was really sinister, though Chu seemed to take it as a matter of course. Little Wang, who saw us before the Singing-Master was aware of our arrival, instantly set down his half-smoked pipe, scrambled off the couch and welcomed us with a bow. He also blushed, but I do not think this had anything to do with repentance for his opium-smoking. He was just a boy who blushed easily, as I had noticed before. When I had introduced Chu to both of them, I tried in vain to persuade Little Wang to lie back on the couch. Instead, he fetched two stools for himself and Chu, insisting that I must obey Mr Hu's invitation to take his place.

'Is Little Wang an addict?' I asked the Singing-Master bluntly. The smile creasing his chubby face vanished abruptly, as he answered in shocked tones:

'Most certainly not. Little Wang is only fourteen. No one becomes an addict before he is sixteen, unless in exceptional circumstances. This child takes a puff now and then, under my supervision of course, for the sake of his voice. How did you enjoy the opera?'

'Enormously, thank you. But what can I say? Mei Lan-Fang is beyond praise. Ask Chu Hsienshêng.'

I was glad I had brought Chu with me, as I could not possibly have discussed the performance in a way satisfactory to the Singing-Master. Chu, whose record of studies at the university was very mediocre, showed himself wonderfully quick and well informed in matters of this sort. He spoke so gracefully and displayed such knowledge of fine points that Mr Hu was charmed with him. They entered upon a technical discussion of which I understood hardly one complete sentence; and Little Wang, seeing me left out, hurried back to the edge of the couch to keep me company. For an instant, his abrupt return from exile on the stool made me fear he was jealous of his teacher's preoccupation with Chu, but not at all. Smiling shyly, he wiped the ivory mouthpiece with a clean cloth and set about preparing a new pill of opium; then, holding the pipe with its bowl close to the flame, he pressed the mouthpiece gently against my lips. I had not intended to smoke, but saw no particular reason why I should not, especially after Little Wang had taken this trouble. During the next half hour I learnt that opium is in one respect similar to brandy. Just as the first glass burns the mouth, the second merely scorches, the third slips down smoothly, the fourth and fifth vanish imperceptibly, so does each pipe of opium pass into the lungs with less conscious effort than the one before. Before I had the sense to begin counting the pipes, I had already smoked a great deal too much; so when the Singing-Master next gave me his attention, I was in something of a daze. Able to understand and to answer clearly, I nevertheless felt so content just *to be*, that conversation seemed tiresomely superfluous. I had passed beyond the loquacious stage without saying more than an occasional word of thanks to Wang.

'P'u Hsienshêng! What has Little Wang been doing to you? Little Wang, you idle bone, you ought to die! Our friend here is not accustomed to such tricks. He doesn't share your capacity for . . .'

At that moment, I knew with absolute clarity that both the Singing-Master and Little Wang were confirmed addicts, yet it didn't seem to matter now—not a copper cash. Why should I bother with moral indignation when the whole world was beautiful? Yes, everything and everybody. Little Wang was beautiful, so was the Singing-Master, and also Chu, and so was the thin man whose face I could not see. A shining memory flashed into my mind. Three years before, my lama had taught me that all men, when their True Nature is revealed, are seen to be gods. Now (as I thought) I knew the truth of this, though at the back of my mind was the disturbing thought that my lama Teacher would have wept to find me confusing Truth with this false ecstasy.

Thus something like the experience described in Aldous Huxley's *Doors of Perception* occurred to me more than twenty years before that book was written, giving rise to much the same thoughts. However, unlike Mr Huxley (for whose opinions on other matters I have long felt admiration), I have now come to believe that the doors opened by the physical action of a drug lead away from instead of towards perception of Eternal Truth. Or, to be more accurate, I know that certain drugs do carry us into one of the lower states of mystical contemplation, while at the same time making it impossible for us to rise to the higher states. Making use of them with serious intent is like locking oneself in a railway carriage and throwing away the key when setting out for a destination *beyond the terminus of the railway*! The highest states, I believe, can only be attained by tremendous efforts and by walking every foot of the way on our own feet.

That night the Singing-Master, who knew from experience that I was in a state when *everything* would seem pleasant to me, would not let me go home. If the rickshaw-puller were to turn round and rob me —not that such things ever happened in Peking—I would find it amusing to let him have his way. If a car should push me into the palace moat, I should rejoice to find myself among the lotus-leaves. If deserters from the army—Peking's most dangerous characters—were to follow me into the house, I should make them welcome to my possessions. So Chu, after angrily protesting that he must see me home, left by himself, deeply offended by our laughter. Then the Singing-Master and Little Wang, placing their hands upon my arms, guided me tenderly back to the theatre where I spent the night in Little Wang's bed, leaving Wang himself to share the bed of one of the Singing-Master's other pupils. I did not sleep for one minute, but the hours rushed by and I desired no pastime, no entertainment, beyond the joy of just *being*.

At about seven in the morning, a girl came in with a pot of tea and a bowl of rice-gruel on a tray. Mistaking the reason for the radiant smile with which I thanked her, she leapt away from my bed with such a show of outraged modesty that I could hardly contain my laughter. Obviously women acted the parts of women much less convincingly than Mei Lan-Fang. However, she was a kind-hearted girl and presently, feeling sorry for the disappointment from which she imagined I was suffering, she treated me from a safe distance to some melting looks and surprisingly racy remarks. After she had taken away the tray and given me a chance to put my clothes on, I left the theatre in excellent spirits and took a rickshaw straight to the Tung Yüeh Temple. There I found Yang Taoshih, who had just completed his morning meditation and exercises; he was breakfasting off sweet rice-gruel. His mode of greeting came to me as a shock.

'I see you've been smoking opium. You need something very sweet. I'll send for another bowl of this gruel, which contains lotus-seeds and dragons'-eyes [a kind of dried fruit], besides plenty of sugar. However, please do not suppose I approve.'

'No, I suppose not. Nor do I, now I come to think of it. Last night I drifted into smoking through force of circumstance.'

'A pretty girl placed the pipe to your lips?'

'Not a girl. Just a boy who is training to become one.'

'Ah, you mean an actor. Bad company!'

'That is what everyone keeps telling me. So far, I like all those I have met.'

'So do I. They are refreshingly free from convention and, to that extent, are natural Taoists. But don't they tend to abuse their freedom?'

An acolyte hurried in with a big bowl of sweet gruel which he placed in front of me. Instead of answering the question, I asked:

'Yang Taoshih, how could you possibly know—about last night?'

'A mirror would tell you, if I had one. Your pupils are no bigger than the eyes of a very small prawn. They are so small as to convince me that you are not used to opium. That I find reassuring. Now I should like to enquire why my humble abode is graced by the light of your presence so very early in the day.'

His glance swept the beautiful cell and came back to rest on me with a look compounded of amusement and concern.

'Last night, in the opium-den, I wondered if I had found Truth—the Truth of Being. I seemed to experience what you and also my Buddhist Teachers have so often told me I ought to feel. But I grant you the gateway was an ignoble one—certainly not the Jade Pass you would have me enter. I realize now that what I saw was only a shadow of what lies beyond that Pass. And yet it seemed perfect. To exist, to be part of Now, was in itself a supreme joy—no need for action of any sort. Wasn't that close to what you mean by *wu wei*?'

'Possibly. I have never taken opium, so I cannot say. If you had really ridden through the Jade Pass, you would still be there. Those who enter, never have to come back, although they may stay with us for a while in their ordinary bodies. The whole universe is changed for them, with light and shadow both seen for ever as perfection. Opium cannot achieve that. To regain your joy, you would begin to smoke constantly. Enslaved to it, you would find its joy-giving power had vanished; while without it you would feel ill. It is no way to lasting happiness. Everyone in China knows that much. I have always thought that giving unasked-for advice is a senseless, impertinent and even a dangerous thing to do, yet now I do advise you not to play with that sort of fire again. It leads to—— Come, the early morning is not time for sermons. If you like our gruel, do make our cook happy by sending for another bowl or two.'

'Thank you indeed, but I can hardly finish this one. I ate one big bowl of savoury gruel at the Singing-Master's.'

'Good. The boy who is studying to be a girl has looked after you well.'

'No, no. He was asleep somewhere. The gruel was brought by a girl who—just a girl.'

'Then have I to felicitate you?'

'I don't quite—oh, no. She is part of the ménage of my host. How could I . . .' I stopped, blushing at the implication.

'Probably you could not. I have been a recluse since I was twelve, so the affairs of actors and singing-masters remain a mystery to me. In an ordinary household, a guest treats his host's *yat'ou* [servant-girls] with respect, but I have always been told that actors have the morals of rabbits. It may, of course, be quite otherwise. And then, everyone's morality is entirely his own concern, is it not?'

'In the West people are often more concerned about other people's morals than their own.'

'Ah, dear, dear! Just like our Confucian scholars. Who would have thought it? How distressing!'

I glanced at him shyly, wondering whether I could put my sudden thought into words. Seeing him bland and smiling as ever, I plucked up the courage to say:

'But you, yourself, have adopted a life of celibacy from choice. I had assumed that you attach importance to sexual continence—more so than the Confucian scholars. Was I wrong?'

'Nothing is really more important or less important than any other thing. I do, as it happens, lead a celibate life, because my Master taught me how to transcend most of my longings. Until a need is no longer felt, exercising forceful restraint merely spoils a man's temper without providing any compensatory gain. People who force themselves to be what they call good easily turn sour. When a child wants to take burning charcoal into his hands, you do not take away the brazier. You take away his desire for it by letting him see how it burns things. Then he grows indifferent to those pretty red toys and leaves them alone from choice.'

'I wish you would teach me how to become indifferent to pretty toys!'

Roaring with laughter, he answered: 'I shall certainly teach you that, *when you are quite sure you want to learn.* Meanwhile, have some more gruel. After last night you need plenty of sweet things to help you recover.'

To please him, I forced myself to eat another bowl and then took leave of him. When I reached home, Lao Chao, though my absence must have made him sadly worried, received me with his usual calm except for one quick glance of enquiry and surprise. A quarter of an hour later, instead of bringing me my usual breakfast, which I had forgotten to cancel, he came in smiling with a bowl of sweet gruel and a plate of super-sweet Chinese dates swimming in sticky syrup!

# 8

# Singing-girls among the Pine-trees

IN MID-SPRING Peking assumes the rôle of a lovely, flirtatious girl who now and then teases her admirers by hiding her face behind a Moslem's veil. Though the season's gifts of flowers and fresh foliage are bountifully displayed, dust-storms thicker than a London fog suddenly descend from the skies, blotting out trees and buildings, filling eyes and throat with painfully sharp grit, penetrating doors and windows, and leaving a pall of yellow behind the glass of tightly shut bookcases. Tempers fray and food is spoiled. At other times, the spring weather is irresistible and beckons people to haunts of beauty scattered in profusion between the city walls and the nearest summits of the Western Hills.

The Spring Festival of Ch'ing Ming had come and gone. Those whose ancestors lay buried within a convenient distance had gone forth in family groups, carrying sacrificial food and wine, to perform the annual ceremony of 'sweeping the tombs'. Naturally, when the spirits of the ancestors had feasted upon the essence of these offerings, their descendants consumed what remained, while completing the solemn rites with a cheerful picnic. Upon an evening some two or three weeks later, I happened to be dining with Dr Chang and several of our friends at a restaurant famous for steamed crabs. Among the shells strewing the table stood three whitish-grey earthenware bottles of *maot'ai*, an ardent grain-spirit from the south-west which stimulates uninhibited conversation. Presently, Dr Chang was inspired to bring forth some of those extempory poems which his compendious knowledge of T'ang and Sung poetry enabled him to compose with scarcely a pause between one line and the next. We had been talking about the Ch'ing Ming Festival, when he said:

'I think the time has come for a real picnic. Everyone whose ancestors dwell near here came back complaining that the weather was too chilly for them to enjoy their visits to the Western Hills, but now—

'The sunlight slanting warmly on the moss
Of ancient gateways peering from the crags
Brings forth recluses from their icy cells
Collecting dew to serve their guests with tea.'

Our exclamations of pleasure were followed by an excited *maot'ai*-stimulated discussion as to the arrangements to be made for the picnic. One of my colleagues, a very young history lecturer called Lin, whose face after a few thimblefuls of *maot'ai* had turned scarlet, suddenly broke his befuddled silence to cry:

'What about girls? Who wants a spring picnic without girls?'

'What an exceedingly *modern* young man you are,' mildly observed his senior historian, Professor Ch'êng. 'Picnics are to admire the moon, to pay respects at the tombs of dead poets, to enjoy any of nature's gentler moods, to visit a secluded temple in search of hermits steeped in mystic lore, to commune with silence in unfrequented places, to revere a waterfall in spate, to drink tea infused with melted snow, to watch for dragons in a pool—what place have women in these things? They are noisy and get in the way.'

'You are right, Professor, but permit me to disagree,' observed a young man surnamed Ouyang, who was still sober enough to make use of this polite formula for introducing a contrary opinion. 'Women of the right kind would add to the poetry of the mountains. Chang Taifu may perhaps know where to find some talented little friends of the sort we need—girls able to play the flute, to sing and, above all, to remain silent when need be. Their company would surely enhance our pleasure in the songs of birds and the silence of the pine forests. Do you not agree?'

His reference to Dr Chang's long-standing affair with a singing-girl and the implication that a secret known to all Peking need be guarded no longer caused my friend's urbane smile to fade, but Professor Lee came to his rescue, saying:

'If we were living in an age when the erotic exploits of Hsi-Mên Ch'ing were openly admired, I should agree with you. As it is, it would not be quite the thing for us to be seen in broad daylight with girls of that sort. Custom has decreed proper times and proper places for all things. Suppose some of our students meet us or Chang Taifu encounters some elderly *t'ait'ai* who is a patient of his? What then? How could we face them? Especially grey-heads like Professor Ch'êng and myself! People would say we are too mean to keep respectable concubines in our homes, yet too careless of propriety to conceal our need for them. If you two young men cannot be content to enjoy the perfume of the pines unmixed with the scent of face-powder, you had better invite a few girl-students or some of the young lady assistants in your departments at the university.'

'Better no women at all than university girls,' exclaimed Lin sulkily, for his usual good manners had been overcome by the *maot'ai*. 'Either they will be like frightened sparrows placating a hawk by chirping "Yes, yes, you are right" the whole day through, or they will be learned females throwing the platitudes we have taught them back in our faces. They might even turn out to be serious and want to discuss politics or *social welfare*! What becomes of Lee Hsienshêng's a time and a place for all things, then? By girls, if you will allow me to be explicit, I mean girls—charming children who care for nothing in the world beyond making themselves decorative and amusing.'

After further discussion, interrupted by the arrival of meat-stuffed beancurd and mushroom-garnished fish-head soup to help us tackle a bowl or two of rice, Dr Chang suggested a graceful compromise. Young Lin and Ouyang were to escort three or four quietly dressed, decorously behaved flower-girls to a rendezvous in the mountains where the older men would join them later. Asked to choose, I elected to go with the latter, as I was more intimate with them. My decision won a smile from the doctor who, nevertheless, must have had some thought that I was making a sacrifice, for he presently took me aside and said:

'Do not be afraid to enjoy yourself. Who is Jade Flute's latest successor? Not Moon Fairy any more, I suppose? No one at all just now? What a pity! I could have arranged for Spring Fragrance to call for her and escort her with the others. By the way, I have long wished you to meet Spring Fragrance. She is almost thirty, so you will not find her beautiful; but she has a warm heart and delicately sensitive intuitions. After knowing her intimately for ten years, I still cannot decide whether I prefer to sit quietly while she sings in that lovely voice of hers or just to converse with her. She is clever at saying just those things which, at a given moment, you most want to hear. There's no

other girl like her.' He was not smiling now. Suddenly, in a burst of
confidence, he added sadly: 'I wish she were my wife!'

So the picnic took place. There was no dust-storm that day, but
early in the morning I sensed the threat of a heavy shower or two of
spring rain. This, as it happened, led me into a farcical, but embarrassing, situation. Having arranged to meet my three friends at the motor-
coach terminus in the west city punctually at eight o'clock, I called a
rickshaw to take me there. On the way, the state of the sky made me
lean forward to ask the rickshaw-puller if he thought it was going to
rain. No sooner was the question asked than the man braked the vehicle
with all his strength, released the shafts so that they thudded to the
ground and, turning on me furiously, shouted:

'Your mother's a ——! I won't stand for it. I'm a poor man, but
nobody has the right to talk to me like that. You can get out now. I
don't want your money.'

He looked so dangerous that I clutched my parcel of food and
leapt into the road, in case he should strike me or tilt me out on my
head; whereat, deaf to my expostulations, he seized the shafts and
stalked away. I found myself standing there open-mouthed, scarcely
aware that other rickshawmen were clamouring laughingly for my
custom. My Chinese pronunciation, though not perfect, was really
very good. There was no possibility of my having made a serious slip
of the tongue. Still shaking my head, I stepped into another rickshaw
to continue my journey and arrived at the coach station full of impatient curiosity. Hardly waiting to return my friends' greetings, I
poured forth my story, which reached its climax amidst roars of
laughter.

'What's so funny?' I asked, struggling with my vexation.

'John, John,' exclaimed Professor Lee, trying to bring his laughter
under control. 'You like to say your appearance is the only un-
Chinese thing about you, but you're still a foreigner after all.'

'But . . .'

'You must never call a man a turtle. It is unpardonable.'

'I know that. It means his wife accepts lovers. Of course I didn't
say anything of that sort.'

'You did, you *did*!' cried Professor Ch'êng, waving his parcel with
unusual abandon and speaking, as always, in Chinese. 'Excuse me, P'u
Hsienshêng, you really did. Who knows when it is going to rain later
in the day, unless he is a turtle and feels some moisture on his back?'

'You mean I can't ask someone if . . .'

Suddenly my indignation vanished in a fit of laughter, echoing theirs. Chinese insults, blunt or tortuous, are always hideous. No doubt that was why my Pekingese friends had to be goaded before venturing more than a cold smile or a mild, ambiguously worded sarcasm. Even that much was rare.

My three friends, although they were carrying sizeable parcels, were in no hurry to reach the rendezvous where Lin and Ouyang had promised to escort the girls; and I found our leisurely journey too enchanting to care whether there were to be girls or not. Beyond the Hsi Chih Gate, the motor-coach carried us past villages with yellow-ochre walls; fields clothed in the fresh green of very young corn and dotted with elms, maples or locust-trees in full new leaf; crimson-walled shrines; straw-hatted peasants in sky-blue jackets, laughing children in red combination garments cut to leave their little behinds conveniently bare; blue-hooded carts, cattle, horses, yellow dogs—a feast of colour beneath a sky from which the clouds were drawing away like curtains.

The motor-coach was in some ways less attractive than the crowded country buses filled with peasants who laughed loudly and smelt unashamedly of sweat and garlic; it had comfortably cushioned seats of green leather all facing towards the front, but our fellow passengers belonged to a section of Chinese society to which I was always trying hard to remain blind. Picnickers and sightseers like ourselves, the men were noisy fellows dressed in parodies of American campus costume, and the girls accompanying them made no secret of belonging to the same 'modern' set. From their un-Chinese behaviour, I gathered they were a party of tourists from the south, or perhaps Shanghai-born students at one of Peking's universities. The girls either had short, waved hair and wore tight gowns cut to expose their thighs far above the knee (even in those days), or else they made blatant parade of being 'serious'—hair severely bobbed, shiny noses innocent of powder, and lumpy, ill-fitting garments purposely unbecoming. In other words, they belonged to two types, each of which claimed to be in the vanguard of progress—well-to-do playgirls steeped in the atmosphere of Hollywood, or intense do-gooders with leanings towards Communism. The distinction between them was not confined to hair-style and dress; the former type, who laughed and giggled if you so much as glanced at them, liked crossing their legs to display as much as possible and to indulge in arch flirtations with people looking on; whereas the latter, humourless and apt to converse with fierce intensity, preferred to comport themselves with prim rectitude so that everyone should recognize them as the sexless, dedicated, politically conscious leaders of the society of tomorrow. As for those delightful girls, at once modest and attractively feminine, whom Old China had moulded with such tasteful care, they were not often to be seen in motor-coaches, nor easy for a foreigner to come to know. Paradoxically, those of my acquaintance who approached this chaste ideal more closely were the girls of the flower-houses, for in those establishments tradition still held sway; the matrons thought too highly of their patrons' good taste to permit any girl in a 'good house' to look or behave like a prostitute. So it had come about that, while the daughters of generals and bankers looked like expensive whores, the girls whose bodies really were for sale avoided indelicacy as carefully as if they had been reared in the houses of conservative scholars.

At the I Ho Yuan Summer Palace, as it was not yet ten in the morning and the whole day lay before us, we decided to enjoy the sights. Strolling through those courts and gardens where everything about us bore the imprint of the Empress-Dowager's hand, I thought of her as a living presence. Almost I could hear the tinkle of the jade and pearl ornaments adorning her golden hairpins; almost I seemed to smell the fragrant unguents she had used in her latter years to embalm her aging beauty. All the marvels to be seen on the hither side of the Hill of Ten Thousand Years had been her own creation. When, towards the end of the last century, the allied troops of Europe and Japan poured destruction upon the imcomparable palaces built by the Emperor Ch'ien Lung on the hill's farther side (burning what they could not loot and hewing what they could not burn, so that scarcely one stone remained upon another), Tzü Hsi wept. She shed more tears then than over all the other humiliations inflicted upon her, including the loss of vast territories and dependencies to piratical Western Powers armed with Bibles, gunboats and business tycoons' morality. For years afterwards she laid plans for building palaces and parks equal in beauty to those so vindictively destroyed. Being Tzü Hsi, she succeeded, but not without diverting a big fund collected for the construction of a Chinese navy.

'How beautiful it is!' exclaimed Professor Ch'êng, nervously rolling back the knuckle-length sleeves of his gown, as he often did

when excited. 'Most people hate the Old Buddha [Tzü Hsi] for diverting the naval funds. How unjust! Does their attitude make sense? Any
navy we could have built in those days would have been destroyed in
the first battle. Which of our enemies would have helped us build a
fleet capable of destroying a single ship of theirs? They would have
sent our fleet to the bottom of the sea and then charged us the costs of
the action, as they always did! As it is, the Old Buddha's palace still
stands—they say there is nothing to equal it in the world! Could
anyone, Chinese or foreign, of our generation duplicate it?'

Gazing at the beauty on every hand, I recognized the truth of his
words. The palaces lapping the slopes of the Hill of Ten Thousand
Years consist of court after court of low, stately halls, multicoloured
pagodas and lacquered pavilions, each one a miracle of grace and
beauty. In front of the hill stretches a wide lake, fanning out from a
series of streams and smaller lakes, a place of blue water, of wooded,
temple-dotted islands and deliciously curving marble bridges, each one
lovelier than the last. Palaces and lake are set about with gardens
containing ancient trees, flowering shrubs and curiously shaped rocks,
as well as ritual urns and birds and beasts of finely sculptured bronze.
Where symmetry was demanded there had arisen courts and buildings
as symmetrical in design as human ingenuity could devise; where the
Old Buddha had thought asymmetry more desirable, her architects had
surpassed themselves in interweaving beauties of art and nature. From
the lake you look upwards to the nests of coloured roofs shining
amidst the trees and see the whole hill gleaming like a jewelled ornament against the dark background of taller hills beyond. From the
great pagoda below the summit you gaze down across the lakes
towards the intricate pattern of fields which have been tilled these
thousand years and more. In the distance lies Peking with its tremendous gateways and massive towers rising above the ramparts.

As we did not have time to visit everything, we strolled along the
covered zigzag walk which runs parallel to the shore of the lake and
separates it from the foot of the hill. Its gaily painted pillars and beams
had been designed, not so much to afford shelter from the rain, as to
frame vignettes of slowly changing, never diminishing loveliness.
This was my fourth or fifth visit to the I Ho Yuan and I was to pay it
some thirty visits more during the years to come, but familiarity never
spoiled my pleasure in being there, nor did I at any time have difficulty
in discovering fresh beauties previously unperceived. Half an hour's

walk brought us to the famous marble houseboat. This, apart from some ludicrous attempts to furnish some of the palace state rooms in Western style, is positively the only thing lacking in taste throughout the I Ho Yuan. Resting upon the lake bottom because unable to perform the primary function of every vessel, it does not even have the merit of being beautiful.

'How is it possible that the Old Buddha, with her extraordinary good taste in all things not foreign to Chinese-Manchu tradition, could have been persuaded to tolerate this absurd pavilion in the form of a clumsy barge?'

My question, addressed to no one in particular, produced a sly laugh from the historian, Professor Ch'êng.

'It is such a good joke. If you recall that much of this palace was built with funds diverted from ship-building, you will see the point. The Old Buddha was always clever at dealing with popular criticism. Surely you can imagine the scene? One of the Imperial Censors, taking his life in his hands, steps forward to offer an admonitary memorial to the Throne on the subject of ship-building. He is a patriot expecting to die for his temerity, but the Old Buddha, speaking from behind a curtain at the back of the Throne, replies sweetly: "Naturally the Lord of Ten Thousand Years *has* employed the money for ship-building. You must proceed to the I Ho Yuan when the Emperor and I are in residence. The Lord of Ten Thousand Years will graciously make special arrangements to receive you on His flagship there." Exquisite, exquisite!'

The parcels of food we were carrying began to weigh heavily, but still we were not tired of sightseeing. From the Summer Palace we took a country bus to the Jade Springs which lie closer to the Western Hills. Here, beneath an outlying spur crowned with a pagoda built of porcelain, was a deep natural pool with waters so crystal clear that every frond of the delicate green water-plants clinging to its bottom could be distinctly seen. At one end was a small temple erected in honour of the Jade Emperor, that mysterious Being who presides over all the deities of the indigenous Chinese pantheon. Otherwise, there was nothing at all to distract the eye from the lavish charms of nature; whatever part the hand of man had played in forming that small green paradise had been too artfully hidden to obtrude.

We sat down by the water's edge, where conversation gradually died into silence as one by one we fell under the spell of the lake's stillness. Had it not been for Professor Ch'êng, whose fondness for Taoistic communion with nature went hand in hand with a robust appetite, we might have forgotten lunch until it was too late to reach our mountain rendezvous. He was already clearing his throat to break the silence when Dr Chang, who had been watching some birds preening themselves close to the lake's edge, intoned softly:

'From hidden springs the waters gush
Into the silence of the pool.
Awed by these jade and crystal lights,
Kingfishers fold their wings in shame.'

'Good, good, very good,' agreed Professor Ch'êng hurriedly, as though fearing that, with the poetic ecstasy upon us, we should be even harder to prize from the grass where we sat, 'But what about this one? I was about to offer my poor lines for your criticism when a greater poet forestalled me:

'The dragons lurking neath these fronds of jade
Appease their hunger with the sacred viands
Cast by the priests on days of sacrifice—
While hungry mortals count their ribs and sigh!'

His poem was greeted with a burst of laughter. Professor Lee, who had been dabbling his feet in the cool water, hastened to withdraw them and reach for his socks.

'Ch'êng Hsienshêng, you seem to have made only slight provision against that contingency,' he said. 'May I ask what contribution you have brought to the feast? Your bundle looks rather small.'

'Nothing edible. My imagination rioted, so I compromised by bringing three bottles of yellow wine perhaps worthy of your acceptance. I brought it all the way from my native Hsiaohsing. When my daughter was born we followed our local custom by filling two six-foot jars with new-made wine and burying them in the ground to await maturity at the same time as the girl herself. On her marriage day, last year, we dug them up. One jar was consumed at a wedding feast attended by some two hundred guests. The wine from the second we bottled and I remembered to bring a few bottles back with me to Peking. My contribution to the feast is small, but not altogether unworthy.'

'Admirable!' cried Dr Chang. 'What else have we?'

'I,' said Professor Lee, patting a parcel concealed in a blue carrying-cloth, 'have brought four chickens which were rubbed with garlic and baked in a wrapping of lotus-leaves. John?'

'I'm afraid my contribution is less imaginative. I have brought three dozen of Lao Chao's homemade dumplings stuffed with minced pork and shrimps. And Dr Chang? Your bundle looks the heaviest of all.'

'Just two little sucking-pigs roasted on the spit,' he answered modestly. 'I had intended to bring four, but to have taken out the bones would have spoiled their appearance and sucking-pigs are rather heavy.'

Meanwhile, we had begun walking back to the road. Another country bus set us down close to a pathway winding steeply upwards through a forest of maples, beeches, cyprus and silver pine which led to eight small temples, each built at a spot chosen for some special beauty of its own. We had selected the remotest of them all, a place people seldom took the trouble to visit. Our search for seclusion was dictated by considerations of propriety—none of my friends contemplated turning our peaceful picnic into an orgy by indulging in actions which, according to Jade Flute, were offensive to the sunlight; but the two professors had nation-wide reputations to preserve. The climb was more arduous than we had remembered and our pauses to admire trees and rocks were so numerous that we reached the temple hours after the time agreed upon with the others, yet there was no sign of them at all. Standing in bewilderment on the mossy threshold, we peered into a courtyard which looked lonely and deserted until two aged monks, black robes swishing and sunlight gleaming on their shaven pates, hurried out to greet us.

'*Namo Omito fu* [Hail to the Buddha of Boundless Light]!' they mumbled, pressing their palms together in greeting.

'*Namo Omito fu*,' we answered, bringing our hands together at our breasts to return their salutation according to the time-honoured custom. Buddhist monks of the Pure Land Sect use these words, not as a Christian might say 'God be with you', but because the Holy Name should be so constantly on their lips as to leave them no time for words like welcome, goodbye or thank you; though in practice most of them have a weakness for gossiping with visitors, especially in remote temples where contacts with the outside world are rare.

'Your Reverences,' said Dr Chang, 'we were expecting to join a party of youths and maidens here. Did they come in to pay their respects?'

'There are no youths or maidens within these precincts, as you can see. Where would we hide them? There is only the shrine-hall you see before you and those poor cells to right and left.'

For the moment, I was too occupied with what lay before my eyes to care especially about the non-arrival of the others. The low single-storey buildings of brownish-grey stone nestled beneath gently sloping roofs curving slightly at the corners; these and the sun-dappled court-yard with its ancient flagstones deep in moss seemed like natural projections from the dark background of lichen-covered rocks and giant cedars, gnarled and twisted by the mountain gales. Everything in sight might have been there since the beginning of time. Through the open doors of the shrine-hall I glimpsed a dilapidated altar furnished with but a single oil-dip and with a solitary stick of incense smouldering in a cracked bronze urn; and behind these were three decaying antique images, their clay forms bared of the last shreds of golden lacquer, their noses and fingers long since crumbled into dust. They were beautiful no longer, but the calm serenity of their poise and of what could still be seen of their gestures and expressions seemed marvell-ously imbued with inner peace.

Suddenly the notes of a metal-stringed lute shivered the silence and a woman's voice soared into the air, making us stare accusingly at the two old monks, who faced us unabashed, hands politely encased in their long sleeves, ancient bodies shaking with soft laughter.

'No youths and maidens within the temple precincts,' repeated the elder significantly; then he pointed, Chinese fashion, with his chin to a clump of pines rising from a knoll above the temple, which half concealed the eaves of a curly-roofed pavilion. Following some steps cut in the rock, we came upon Lin and Ouyang seated on the ground in the company of just two girls, one of whom was certainly Dr Chang's Spring Fragrance, for she was singing to her own accompaniment while the other girl gazed at her in admiration. Spring Fragrance, as Dr Chang had said, was neither pretty nor particularly young, but she was one of those people whom it is impossible not to like from the moment you first see them. The smoothness of her skin was very slightly blemished by faint pock-marks which she had not made the mistake of disguising beneath thick layers of powder. Her hair was coiled round her head in a simple plait and she had dressed for the occasion in a starched white jacket and narrow blue trousers which made her look rather like a prosperous farmer's wife. Nothing could have been more appropriate to the surroundings or to the older men's sense of propriety, but it was odd to see a farmer's wife plucking the strings of an ornamented lute with such expertise.

The other girl, who seemed about eighteen and sat very close to Lin, was less striking. Her bobbed hair framed a thin white face, amiable and showing signs of beauty that would ripen when she reached full maturity at the age of twenty or so. Her gown of dark-maroon cloth worn beneath a yellow hand-knitted sweater suggested a university student dressed for some mild festivity. Had we travelled in the company of such girls, only the lute would have given us away.

Lin and Ouyang's contributions to the lunch were two dozen leaf-wrapped mounds of savoury rice cooked with diced chicken and ham, and a similar number of red, spicy Cantonese sausages, together with some pastries stuffed with what they alleged was minced goose and black mushrooms. Professor Ch'êng refused to believe this on the grounds that no cook would waste goose-flesh on pastry-stuffings.

'Minced duck, perhaps; minced goose surely not.'

Only when Ouyang confessed to having sat up half the night preparing the novel stuffing with his own hands did the Professor accept his statement.

'That reminds me of something,' said Spring Fragrance in a speaking voice as melodious in its way as her singing had been. 'Long ago, in T'ang times I think, a barbarian chieftain held captive in Ch'angan won his freedom by cooking a mess of minced squirrel. The Emperor —was it T'ang Ming Huang or another?—had ordered him to produce a novelty able to tickle the jaded tastes of his favourite concubine. She praised the minced squirrel with such fervour that the Emperor released the prisoner and had him escorted with honour back to his own country in the wild mountains of the south. So, today, if the minced goose and mushroom stuffing wins our applause, we must be sure to reward Ouyang Hsienshêng suitably.'

The pastries did win unfeigned applause and Spring Fragrance asked Ouyang to name his reward. Blushing with pleasure, he replied:

'I should prefer something we can all enjoy together. What can this mountain forest provide that is more desirable than a song from Spring Fragrance?'

'Nonsense! You flatter me,' she replied, laughing. 'I am sure Snow

Plum here sings much more sweetly than an old lady of twenty-nine like me.'

Snow Plum blushed deep red and hid her face in her hands. I was not sure that she could sing at all. Perhaps Spring Fragrance had only wished to avoid slighting a girl who, though younger and more beautiful than herself, had so far been eclipsed by superior wit and charm. But Spring Fragrance carried her charity beyond these formal words. Plucking gently at the lute-strings, she played the introductory bars to a folksong written in praise of southern beauties, repeating them again and again until Snow Plum, recovering from her shyness, began to sing. Her tact in choosing a well-known easy melody was rewarded, for Snow Plum had an unexpectedly sweet voice which, as her courage grew, rang out gaily through the pine-grove.

The rest of the afternoon passed quickly, with the girls singing turn and turn about during pauses in the lively conversation led by Dr Chang's enchanting friend. I was by that time no stranger to wine, good food, music and gay company, but the eerie silence of the pine-forest endowed these things with a strange piquancy, a feeling of being lifted up for a space into the world of Taoist dreams. Everything was spiced with novelty. The only disharmony was provided by Lin. Soon after lunch, during which he had as usual been too easily affected by the wine, he lurched to his feet and walked over to a dense clump of pines, as if to relieve himself. From there, he shouted peremptorily to Snow Plum, telling her to come and see some marvel he had discovered on the ground there. She obeyed with reluctance and they disappeared among the trees. A moment later she came running out with scarlet cheeks and ready to burst into tears. The drunken Lin came swaying after her, seized her by the shoulders and began propelling her back towards the trees. Everyone was shocked, but we were tardy to intervene because we remembered that she was 'his girl' and we could not be absolutely sure that her modesty was not simulated. It was left to Spring Fragrance to come to her aid. Speaking courteously, but in tones which made Lin first hesitate and then reluctantly withdraw his hands, she said:

'Lin Laoyeh, please. We are so grateful to you for today and do not know how we shall ever repay your kindness. Sitting here among the pines is happiness indeed; but we are here with you as *friends*. Will you not permit us to enjoy that honour a little longer?'

No one else spoke, but something in her eyes compelled Lin to return sulkily to his place, allowing a frankly tearful Snow Plum to make her way back to a place of refuge between Ouyang and Professor Lee. All of us were feeling embarrassed and the silence which followed weighed upon us until it seemed impossible to break it, but again Spring Fragrance came to the rescue.

'Thank you, Lin Laoyeh. You will be more ready to forgive my interference if I tell you a story which Chang Taifu has known for— oh, many years. When I was fourteen I was married off to a boy two years older. Coming to him as a stranger, I nevertheless learnt to love him as deeply as if all our former lives had been spent together—as perhaps they were. But a year later, the boy caught the heavenly flower sickness [smallpox] and died. Of course, after nursing him night and day, I also received the heavenly flowers, but did not have the good fortune to accompany my husband to the Yellow Springs. By bad luck, I recovered. My face was not much disfigured and, as I was still young and attractive enough to be interesting, my mother-in-law sold me cheaply to one of those ever-watchful men who keep the flower-houses supplied with girls. She was not a bad woman, but she believed her son's death had been due to his marrying a girl of ill-omen. It was natural for her to hate me.

'At that time, I was fifteen. Now I am twenty-nine. For fourteen years I have had a lot to endure. I have had to be intimate with all sorts of men—even those who made me shiver with disgust. Lin Laoyeh, if you can imagine yourself forced to endure the embraces of women, some of whom are old, ugly, lewd or sadistic, you will understand me very well. Whatever happiness I have enjoyed has come to me from Chang Taifu here. Today, thanks to him and you, Snow Plum and I have been allowed to join you 'Six Immortals of the Pine-Grove'— for I am sure you are all incarnations of the Poet and his friends. Who, but Li T'ai-Po, was ever able to compose poems which come pouring out like Chang Taifu's? Believe me, days like this one are as rare for us poor girls as rabbits' horns. Snow Plum's story I do not know; I have never had the pleasure of meeting her before and it would embarrass her too much if we asked her to relate it now. Still, it is not difficult to imagine. It may be a little more or a little less painful than mine—it is surely not a happy one. You must think of us as people released from a cage for a single day and not be in a hurry to remind us of its bars.'

For fear that her story might have a permanently dampening effect on our spirits, Spring Fragrance had begun running her hand up and down her lute even while she was speaking. The notes, at first soft and random, now quickened into a robust folksong full of peasant humour, which the girls presently sang together. At the third verse, Ouyang, who had never before been heard to sing, began joining in with noises like the mooing of a calving buffalo and, amid general laughter, we recovered. Towards evening the mountain air grew chilly, reminding us that it was never safe to be abroad in those hills after dark. We had heard grim stories of deserters, escaped convicts and wanted men emerging from their lairs deeper in the mountains to rob or kidnap travellers encountered after nightfall. There were also rumours of bands of Communists and others preparing in secret to harass the expected Japanese advance on Peking. However, although Professor Ch'êng kept anxiously urging us to hurry, he was too courteous to refuse the tea offered by the two old monks when we called in at the temple to say farewell.

The tea was too hot to be gulped down; while we were waiting for it to cool off, Dr Chang unobtrusively slipped away, which caused Professor Lee to give me a peculiar smile. The agnosticism derived from his father, a strictly orthodox Confucian scholar-official of the old régime, and the effect of spending some years at Oxford had made him incapable of understanding his friend's attachment to Buddhism. That the well-educated and liberal Dr Chang should feel it discourteous to leave a temple without prostrating himself and offering incense to the Supreme Buddha was to him irritatingly incomprehensible. He knew that I shared what he called Dr Chang's outrageous superstition and laughed at me for it, though we were otherwise good friends. More than once he had laughed away my contention that, while scholars focus their minds upon one or other tiny segment of the universe's outer rim, mystics by their intuitive wisdom penetrate directly to its hub.

I, too, found Dr Chang a surprising person, but in a different way. At first I had taken him for a charming and gifted man who nevertheless frittered away enough time and energy on wine, women and song to make someone of his age seem faintly ridiculous. My upbringing had taught me to classify people as serious or otherwise; it had not prepared me for genuinely religious individuals who, like my friend, followed a middle path of acceptance. Very much less profligate than I had at first supposed, he certainly did manage to enjoy the good things of life. If I had known my Wordsworth better, I should have recognized in Dr

Chang a spirit closely akin to the Lake Poet's, but less inhibited; for he combined sincere spiritual piety and insight with an appreciation of the rôle played by the senses in affording intuitions of all-embracing divinity. It was striking how unerringly he had picked Spring Fragrance from among all the thousands of girls in Peking's flower-houses; I have never met another woman who better exemplifies what is meant by the Buddhist symbol of a perfect lotus rooted in odorous mud. Since the death of his wife, a dozen years before, he had bestowed most of his affection on this girl, who was now neither young nor beautiful; but who, in Dr Chang's meaning of the words, was supremely virtuous. Other people now and then spoke scornfully of the doctor as a man who thought himself religious and yet made frequent visits to the willow-lanes; but, as far as I know, he only went to houses other than that where Spring Fragrance lived to keep company with his dinner-companions. He was, I imagine, at least more faithful to her than many men are to their wives; the only reason they were not married was that she had resolutely refused to compromise his reputation by becoming his wife. A genial person, always willing to go anywhere his friends wished to take him, he liked best to take them to visit Spring Fragrance, rather as a Westerner, proud of his wife's musical or conversational talents, invites friends to spend an evening at his home.

When Dr Chang returned from his devotions in the shrine-hall, we bade the monks goodbye and began walking down as briskly as we could. Only Lin and I were in Western dress; the other men wore long ankle-length gowns which, though made of materials sensible for country walks, looked altogether cumbersome; yet, however fast we walked, the slits at the sides of these gowns enabled them to keep up without inconvenience. Indeed, even the partially Westernized Professor Lee claimed that Chinese dress was superior to ours, because the softness of the material and the loose cut of every garment, including the pyjama-like underjacket and trousers, constricted movement much less than tie, collar, closely fitting jacket and braces or leather belt. (Later, when I had grown accustomed to wearing them myself, I discovered the added advantage that four complete sets of Chinese clothes occupied the same luggage-space as a single one of my English suits, not to mention the additional space required for shirts, ties and leather shoes. This did not apply to the thickly wadded Chinese garments used in winter, but these compensated by extreme lightness for their extra bulk. A winter gown consisting of two layers of silk padded with an inch and a half of silk floss was as warm as the heaviest overcoat, yet scarcely one-fifth of its weight.)

Emerging from the wooded path on to the plain below, we saw the last bus disappearing in a cloud of yellow dust, so we were compelled to return to Peking in a couple of hooded carts. With their wooden wheels and ungreased axles, they bumped and screeched their way along the uneven road so ponderously that it was midnight before we reached the city gate, aching and bruised. By contrast, the dilapidated rickshaw which carried me on to my house seemed both swift and luxurious!

.        .        .        .        .

A few weeks later I encountered most of the picnic-party again at the wedding-party of Professor Lee's niece. This time they all wore their best gowns of plain or figured silk and, for once, the ladies of their families, who were wearing splendid brocades for the occasion, accompanied them. Even so, men and women tended as though by instinct to keep apart; at the banquet, which followed immediately upon the ceremony, very few women ventured to sit at the same tables as the men; and it was not until the majong tables were brought in that any real intermingling took place.

The wedding ceremony, which was attended by about a hundred guests (with Bill Luton and myself as the only Westerners), was of the modern kind and thus *relatively* economical. It took place in the southward-facing hall of the bridegroom's family residence. The parents and some family elders occupied three rows of chairs behind a table spread with a scarlet cloth, so that they faced the central doorway, sitting with their backs to a curtain of scarlet silk embroidered in gold with a *shuang-hsi*—a stylized pattern formed of two identical characters for happiness intertwined, symbolic of connubial bliss. Each of the brass holders in which the huge red marriage candles spluttered had been cast in the same *shuang-hsi* form. Otherwise, not much attempt at conformity with tradition was made. The bride and groom both appeared in Western-style wedding garb instead of the marriage robes and bride's scarlet veil which I had been looking forward to seeing.

We guests stood facing the seated elders, some of us in the hall itself, others crowding the wide steps leading up from the courtyard in front. When the ceremony began, bride and groom took up their stations in a space reserved for them in front of the table, with the master of ceremonies standing to their left, from where he issued instructions in the high-pitched, long-drawn-out tones appropriate to solemn rituals.

'Bride and groom will bow to the elders.

'The elders will return their bows.

'Bride and groom will bow to the guests.

'The guests will return their bows.

'The presiding elder will admonish the bridal pair.

'The groom's father will speak.

'The bride's uncle will speak.

'The bridal pair will proceed to the table and affix their seals to the nuptial bond.

'The presiding elder will affix his seal.

'The parents and guardians will affix their seals.

'The go-between will affix her seal.

'The witnesses will affix their seals.

'Bride and groom will face each other and perform three bows.

'The ceremony is complete.'

This simple ritual began at five in the evening. By six, we were all seated at ten big tables brought in by the servants, six in the hall, four in the adjacent room to the east. During the banquet a great deal of wine was drunk but, as usual, without ill-effects because of the richness of the food. Towards the end we were entertained by singers and musicians who took it in turns to mount a small dais to one side of the hall. Spring Fragrance, whose presence among the musicians I first noticed with a start of surprise, presently drew loud applause from the guests. Each time she sang the room echoed with our shouts of '*Hao, hao! ha-a-ao!*'

Meanwhile, the bride and groom were kept busy going from table to table to receive the toasts of their guests. When they reached us, we all rose to our feet and, raising our cups with both hands, emptied them at a gulp, the bridal pair responding according to custom by drinking simultaneously with us. Immediately afterwards, individual toasts offered by various people seated at our table followed. The groom, but not the bride this time, was forced to down one cup after another. As he had already suffered this fate at several other tables, I expected the poor fellow to fall flat on his face at any moment, but he still looked reasonably sober in spite of thirty or forty cups of spirit!

'Good Lord!' I said to Bill, who was sitting next to me. 'The wretched bridegroom will be finished if he goes on like this. His bride will have to spend her wedding night alone.'

'That is more or less the idea. Don't worry, though; he's been too clever for them up to now.'

'What does that mean?'

'Why do you suppose the guy following him round from table to table is carrying *two* wine-pots? I guess one of them is filled with weak tea, the same colour as the stuff we're drinking. If you watch carefully, you'll see the guy filling the bridegroom's cup from one pot and replenishing the pots on the tables from the other. There, do you see?'

'So that's it. Still, isn't it a bit mean of us even to try to get him drunk on his wedding night?'

'Why not? Why not? They're only kids. They've got years and years in front of them yet. The bride's not a snow-maiden who will melt away in a single night.'

'All the same, I'm glad they've failed to wreck the wedding night.'

'Failed? Don't be too sure. They'll have other tricks up their sleeves.'

Bill was right. After the banquet the guests were in no hurry to go. Instead, they settled down to an evening of music, cards and majong. Presently the bride quietly disappeared, but the groom was still running about bringing us wine, tea or fruits with his own hands. By two in the morning, with about thirty guests remaining, the majong players were still indefatigably slapping down their ivory cubes on to the hardwood tables; and even I had been induced to play in place of someone who had broken up a four by going home earlier.

At about six o'clock, with the dawn light filtering in through the paper windows, I realized I was very tired. I had been losing consistently, which probably increased my feeling of weariness; but, as Bill and all the other people I could have asked to replace me had slipped away, I was forced to continue playing until the end of the round was reached. Then, scarcely able to place one foot in front of the other, I stumbled towards the door.

The watchful bridegroom, though he had never seen me before and probably wondered who on earth I was, came hurrying over with a smile and urged me to stay longer—surely I would not deprive them of the pleasure of my company at breakfast? Unable to detain me, he followed me all the way to the outer gateway murmuring expressions

Gilded Peking shop-front

Temple at the foot of the Western Hills

A canal in the grounds of the Summer Palace

Lake scene at the Summer Palace

of regret. When I turned to make my farewell bow, he exclaimed softly:

'It is really a pity you have to leave so early!'

'*Early!*' I answered in astonishment. 'I should have thought my conduct in staying so long would seem unpardonable.'

'Oh no. Why should you think that? My family and I had been hoping that all our guests would stay with us for another day or so.'

I imagined his bride, alone and possibly tearful in a strange bed, watching the burnt-down wedding candles guttering in the early-morning breeze. I could not believe she joined him in this hospitable desire for more of our company.

# 9

# A Laughing Taoist and a
# Doubtful Confucian

THE summer heat weighed upon the city. Doors and windows gaped widely towards courtyards protected against the sunshine by roofs of matting supported on tall wooden poles. Men of leisure like Chu's father spent the long daylight hours reclining half naked against the cool polished wood of heavy chairs built to slope backwards like the deck-chairs of the West. Fluttering their silken fans, they sipped pale-green Dragon's Well tea or a sugared infusion of chrysanthemum petals, both of which have cooling qualities. Professors in white gauze gowns with rolled-back sleeves sat over their piles of examination answer papers, keeping a cloth between wrist and paper to prevent their sweat smudging the ink. Vendors of iced water-chestnuts and sweet lotus-seed broth patrolled the lanes. The steam-heated bath-houses were almost emptied of their customers. At the theatres, second-rate actors performed to dwindling audiences. Only the restaurants were unaffected; for, come sunshine or snow, the Pekingese never lost their appetites. Peking ducks and sucking-pigs still sizzled on the spits, tended by half-naked cooks; but the heavy chapati-like bread, steamed rolls and stuffed dumplings, which during most of the year formed the staple middle-class diet, had largely given way to thin, wheaten pancakes called *paoping*. These were eaten wrapped around light oddments taken from dishes in the centre of the table—shredded omelet, sliced ginger, fresh celery, diced cabbage and small slices of smoked meat. Rolled with the fingers into a small sausage-shaped bundle, they formed one or two mouthfuls apiece.

It is typical of the way Peking affects people that a chapter to be devoted to religious topics somehow begins itself with a paragraph concerning food; yet this juxtaposition would have struck few

Pekingese in those days as strange or undesirable. The Taoist poet drunk on moonlight, the learned scholar engaged in preparing his comments on a commentary elucidating the works of the traditional commentators on the Confucian classics, the dealer in Han jades lovingly fingering his wares, the singing-girl caressing her lute, the painter delineating mist-enshrouded mountains with masterly down-ward-sweeping strokes of his brush—all had this in common, that they were replete or about to eat or dreaming wistfully of the time when they would be able to afford good meals.

One clammy summer's day when Lao Chao had just set the table with my lunch, he reappeared with a note brought to the house in a sealed envelope by a man who would not give his name. It was from Pao, whose visits had inexplicably stopped about a month before. Surprisingly, he had written in Chinese, which suggested he was living somewhere where a Chinese brush and soft local paper were the only writing materials available, for the language used between us had always been English. The pith of the letter was sandwiched between some formal introductory sentences appropriate to the time of year and a sentence assuring me that my brother, Pao Yiu-Kuang, bowed his head in humble token of respect. It consisted of four terse sentences:

'I am with Younger Sister travelling for pleasure. Here in the hills, the heat is not severe. In the Monastery of the Held Forth Flower lives a layman, Têng Chêng-Chung. When you have leisure, you may go to him for further news.'

Even if Pao had possessed a sister, it would have been obvious that the first sentence referred to Kuei-Hsiang. The second suggested that they had gone into hiding somewhere in the hills. The other two presumably meant just what they said. Though there was no sense of urgency about the message, I left my after-lunch pot of tea untouched and hastened to the Nien Hua Monastery in the north city.

This monastery, like most others, had been allowed by the Nationalist régime to fall into decay. Its Abbot, later to become my friend and Teacher, was still unknown to me, so I decided to ask one of the monks to direct me to the living-quarters of Layman Têng. The outer gate stood open and unwatched; the first courtyard was such a wilderness of insect-infested weeds and unswept leaves, its silence so profound, that I began to fear the whole place was deserted. However, inside the second gate I came upon a tall, thin monk beating a 'wooden fish' as a signal to other monks to assemble; and, surely enough, while his stick was still raining blows upon that archaic prototype of a bell, seven figures similarly garbed in faded black gowns marched in procession from their tumbledown cells to a hall where birds and weeds had made their homes amidst gaps left by fallen tiles. When they had passed, he laid down his stick and, with a questioning glance at me, courteously inclined his head.

'Reverence, may I know where to find Layman Têng?'

'Layman Têng stays in the west wing of the small courtyard beyond the gateway to the Abbot's quarters. There! Will you be able to find your way? I regret I am not now at leisure to accompany you.'

I came upon the layman seated by a fish-pond. Dressed in a sleeveless inner jacket and patched trousers of dingy white, he was peering near-sightedly at an old-fashioned block-printed Buddhist text held close to his eyes, while his left hand moved slowly up and down the body of a black cat as sleek and well fed as its master was thin and undernourished. He neither saw nor heard me until I had approached within arm's length. Then he glanced up without surprise and rose to his feet.

'You are looking for the Abbot, Hsienshêng? I'm afraid he will not be back for about a month and——'

'No, I am looking for Layman Têng. Pao Yiu-Kuang sent me.'

'Ah, just so.' He allowed his eyelids to droop as though wishing to lower a curtain between himself and some hidden watcher. 'Softly, Hsienshêng, if you please. Please take this stool. I shall sit on the parapet of the fish-pond. There! Have you brought Pao Hsienshêng's letter?'

'No. I didn't think to do that.'

'Your honourable surname and distinguished cognomen?'

'My humble surname is P'u, my worthless cognomen Lo-Tao.'

'And your age? Your native town? Do you happen to know the name of Pao Hsienshêng's uncle? His address? The profession of Miss Kuei-Hsiang? Did she strike you as a tall girl or short? Do you remember any distinctive features? Her eyes, for example?'

Finding that I answered all these questions to his satisfaction, he suddenly relaxed and made a smiling apology.

'So you have come for news of your friend. I cannot tell you much. He is married, which is good news, is it not? Now he and his wife are living *there!*'

He gestured to the corner formed by the northern and eastern walls of the courtyard. For a moment I thought they were actually living in the compound, until it dawned on me that he meant the north-eastern provinces—otherwise Japanese-occupied Manchuria! I nodded, waiting for him to continue.

'As far as I know, both of them are well; but people's health there is uncertain. There can be changes from day to day.'

Again I nodded.

'Our friend did not write to you only for the sake of friendship, you understand. Such risks could not be allowed. He wished you to come and see me because he hopes that, if an emergency should bring one or both of them to Peking, you will be good enough to offer them, very discreetly, a single night's hospitality. Think well before you answer, Hsienshêng. Your friend is asking of you more than you may know.'

'I don't need to think. I am a foreigner here and not at all anxious for trouble with the authorities; but an old friend can surely count on me for occasional passive assistance of that sort. They must tell me nothing so that, if anything untoward happens, they can swear I provided them with shelter in all innocence. Is that good enough?'

'Thank you. That is good and also wise.'

Though unwilling to say more about my friends, Mr Têng seemed in no hurry for me to go, nor was he specially guarded about his own affairs. Assuming him to be a secret agent of the anti-Japanese activists, I had expected him to seem a politically minded person using Buddhism as a cloak for his underground activities, but I found this to be true only in a limited sense. What he told me in the course of that hot afternoon came as a surprise. Far from being interested in Communism or any other kind of political creed, he had devoted the last thirty years to practising the mystical means leading, via self-mastery, to emancipation from the aeon-long round of birth and death. Politics could hold no interest for a man who saw struggles for power always as symptoms of stupid egoism pitted against stupid egoism. However, when Mukden, his native city, had fallen into Japanese hands a few years previously, he had incurred the enemy's wrath by refusing a post in the Manchurian puppet government. He had told the Japanese bluntly that he could not bring himself to serve under Hsüan T'ung, the deposed Emperor of China whom they had decided to put on the throne, until it became clear that he was a fully independent monarch. At such a time, criticism of the Japanese-sponsored régime meant death, so Mr Têng fled from Mukden to Peking just in time to escape arrest and probable execution.

Since then he had been living under the assumed name by which I knew him in the seclusion of this little-frequented monastery; but he had had to pay a terrible price for his freedom. His wife and three children, while attempting to join him in Peking about a month after his flight, had been seized by the *Kempetai* (Japanese secret police) and, in a spirit of pointless vengefulness, shot 'while trying to evade the guards'. Thus it happened that the former unworldly Buddhist scholar had—to what extent I never discovered—been driven to throw in his lot with the anti-Japanese activists.

Presently a tall, shaven-headed figure in a black gown with butterfly-wing sleeves entered the courtyard by the south gate and, pausing to give Mr Têng a friendly greeting, swept through into the Abbot's quarters, behind.

'That was the Venerable Hsiu Shan who is in charge of the monastery during the Abbot's absence. If you care to call on him for a little while, you will find his company rewarding. I shall wait here for your return.'

I followed the Assistant Abbot into the innermost courtyard, prostrated myself at his feet, and was courteously bidden to take tea with him. He was an exceedingly thin man whose austere features were sometimes lit by an attractively wry smile. At the time I put his emaciation down to deliberate asceticism, for I did not then know that the whole community was forced to live chiefly on *wot'ou*, a very cheap, coarse bread made of millet which was sometimes mixed with powdered peanut shells to make it go farther. The monastery's few patrons could none of them afford more than occasional token gifts, so the fifteen monks and novices had to live on the poor income derived from the rents of half a dozen small houses, the very last property left in the monastery's possession.

The Venerable Hsiu Shan, on discovering that I thought myself a Buddhist, managed by a few adroit questions to discover how little of Buddhism I really knew. The questions were courteous but framed to penetrate to the heart of things. Presently he asked:

'Layman P'u, what do you regard as the supreme object of all Buddhist endeavour?'

'Enlightenment,' I answered promptly.

'Which is?'

'An intuitive understanding of our own True Nature.' Again my response came patly, but the Assistant Abbot handed me no laurels.

'Which is?' he persisted.

'Well—er—a sort of—a universal Nature shared by all sentient creatures. Shall we say a sort of ocean in which individuals are the component drops?'

'Excellent,' he answered in a tone so unconvincing that I knew he was not impressed. He might just as well have said frankly that my answer had been banal and inaccurate. To avoid being plunged even deeper into the bog of my own ignorance, I said hurriedly:

'Reverence, what should my answer have been?'

'Silence,' he said. 'Just silence. The answer you gave could have been made to sound more learned or more logical or more something —but it would still have been a pretence of holding the moon in your single pair of hands. Why seek to confine the illimitable, the inconceivable, in words? Besides, a reply based on hearsay, instead of on intuitive understanding arising spontaneously from your own experience, is a poor sort of coin. But do not let me discourage you. You are, if I may say so, over-young to concern yourself with such matters. At your age most people are too nearly satisfied with the world to recognize its prizes as wisps of cloud. I can see that, in your case, life has not yet let you down often enough to teach you Wisdom. I do not mince words, you see.'

I smiled a foolish, happy smile.

'Ever since I came to Peking, Reverence, I have been in love with life. My mind and senses respond to undreamt-of delights and my days are so short that it is actually a pleasure to rise early in the mornings. But I am not blind. My boyhood was not too happy; I can see misery around me even now; and I know that a sudden jerk of the wheel can plunge me into grief, accident or death in a single moment.'

'So? That is what you tell yourself at this moment, but are you really so thoughtful? In any case, do not despise your rare good fortune. Not many people find their days too short. You must have stored great merit in some previous existence; do not turn away from your happiness until it turns away from you. You must be disappointed before Wisdom can root itself in your mind. When the shining gold shrivels in your hand to the dust of yellow autumn leaves, then the Ocean of Scriptures will begin to yield up its hidden treasures and the Buddha's Wisdom mean more to you than a donkey's fart. Now, sermons and farts are really all one to you, scriptures an arid waste of dusty theories —even though you persuade yourself it is otherwise. Why bother with them? The secret boredom they inspire in you dishonours them and leads you into building stocks of evil karma. Leave them alone and, meanwhile, when your conscience bothers you, you can always soothe it by tossing some gifts to the needy. Such charity will not help you in any real sense, but it can make you feel better.'

'What sort of gifts?'

Stupidly imperceptive, I thought that he was angling for a donation. He must have read this in my eyes, for his lean face crinkled into a smile. (I think he liked people when they were being naturally stupid better than when they were pretending to be wise.)

'If you are thinking of bestowing your charity upon me, or upon the Abbot when he returns, I accept for both of us. An occasional packet—a very small one—of tea will be most acceptable.'

.        .        .        .        .

When I told Yang Taoshih about my conversation with the Assistant Abbot of the Nien Hua Monastery, he declared I needed an antidote for so much solemnity and, smiling at some private thought, wrote down the address of one of his fellow Taoists. The Peach Garden Hermit was a recluse inhabiting the upper storey of a pavilion situated on an island in one of the lesser lakes to the north of those adjoining the Forbidden City. Yang Taoshih did warn me that the hermit might appear frivolous and unconventional, that his conversation ran on such trifles as gods, demons and the search for the drug of immortality instead of dealing with Action in Non-Action and the Attainment of the Way, but his mild criticism had not prepared me to meet a glorious madman, drunk with *being*!

Lotus-leaves lay so thickly upon the water between island and shore that it resembled solid ground. As soon as I reached the red zigzag wooden bridge spanning the space between the two, there burst from behind the willows on the island an astonishing young man who capered rather than ran towards me, waving his hands and letting forth peals of happy laughter. (This strange manner of welcoming me he chose to explain later by assuring me he had spent half the day attempting to conjure up a demon and that, at first, he mistook me for the fruit of his conjurations!) His tattered sky-blue robe had been thrown on so carelessly as to leave his chest and the upper part of his stomach completely bare. His long hair, instead of being confined in a prim Taoist's bun atop his head, danced on his shoulders like the tresses of a forest nymph; indeed, he so resembled a girl or, at any rate, an immature boy that I should have taken him for an acolyte if his behaviour had been more restrained; but no one could have supposed this wild creature was living with his Master.

In response to my formal bow, he laughingly seized my hands and, running backwards, dragged me across to the steps of his pavilion. Next, he pushed me into one of several chairs scattered about the open-sided lower storey and began vigorously fanning me!

'Such exertion! Such exertion! All on a hot day, too! So, in response to my incantations, you have come all the way from the Western Regions to visit me. Come now, confess you rested on the way. Ha, ha, ha! So you speak *jên hua* [human speech] even though you are an Ocean Devil. D't, d't, d't! I've had so much to do with devils in my life. It is really a pleasure to meet one like you. Most of them know only how to make brutish noises or how to scream Chinese oaths when we exorcize them too roughly without regard to their natural feelings. But there, there, don't be offended. Are you solid enough to—I mean do you sometimes drink tea? Excellent, excellent! I have a little canister of leaves from the Seven Stars Terrace and I myself gathered every drop of water from the lotus-leaves around here after yesterday's shower. Almost as good as dew. You need not be afraid I'll give you common water from the lake. Not to you, dear demon.'

A toy-like earthenware stove with live charcoal embers embedded in the ash stood upon a rickety bamboo table, supporting a bronze tea-kettle with a camel's-mouth spout and lizard-shaped handle, beautiful but sadly battered. The precious water, which he poured from a jar taken from a nearby shelf, was just enough to fill half the kettle. My pleasure at the thought of tasting this rare tea was not half so great as my relief when he transferred his fanning operation from me to the stove. Being fanned by my host had been too embarrassing. The water soon boiled and some of it was carefully transferred to a teapot no bigger than an English cup. It was a pale tea more nearly amber than green and pleasantly fragrant, but I was not experienced enough to detect any marked superiority to the excellent tea I drank at home. However, I could see the Peach Garden Hermit gazing at me expectantly as I put the diminutive cup to my lips, so I assured him it was superb, taking care to demonstrate my appreciation with noisy sips.

'Superb!' he exclaimed. 'Do you mean that?'

'Why, certainly I do.'

'What is superb—the taste as the tea enters your mouth, passes through your mouth or reaches the throat? Or are you referring to the after-taste echoed back from the throat's entrance?'

Reflecting that this question implied something very unusual about this tea, I plumped for the 'echo'.

'Wrong,' he laughed. 'Wrong, wrong, wrong, wrong! This is a tea which yields its fragrance at the moment it reaches the tip of your tongue.'

His emphatic 'wrong, wrong, wrong, wrong' could not possibly cause resentment. Indeed, it was a refreshing reminder of manners of speech among the ruder peoples of the Western Ocean whence I had come. All the same, it was unexpected. I suppose that no one in Peking had, before attaining the status of intimate friend, ever told me point blank that I was wrong. The usual formula for indicating a contrary opinion was: 'You are absolutely right; on the other hand I also think that perhaps . . .'

Over the second cup of tea I asked how he had happened to have had so much to do with devils.

'Oh, that! I am an expert exorcist, but your friends still have a lot to teach me. Only last week I nearly came to grief! Someone had promised to bear the whole cost of my current medical experiment, if I succeeded in destroying a malevolent demon which had recently taken up its habitation in his wife. I believe it had chosen her left kidney: but his reason for objecting to it was that it had made her shrewish. Thinking this a very ordinary request, I accepted the challenge without giving much thought to the matter until I reached their house. On the appointed day, I went there early in the morning and helped him give his wife a mild beating which continued until the devil, using really disgusting language, emerged from her left nostril. Then, telling the husband to get her quickly out of the way, I remained shut up with it in the kitchen. You can understand how angry I was with it for swearing at me in front of the whole household. I was in a rage and imprudently decided to finish it off quickly. No bargaining for its life or anything of that sort. After reciting a peculiarly powerful spell, I formed the fingers of my right hand into the gesture which transforms them into an irresistible magic sword. Then I struck. Three times I struck at the very place where I sensed it was sitting. That should have finished it off! I expected it to tumble dead at my feet in the form of a noxious insect or small reptile.

'But what happened? I was seized by a pair of red-hot iron hands which burnt my clothes, lifted almost to the ceiling and hurled down upon the floor! My head hit the boards with such a crack that I lost consciousness and people came running in to see what was the matter. Imagine! Instead of a dead devil, they found a half-dead Taoist! My reputation may never recover. Then a thin high voice began laughing in the middle of my brain, as though that turtle's egg of a demon had bored right into me. The voice said: "Who, but you, would dare to use that powerful spell without preliminary fasting? And then, your discourtesy! First you beat me; then you take a sword to me without so much as asking, friend to friend, if I will oblige you by leaving the wretched woman alone. Away with you!" That demon spoke the truth—no doubt of that. Such carelessness would rob any of the more potent spells of their efficacy. In the end I had to *thank* it! I thanked it for sparing my life and promised to let it stay in the woman's kidney until next full-moon day. If it doesn't leave peacefully then, I shall have to fast and put myself to a great deal of inconvenience to get rid of it. My reputation is at stake, which is serious because I entirely depend on it for my living.'

Was he making fun of me? Did he believe his own story? Had these things really happened, perhaps? I shall never know. And when I enquired about his medical experiment, he replied, laughing:

'We doctors don't give away our secrets so easily. Otherwise our rivals would put us out of business.'

Later in the afternoon we walked out on to a rough wooden platform projecting like a pier into the middle of the lake.

'Look at those carp,' he cried, pointing to a place kept free of lotus-leaves where a shoal of fish, attracted by our coming, threshed around pushing their snouts out of the water in expectation of a feed. 'Would you believe it? Last month the mother of the mayor's accountant died. Everything that could be done for the spirit of a mean old woman was done. Chapters of Buddhist monks and bands of Taoist adepts were called in to recite their respective scriptures and incantations on alternate nights; Mongol lamas came separately to placate the hungry ghosts and thus win for her a little much needed merit. For all I know, the family may even have called in some Christian missionaries on the sly, just to make sure that the old wretch would get to some kind of heaven. So far, so good. Her sons are thoughtful men. Among the usual offerings—flowers, candles, incense, wine and food—they also placed her favourite water-pipe. Then came the night after the seventh-day rites, when they all retired to bed weary from grief or, anyway, from the strain of too many ceremonies. It was, by the way, one of those houses with a high-walled compound and a gate that was always properly barred at night. So, next morning, the servants got a shock. When they came in to clean the room and tend the altar, they found the old woman's water-pipe surrounded by burnt spills and tobacco ash for which they had forgotten to provide a spittoon, and there was nothing on the plate of sacrificial carp but clean-picked bones! What a to-do! The servants would certainly have been dismissed, so they came to me and begged me to assure the family that the old lady's ghost was responsible. At first, her sons would not believe me. How did I know? Their honoured mother had been a vegetarian ever since the death of her husband twenty years before. It was inconceivable that her ghost should have eaten fish! And so on. "Well," I said, "it is quite natural for an old woman, on waking up as a ghost and finding that all her years of pious practices have failed to gain her admission to Heaven, to make a grab at the fish, having uselessly denied herself of it for so long. As for her smoking the pipe, it was pure force of habit. She has yet to grow accustomed to living on the essence of food and the essence of tobacco alone." I put it a bit more gently than that and made them see the truth of my words. Ha, ha, ha! They've fed her with carp every day since then.'

I joined in his laughter without the smallest difficulty, but I was still uncertain as to whether he was joking or serious, for the Peach Garden Hermit was a man who would have laughed in the faces of his own executioners.

'You know,' he said presently, 'when I was training to become an Immortal, I had such faith in the efficacy of abstinence that I lived on a diet of candles, peanut shells and fruit peel. What did I gain from such foolery? Nothing! Far from achieving immortality, I nearly finished myself off. Then, one day, I passed a cookshop and smelt a ravishing scent of roasting pig. My Master allowed me no money at all—he was a severe man aiming at nothing less than transcendental bliss, who died recently when a beam from the temple he was building in honour of his guardian deity fell on his head. Mad with hunger, I rushed into the shop, banged my jade hair-ornament down on the counter and shouted: "Give me all the roast pork I can eat plus twelve ounces of *Kaoliang* spirit and the jade is yours." On that day I left my Master and have since then earned my living as a doctor with a hard-earned reputation for knowing how to deal with every sort of demon. After discarding the jade symbol of my austerities, I came near to becoming an Immortal on the spot. I even gave myself a title, the Peach Garden Immortal, but people still refer to me as the Peach Garden Hermit. Perhaps, at twenty-nine, I am too young to convince anybody of my immortality. A beard would help, if I could grow one. Impossible. As you see, my chin is as smooth as a child's bottom.'

Before I left he told me one other curious story. It concerned a thick brown birth-mark running half-way across the back of his left hand, the one blemish to his rather childlike and unkempt beauty. Again it was impossible to know if he meant it seriously, because his laughter was so much at variance with the factual appearance of the story itself.

'You see? It's a burn carried over from a previous existence. In my last life, I was the son of a merchant in Paoting. My then mother (not my present one, of course) died in childbirth and my then stepmother, jealous because she had no sons of her own, mistreated me abominably. One day, enraged at my laughing at her, she beat me across the hand with a pair of charcoal tongs hot from the fire. It was shortly after the Mid-Autumn Festival in the sixth year of my life. That night I was attacked by a fever and knew I was going to die. Remembering how much she hated a certain Liu Hsienshêng, a cloth-merchant in our town, I said: "Ma I'm leaving tonight. If you want to see me again (which I doubt), look for me in the Liu family." By morning I was dead. I must have passed quickly into the womb of Liu Hsienshêng's concubine, for nine months later I was reborn as her son. Everyone recognized me and tried to persuade my former stepmother to come over and examine the mark on my hand. She never did. Nothing would induce her to come.'

'Do you *remember* your past life?' I cried, opening my eyes wide.

'No, not that. The neighbours knew the story from a maid who had overheard what I said to my stepmother, so they were all anxiously awaiting a birth in the Liu family. When I was reborn there, they saw the mark on my hand and decided it was identical in shape and position with the burn from the hot tongs, which three or four of them had seen before I was put into my child's coffin. How could they doubt who I was? Can I doubt it myself?'

The Peach Garden Hermit was so talkative that it was difficult to find a suitable moment to take my leave. When, after several ineffectual attempts, I persuaded him that I really must go home, he laughingly accompanied me to the bridge, holding my hand affectionately all the way. Exactly in the middle of the bridge, he dropped my hand abruptly, turned round and tripped back towards the pavilion still laughing and without a word of farewell. By such inexplicable actions, he had given me the impression that he was mad; on the other hand, his conversation, though running on bizarre subjects, had been entirely coherent and revealed the workings of a lively puckish intellect. Puzzled and amused, I took the first opportunity I could find to visit Yang Taoshih, to whom I reported the whole of that extraordinary conversation. Naturally he laughed a good deal, but when I asked him point blank if the Peach Garden Hermit was mad, all he would say was:

'There are plenty of people who think so.'

'And *you*?' I asked, determined to make him express an opinion. 'What do *you* think?'

'Thinking is a dangerous and fatiguing pastime,' he answered lightly. 'It seldom does much good.'

.        .        .        .        .

My student, Chu Tê-Ku, was not of unadulterated Manchu stock. He had inherited a quantity of Mongol blood from his mother, whose own mother had been a minor princess—the daughter of a Mongol chieftain from the region of Urga. During the last years of his mother's life, Chu had acquired from her a fair acquaintance with the Mongol language and was thus able to introduce a few Mongol friends to me. Once, using him as an interpreter, I asked one of them, who had just made a passing reference to Father Vassily, what standing the Russian priest enjoyed among the Mongol community. My question produced the following extraordinary tale.

When Father Vassily, or the Ruski Lama as the Mongols called him, had first arrived in Peking dressed altogether as a lama, his claim to be the pupil of a famous Grand Lama from Kokonor had won for him immediate respect and made him welcome to take up his quarters in the Yung Ho Kung Monastery. Moreover, his casual display of unusual powers—spiritual, magic, hypnotic or whatever people chose to call them—had enhanced his reputation among the more ignorant Mongols living there. Advanced Lamaist initiates, on the other hand, took such powers for granted and were no more astonished by them than Catholics are astonished by a priest's fluency in Latin. Believing in the infinite power of Mind and accepting the doctrine that time, space and the apparent individuality of objects are all, in one sense, illusory, they were not easily impressed by evidence of mastery over material phenomena. By them, such powers as levitating, transposing or transforming objects or causing them to vanish and reappear, together with telepathy, foreknowledge of the future and so on, were not even classified as miraculous; they were regarded as calmly as chemistry students regard the simple feats of changing liquid into gas or separating a substance's component parts. Father Vassily's powers they accepted entirely as a matter of course. However, for more than a year he had continued to enjoy the special regard accorded by the followers of almost any religion to converts from distant corners of the world. The Mongols made as much fuss of him as proselytizing Christians would make of a converted mullah; but, unexpectedly, there came a day when he forfeited the greater part of his claim to their regard.

Shortly after the Anching Sacred Incarnation arrived from Lhasa on a visit to Peking, a ceremony was held for the bestowal of a high and rare initiation upon specially qualified monks and laymen. At some point in the preliminary section of this ceremony the candidates for initiation, now blindfolded, had to come forward one by one to cast a flower upon the Mandala. This Mandala, large enough to cover the whole surface of a fair-sized table, was a coloured drawing in the form of a many-petalled lotus with a different symbol painted on each of its petals. In accordance with the symbol nearest to the point where the flower came to rest, the Sacred Incarnation would decide the particular form of the individual initiation to be bestowed on each candidate.

When Father Vassily, supported by his Mongol friends, pleaded to be allowed to enrol himself among the candidates, he was able to produce some documentary evidence of his spiritual qualifications which inclined the Sacred Incarnation to assent. The flower-casting rite, watched eagerly by those who had just cast their own flowers or were still waiting their turn to be blindfolded, proceeded normally until it came to Father Vassily's turn. He submitted to blindfolding with a red cloth and was led forward to stand in a place less than three feet from the Mandala. At the proper moment he lifted his flower between the finger-tips of his two hands, touched it to crown, mouth and heart to symbolize purified body, speech and mind and, raising it above his head, cast it lightly towards the table. His first intimation that something was terribly wrong must have come to him from the sighs and gasps of those around him. More than twenty people saw what happened. The flower moved through the air in an arc, almost reached the centre of the Mandala and then, inexplicably, *reversed its direction* and fluttered down to the floor. Gasps, sighs, murmurs of horror and indignation rose all about him. The Ruski Lama had been revealed as a fraud!

The Sacred Incarnation, crosslegged upon a high throne which faced the Mandala from the opposite side, signed to the others to be silent and calmly continued the rite until every one had cast his flower. When this point was reached, he quietly gestured to Father Vassily to leave, so that the initiation rite itself proceeded without him!

At first sight this story might seem open to one of two prosaic explanations. Either the flower fell to the ground for a natural reason, such as Father Vassily's failure to throw it hard enough, or else my informant was not speaking the truth. Both explanations occurred to me, but I was forced to reject them. The Mongol layman who had told me the story had himself witnessed the scene. He was too intelligent to mistake a short throw (almost impossible under the circumstances) for the elliptical movement he had described, and he was much too much in awe of sacred matters to profane them with a deliberate untruth. It follows, therefore, that everything occurred very much as he had described. Moreover, I discovered later that Father Vassily, who had previously called himself a Buddhist, dressed as a Buddhist monk and proclaimed his total break with the Orthodox Church, had made a half-turn back towards Christianity and commenced his synthesis of the two religions at just about that time. Happily for him, he had won plenty of Russian devotees to take the place of the Mongol friends he had lost. This explained why, when I first came to know him, he had struck me as having a good deal more in common with Rasputin than with people like Bemaiev.

One day I told this story (as tactfully as possible) to Shura, interested to discover his reaction. I think now that it was criminal of me to risk weakening his faith in a priest whose ascendancy over him gave him such happiness, but fortunately no harm was done. Shura merely smiled and said:

'Father Vassily is a man of God, Vania. Even if you tell us he get

Porcelain pagoda overlooking the
Jade Spring

Marble pagoda close to
the Jade Spring

Tomb of Confucius,
glorious in its simplicity

The Marquis K'ung Tê-ch'ên,
lineal descendant of Confucius

drunk or go to bed with someone, it make no difference for us. Maybe God think Father Vassily too holy to be with those lamas some more.'

.      .      .      .      .

'What can I possibly call myself? Christian? Confucian? Atheist?' Professor Lee looked up from the printed form with a puzzled smile. He had been invited to give a course of lectures in America during the coming long vacation and was engaged in filling up a lengthy questionnaire. His dilemma was a typically Chinese one.

'Christian won't do, though I could easily get away with it, because I received part of my education in Christian institutions. Christians are nice people, but if I decide to worship any God, I shall probably choose one with a yellow face like my own. Buddhism I've never had time to study and no university man would dare call himself a Taoist these days. You might as well be seen throwing spilt salt over your shoulder or making detours round ladders. Your Western pundits have assured us that Confucianism is not a religion at all, so that won't do—indeed it is quite true that the sort of Confucianism which has survived the overthrow of the dynasty is what someone called "a system of agnostic belief inclining towards a vague Deism and encumbered with a too minutely ordered morality". Think of that, now!'

'Why not write atheist or agnostic or leave a blank?' I said, smiling.

'Atheist? You don't know the kind of Americans who have arranged my trip to the States. They would be shocked and put me down as an anarchist, or a satyr glorying in his lack of morals. Besides, I'm not an atheist. There is, as far as I know, no proof or disproof of God's existence; to affirm or deny it would be equally illogical; but I feel in my bones, as you say, that there is a Something. The trouble is to know what to call It or Him—or why not Her? Agnostic makes people sound too smug, too convinced of their superior wisdom. Leaving a blank would be better than either of those, but why should I go among those people pandering to their belief that white men have got something we haven't got? Certainly I must have a religion in a country where to be without one is almost as bad as going to a formal garden-party without a hat.'

He sighed dramatically and, as he had no doubt intended from the first, wrote down Confucian. Of course his remarks had been facetious, but they skirted the fringe of a very real difficulty. Probably the majority of his Chinese colleagues would have been puzzled to find the name of a sect or a religion that fitted their actual beliefs; yet they could not justly be described as irreligious. For generations the Chinese literati had, by and large, adhered to a type of Confucianism denuded by the great Commentator, Chu Hsi, of its more mystical implications. Apart from the formal public ceremonies conducted by the scholar-officials of the empire upon set occasions, it had been reduced to a code of ethics, manners and self-control aimed at the well-being of family and state. Its adherents held that the educated élite must set an example of high morality to those they governed, that harmony within the state must be achieved by regulating the conduct of individuals, families and clans, and that superiors (in age, learning or status) deserved deference and obedience from their inferiors only in so far as they faithfully carried out their responsibilities to the latter and behaved loyally towards their equals. Many Confucians had always regarded the public ceremonies and private sacrifices to ancestors merely as a useful means of regulating the people's behaviour. Without going as far as total disbelief in the supernatural, they had thought of it as something too vague to come within the scope of human activity.

Since the collapse of the empire and consequent discontinuation of the public ceremonies there had been a tendency in some families to neglect the sacrifices to ancestors as well. On the other hand, a vague but tenacious belief in immutable Moral Law had continued to govern the lives of otherwise agnostic scholars, causing the best of them to honour scrupulously their obligations to family, colleagues, official superiors and subordinates, students and persons placed in their care. The really fundamental difference between themselves and their ancestors was that they had grown somewhat nationalistic. (Former generations of Chinese, calmly and rightly confident of their moral and cultural superiority to the peoples of the world then known to them, could not have imagined that a day would come when nationalism—implying, as it did, a recognition of barbarian superiority in certain respects—would have a part to play in China's resurgence.) However, in Peking of the nineteen-thirties, with Japanese control of North China being ceaselessly extended, the new nationalistic feelings had to be carefully hidden. Chinese certainty of the innate inferiority of all barbarian races to the people of the Middle Realm must have been a comfort to them then.

Next to Confucianism, Buddhism and Taoism were still the most important religions; and each presented itself in two widely differing aspects. In their popular form, they served the needs of the masses whose illiterate state put Confucian learning beyond their reach; in their purer form they appealed only to a small minority, who still pursued the world-transcending goals set by their founders. Even of this small minority, very few indeed clung exclusively to the tenets of one religion only; the rest remained Confucian in their relations with society and relied upon Buddhist or Taoist methods (or both) for their inner spiritual development.

To me, as a foreigner with no well-defined place in Chinese society, Confucianism made little appeal. It was not until years later that I came to perceive how *vastly* superior were the Confucian scholars encountered in my youth to the amoral, cynically corrupt Chinese leaders of later days. Those old men, a little tiresome in their insistence upon formality, had been fully developed human beings with a wisdom and urbanity unmatched throughout the world.[1] Men like Professor Lee, products of a modern education built upon Chinese classical foundations, formed a link between old and new; they, too, were admirable in their way, but small in stature compared with men of an older generation who had received their education before any serious break with tradition had occurred. Dr Chang, of course, was one of the Buddhist minority.

.        .        .        .        .

'Is Chang Taifu at home?'
'Yes, Please come this way.'
As I walked across the courtyard to the doctor's consulting-room, I saw gardeners carrying away some of the massed pots of oleanders to make room for the first batch of autumn chrysanthemums. The oleanders were still in bloom, but their waxy pink and white would have clashed with the more sober yellows, purples and dark reds of the friends of autumn. The doctor, having put away his summer gowns of thin gauze, white or duck-egg green, was wearing a dark-blue gown of heavy silk suited to the sudden change in the weather. I was less protected against the sharp, cold wind, which had arisen since the morning; yet I had only myself to blame, for the change had been accurately predicted by the lunar calendar which, as far as the region around Peking was concerned, was seldom more than a day or two out

[1] See page 197 ff. of my *Wheel of Life* (Rider).

in its forecasts of heat, cold, rain or snow. Apparently the local weather gods had been so impressed by the symmetry of Peking's lay-out that they tried to vie with it, though working in a more difficult media.

'Are you busy? I hope I'm not disturbing you.'

'Not at all. This wind has either cured most of my patients or prevented them from coming. Scarcely half a dozen have come in this morning. Two were old ladies whom I have been treating unsuccessfully with medicines ever since I set up practice. The fire element predominates in them so persistently that I despair of reducing it by ordinary means. Both were widowed in early life when their husband died, as I suspect, of overreaching himself in trying to satisfy two such grasping, jealous wives. Naturally the balance of their body-elements was disturbed, first by grief and, since then, by boredom and repression. You know the sort of hemmed-in lives our widows have to lead. Well, I have recommended them to stop coming here for prescriptions and to spend an hour or more a day contemplating cool and soothing objects—the moon, still water, scentless flowers or, best of all, the flame of a very small candle burning before their household altar on a windless night. I hope *you* haven't come as a patient?'

'No, no. I have been thinking about something I don't understand. I hope you will let me ask you a rather personal question.'

'You may ask. There are not many questions I should be unwilling to answer.'

'You and Professor Lee are excellent friends; there is not a great difference between your ages—indeed he is older, which makes the problem more mysterious—and you both come from very much the same sort of background. What is it, apart from the few years he spent in England, which makes you so different? Last spring, during our picnic to the Western Hills, I was impressed by your slipping away from us to burn incense in the temple shrine-hall; it was disappointing to find that Professor Lee thought it rather funny. He cannot understand such things at all. Why?'

'That is not difficult to explain. As a Chinese doctor, I practise an exceedingly ancient art which inevitably helps to strengthen the bonds of tradition. Lao Lee, on the other hand, has to spend a lot of his time with the younger professors and with students who, thanks to the Government's policy, have been deliberately mistaught. Buddhism, for example, has been represented to them as superstitious nonsense by teachers who know less about it than a farm-boy knows of camels.

There is also the matter of karma arising from past existences. Though all of us have *Fu-Kên* (which means Buddha-root, the potentiality of gaining Enlightenment), while one is born with it highly developed, another is unable to perceive his at all, because it is still in an embryonic state. Look at me—my father and grandfather, both strict Confucians, never concerned themselves with other worlds or other states of consciousness; they felt that this world and this so-called normal state of consciousness present enough problems of their own. As a boy I knew nothing of Buddhism; yet when someone persuaded me to study a book only four pages long—the Hsin Ching, which you must know quite well—I thought about it for less than a week, by the end of which I found myself a convinced Buddhist. Though no other book I have seen contains so much wisdom in so small a space, it would have been wasted on me if my *Fu-Kên* had not been watered daily in previous existences.'

'Professor Lee told me once that he would not find it too difficult to believe in one universal God, but he cannot understand how you can believe in all the Figures of the limitless Buddhist pantheon.'

'Certainly I believe in Them. From a certain point of view, all is one, just pure, quiescent Mind. From another equally valid point of view, every single thing is uniquely itself. The number of inter-penetrating forces which make these two states simultaneously possible is naturally beyond compute. If people intuit some hundreds or thousands of them and give them particular names, why not? Whether you believe that the petals of the chrysanthemum standing there by itself on that table—a rare and lovely species, by the way—are yellow or orange, existent or non-existent, the petals are still what they are and the colour exactly what it is; both will be serenely un-affected by the names you give them. Now, suppose you insist that the chrysanthemum in your own sitting-room is purple, though it may not seem at all purple to me, I shall have no objection to calling it "your purple chrysanthemum", for that is how I must identify it in talking to you. Similarly the names of our Deities were undoubtedly coined by human beings to describe something they had discovered in their own minds. Call Them by any names or none, personify Them or not as you like, They are still there and exactly Themselves. Names are conveniences; differentiating a million separate Buddhas and Bodhisatt-vas to symbolize Compassion, Wisdom, Activity and all the rest, is also a convenience. They are separate if you see Them so, One if you see

Them as One. People like Lao Lee know nothing of this; they are too busy and too uninterested; so they laugh at our superstition in prostrating ourselves before this altar or that. They do not notice how often they prostrate themselves before all sorts of different altars—the altars of Nationalism, Internationalism, Anti-Japanism, Socialism, Rationalism, Sanminchui-ism, Commerce, Logic, Vitamin-Worship, Protein-Intake, Progress, Tradition and how many, many more besides! Theirs are short-lived gods, rising and waning like the autumn moon. Our Deities are reputed to have lasted for several aeons and may be depended upon to last several more, though even They are not to be thought of as eternal. There is this, too—when Lao Lee spends an hour patiently guiding a dull student, he feels virtuous; when he goes to a flower-house, he may, for all I know, feel just a little naughty. Everything he arranges in categories of opposites like that.'

'And you?'

'Nothing short of Enlightenment can possibly be good in any important, lasting sense. Similarly, though I must avoid making others miserable or allowing distractions to blind me to my own True Nature, nothing I can do is really worth the name of bad.'

'Should not a Buddhist cultivate austerity—at least to some extent?'

'It all depends. Desires and their satisfaction do lead to folly more often than not. Still, under certain circumstances, they can also be very useful, very improving.'

'How so?'

'If, while desiring and giving way to desire, you can stand back and watch your own ridiculous behaviour; if you can perceive the futility of hoping to grasp those wisps of cloud; if you watch the whole process as something alien to yourself like the movements of a ship which goes on sailing once you have set the sails; if from the first minute of desire's awakening you remain aware of the various sorts of disappointment, boredom and pain attending fulfilled desires; and, above all, if you come to feel compassion for those compelled to minister to your desires at some cost to themselves—then giving way will certainly not do you much harm. You may even gain some useful experience, a better knowledge of the workings of yourself.'

'Dr Chang, do these things come into your mind every time you eat pigeons' eggs in lotus-seed broth or visit a girl?'

'On the whole, no,' he answered. 'You were asking about what Buddhists *should* do. You did not ask me what I *do* do.'

# Girls, Peaks, Tombs and Hermits

A T THE time of the Mid-Autumn Festival in honour of the Moon, the full beauty of Peking's gold-red autumn blazed forth. On the actual night—the fifteenth day of the Eighth Moon (late September)—altars were set up in the courtyards and piled with moon-symbols in the form of round white cakes made from pounded glutinous rice. Upon each altar, in the place of honour, stood an image of the Immortal Hare who, in his Moon Palace carved from ice, compounds pills of immortality according to a recipe for which Taoist recluses spend several life-periods searching in vain. At night, hymns were sung to Tsang O, that pure and unapproachable Moon Goddess whose cold snow-beauty drives amorous mortals to despair. It was in honour of this loveliest of goddesses that, fifteen years later, I gave my new-born daughter the name of Hsüeh-Ch'an (Snow Beauty).

At this season pots of chrysanthemums with petals broad and narrow, thin and thick, large and small, elongated and well rounded, displaying every shade and hue from white to near-black, filled court-yards and halls with their grave and sometimes saddening beauty—tokens of the last years of placid enjoyment before the winter of old age, after robbing men of their faculties, extinguishes life's spark. The pathos of this symbolism was softened for the Chinese by their way of life which, though hard upon the young, freely indulged greyheads of both sexes who had attained the age of dignified maturity. Indeed, one of the ironies of the Communist Revolution that was to take place later was that a whole generation of Chinese who, in their youth, had sacrificed their pleasures for the sake of the elders were to find that, when their turn came, filial piety had become an anachronism and could no longer be counted upon. Fated to live in two contrasting worlds, they were to experience the worst of both. Now their children and grandchildren are too busy manufacturing pig-iron in the back garden to have time to scratch their aged backs, sponge their faces or bring them cups of especially fragrant tea.

One day, after spending an idle morning wandering through the marble-terraced, crimson Halls of State in the centre of the Forbidden City to enjoy the enhanced splendour lent them by a turquoise autumn sky, I decided to visit the T'ai Miao—the Temple of Imperial Ancestors. Alone in that solemn hall, I gazed at the spirit-tablets of successive generations of Ch'ing (Manchu) emperors and their consorts, all of whom were represented except the very last. That poor prince, variously known as Hsüan T'ung and P'u Yi, has the misfortune to have outlived his era. Forced to abdicate the Dragon Throne while still a child, he later allowed himself to be made puppet emperor of Japanese-occupied Manchuria. Then came the Second World War and his capture by Russian troops. For years he languished in a Russian prison; but now, having confessed his 'crimes against the people', he is permitted to work as gardener in a public park. Born to be tended by princes and eunuchs as Heaven's Son, he now tends the flowers and cuts the grass. When his turn comes to 'ascend the dragon', who will make sacrifices to his departed spirit wandering unrecognized through the realm of ghosts?

Hsüan T'ung's imperial ancestors are now in much the same forlorn condition, nor did the Nationalist Government of the nineteen-thirties take more heed of their spiritual welfare than do the Communists today. Before each spirit-tablet I saw a cold, bare altar untouched by flame or sacrificial offering for more than twenty years; and behind each of them was a yellow-curtained bed, dusty from neglect, where the August Departed, summoned in former days to partake of the sacrifices, could rest between the various phases of the rites. I stood longest before the tablet of Tzû Hsi, born Yehonala, later styled Hsi T'ai-Hou (Dowager-Empress of the Western Palace) and called by her intimates Old Buddha; as I stood there silently evoking scenes from the life of that iron-souled woman, whose hand had wrought so much weal and woe that Peking had never lost its imprint, the yellow bed-curtain stirred. No doubt the wind often twitched impiously at those imperial hangings of brocaded satin, but I allowed myself to feel a pleasant twinge of alarm. It pleased me to imagine that this Old Buddha had woken from her sleep. Though, for a hundred excellent reasons, she had detested foreigners all her life, she had nevertheless lifted one slender, ring-encrusted finger to acknowledge the greeting of a barbarian who esteemed her more greatly and perhaps more justly than did the descendants of her own loyal subjects.

Strolling out of the T'ai Miao into the great avenue leading from east to west of the city at the place where marble bridges and sculptured marble monoliths stand guard before the main gate of the Forbidden City, I almost stumbled into Pao! He was alone and hastening towards Wang Fu Ching Street too preoccupied to steer clear of passers-by drunk with the beauty of white marble gleaming beneath a cloudless sky. His face was leaner and his expression more mature than I remembered, but he was dressed in the same kind of cloth gown he had always worn, only it was rumpled now as though not ironed for days.

'Pao!' I cried delightedly, reaching for his hand. He jerked up his head, allowed his eyes to meet mine for the smallest imaginable fraction of a second, blushed noticeably and, ignoring my outstretched hand, brushed past me as though I were an importunate stranger. I had not seen him for months and, though neither of us knew it then, was not to see him again during all the years of China's life-and-death struggle with Japan. My first feeling of hurt was swallowed in the realization that his cutting me had probably been more for my sake than for his own. Layman Têng, to whom I went as fast as I could for news of him, not only had nothing to tell me, but made it clear he would rather I kept away from him in future. Obviously he knew of Pao's secret visit to Peking and was disturbed for his friend's safety and his own. So, though I often returned to the Monastery of the Held Forth Flower to visit the Abbot and Assistant Abbot, who had become my teachers, I never again did more than bow to Layman Têng when passing through his courtyard on my way to theirs.

That autumn I also encountered Jade Flute. The thought of meeting her embarrassed me, because I did not know how to behave to a girl who not long before had been the object of my single-minded passion, of which not a jot remained. Bill Luton had invited me to a party at a restaurant which he patronized for the sake of its carp. It was one of the places to which fish were brought alive and displayed in a glass tank near the entrance, where they swam about until a customer, by pointing to some of them, virtually pronounced their death sentence. Then they reappeared crisply fried and garnished with a sauce of vinegar, sugar and pickles; or steamed with some sort of light dressing such as ginger slivers, bamboo shoots and shredded ham; but carp were generally stewed in a thin soup containing celery and giant black mushrooms. (My pleasure in eating such fish was not unalloyed as I had never got used to having things specially killed for me; though I recognized my squeamishness as indefensible in that, morally, there can be no half-way house between vegetarianism and flesh-eating.) The Chinese guests, none of whom were very intimate with Bill, presently bowed their thanks and departed to various theatres and other places of amusement in the vicinity, leaving us two Westerners alone.

'John, I guess you are not too tired for a little walk? Or are you? I've discovered a swell place called "The House of Springtime Congratulations". Ever been there?'

'Indeed, yes. It was the scene of my grand passion. At one time I used to think it contained all I desired in heaven and earth. You know how one gets carried away. Since Cupid was blinded for Campaspe's sake, it has ever been so.'

'H'm. Does that use of the past tense mean you've quarrelled with your little friend? It wasn't by any chance my Golden Cicada? Good. I'd love you to meet her; she's a swell girl; but I'm glad she never was yours. Otherwise we could hardly visit her together. They'd call that improper, bless their hearts. Say, some people back home would open their eyes if they knew what moral lessons the girls here have to teach us poor benighted Westerners. That's one thing I never have got used to. I like to have fun with a girl without having to mess around with a couple of hundred rules of can-do and can't-do. That's what you'll like about Golden Cicada. I've taught her a thing or two, as you'll see.' She's a honey. Coming?'

Inwardly ashamed to face Jade Flute after my long dereliction, I agreed without enthusiasm. We went on foot. Again I heard music and laughter all about us as we walked through the lanes, but I could not recapture the carefree mood of earlier days. The music seemed jarring and the laughter, so I thought, had a cruel edge. When we arrived at the House of Springtime Congratulations, though the Big Teapot and the matrons greeted Bill with smiling warmth, they seemed not to recognize me at all; for, in the haunts of pleasure, a year is an age. At the top of the staircase, I turned from old habit towards the corridor leading to Jade Flute's room, but was diverted and followed Bill into an unfamiliar room belonging to Golden Cicada. This young lady, who at twenty-four was older than most girls in first-class houses, had clearly taken pains to learn Western manners from Bill—or some other foreigner—for her mode of welcoming him was to rush forward with a scream and throw her arms round his neck. The shock I received was no less than if a girl, hitherto chaste, had suddenly revealed brazen immodesty; for it had never occurred to me that flower-girls might sometimes behave indecorously. However, she was a good-natured, amusing creature who soon had both of us roaring with laughter at her delicately indecent sallies—echoes, perhaps, of cruder sallies learnt from Bill. Before we had been there more than a quarter of an hour she started giving him long kisses, just as if nobody else had been present, and clinging to him like a Western farm-girl hugging her swain in the darkness of a village cinema-hall. This went on for some time: but presently she noticed my expression of distaste (which must have resembled that of Dr Johnson suddenly confronted with impropriety) and, mistaking it for jealousy, cried:

'*Aiyah*! Excuse me; excuse me, please. I am such a stupid girl. Everyone knows that. Bi-lly Laoyeh, please wait for me. I shall run and ask Ma to find some pretty, pretty girls for your friend. He's lonely, poor young gentleman! It's not fair.'

Pulling herself away from Bill's embrace, she jumped up and ran from the room. A few minutes later she returned breathless with two other girls, one of whom—as I had much feared and a little hoped—was Jade Flute; she was looking as lovely as ever. I smiled at her guiltily; but she, far from displaying expected petulance, greeted me with such absence of rancour that it seemed as though my last visit had taken place only a few days before.

'Third Father Wang! You have come! If Ma had told me, I should have been here to greet you. Do please excuse me. This girl is Lao Wu (Number Five); I don't think you've met. She is a Soochow girl as you can see from her lovely skin, but she was born here and speaks like a true Pekingese. Her name is Purple Cloud.'

'Third Father Wang, I think I have heard of you,' said Purple Cloud, laughing. 'And Bi-lly Laoyeh I have seen before. I shall always envy you, sister. He has such a handsome nose.'

The girls went off into peals of laughter—not the gay laughter I was used to, but of a kind which underlined the bawdy allusion hidden in her words. Bill, always ruefully conscious of his outsize nose, was quicker than I to recognize the outrageously indelicate point of the joke and roared his appreciation. As for me, coarseness from girls was a new experience which I did not like well enough to be able to laugh at very convincingly. I was puzzled, too. I could not make up my mind whether flower-girls, whose affectation of innocence had always seemed to me one of their principal charms, were in fact cynical actresses ready to be all things to all men, or whether they just found it amusing to treat barbarians barbarously. With Dr Chang, Professor Lee or even Pao present, nothing of the sort would have happened, and in the past I had always been treated with the same delicacy. I decided that as Bill, despite his thirty years in China, still retained an affection for the frankly bawdy prostitutes of his own country, these girls, having divined his tastes, were willing to indulge them, partly because they were essentially good-natured people and partly because they derived a secret satisfaction from the feeling that they were playing down to someone inferior to themselves. (It is possible that I had come to idealize them beyond their deserts. Perhaps some of them shared his bawdy inclinations, but hid them from people like Professor Lee and so on, who would have deserted the willow-lanes in disgust if the houses there had been unable to afford entertainment more aesthetically appealing than that provided by straightforward brothels.)

However, that evening was not a time for me to feel superior to Bill or anybody else. I had good reason to be ashamed on my own account. Here, sitting beside me, was the girl I had 'loved with all my heart'—pretty, clean, fragrant from the jasmine in her hair, amusing, intelligent and still smiling her well-remembered smile, yet I could feel nothing for her beyond the pleasure of chatting with an old acquaintance coupled with a placid admiration of her poise and good humour. Of love not a glimmer remained.

'You know, Bill,' I said in English, 'I used to think myself madly in love with this girl. I should have been furious with you then if you had suggested that what I felt for her could die so quickly.'

'But that is how it was, of course. How is it possible to *love* anyone until you have lived with her for years and know her inside out? I guess there's a good case to be made for the old Chinese system of arranged marriages, isn't there? The feeling we call "being in love" may or may not result from an intimacy *begun* on the wedding night, but so what? Even with us it seldom survives the test of marriage for long: and love with a capital L is just as likely or unlikely to come later whether the marriage was a so-called love-match or not. Our kids at home almost always marry because they believe they are "in love". When "in

love" is over, unless they are very lucky, they feel let down; sometimes a couple find they've lost the only thing they had in common; the
marriage either goes on the rocks or becomes a test of stoical endurance.
The old Chinese system had—or has—two advantages. One is that a
pair of strangers, wed to please their families, must surely expect too
little of each other for any feeling of let-down to be possible; the other
is that parents selecting mates for their children probably have enough
sense to find young people with more enduring qualities than the kids
would think of seeking for themselves. It could be that an old-fashioned
marriage has a better rather than a worse chance of——'

'Bi-lly Laoyeh,' cried Golden Cicada, slapping him. 'Why don't
we all talk Chinese? It's no fun for us listening to your *lulu dudu jeelee
gala* noises. If we girls are such dull company for you, why have you
come here?'

'We only came just to take a peep at your beautiful eyes, you little
devil,' answered Bill in Chinese.

'Ha-ha-ha-ha,' laughed Purple Cloud, making a face at Golden
Cicada. 'Your eyes are the only thing Bi-lly Laoyeh likes about you.
We should ask Ma to charge half-price to a customer so easily pleased
with the melon's pretty skin that he forgets to eat the fruit.'

As though summoned by sympathetic magic, the matron came in
for the second time since our arrival, carrying two more saucers of fruit
and nuts to indicate that we had now had four *yuan's* worth of conversation, instead of two.

'Don't worry. I'll eat the melon, all in good time,' laughed Bill. 'It
seems I'll have to pay for it whether I eat it or not.'

'Some fruits cost more than others,' put in Golden Cicada darkly.

Jade Flute took my hand between her own and squeezed it gently;
but I, needlessly afraid that she was going to emulate Golden Cicada's
public demonstrativeness, snatched it away and sat listening sulkily to
the lively conversation which now sprang up among them all. When,
towards midnight, I got up to go, angry with myself for being so
irresponsive to their mood, and still feeling guilty towards Jade Flute,
she made her first and only reference to the past. Perhaps remembering
the night when, bursting with affection, I had begged her to stop
calling me by the silly name Pao had used to introduce me and to
substitute Chu Fêng (Bamboo Wind), the name by which some of
my more intimate Chinese friends called me, she exclaimed:

'Goodbye, Third Father Wang. Next time you come, please

remember that jade and bamboo are not the same. Bamboo splits and warps with time: jade, unless dropped, is eternal.'

Though it was said in a matter-of-fact voice, and without bitterness, I felt myself flush and had difficulty in restraining myself from leaving the room at a run. The mocking laughter of the others followed me past the door-curtain and on to the landing.

On the following day it occurred to me to visit Pao's uncle, Professor Yü, in the hope of getting some information about my friend. Except for a few additional tubs of goldfish, I found everything unchanged since my visits of the previous year. The Imperial Tutor still struck me as a courteous but unsympathetic man who could bring himself to be polite to foreigners without ever going so far as to seem cordial. His wife, coming in at the right moments to replenish our teacups, hastened to efface herself exactly as before, and my conversation with him followed the same stilted track as ever. Before coming to the subject uppermost in my mind, I had to go through the whole rigmarole of questions and answers about the healths of our respective families, the state of the weather, current events, people and places familiar to us both, the progress of his children at school, my impressions of Peking, my work at the university and a great deal more besides. Everything belonging to or closely connected with the speaker had to be designated 'humble', 'worthless', 'miserable', 'unworthy' and so on, while the opposites of these words had to be applied to everything closely concerning the person spoken to. This sort of conversation could, in Peking, sometimes seem a graceful and even a diverting pastime—but not with the coldly smiling Professor Yü as one of the protagonists. It never occurred to him to make of it a sort of competition in skill, even though he would surely have been able to win hands down, for some of his compliments were so high-flown that I failed to understand them and said 'Yes, yes' when a courteous disclaimer was appropriate. However, I had by that time become so nearly expert in the art that I managed creditably for a man of barbarian origin and upbringing. The one genuine compliment he paid me concerned my improved knowledge of the Chinese language. After about an hour of this dull fencing, I said casually:

'It is a long time since your honoured kinsman, Pao Yiu-Kuang Hsienshêng, gratified me with a visit to my poor house. I trust he is well.'

Instead of producing a conspiratorial look, or a discreet change of subject, my mentioning Pao merely made the Professor petulant. I realized then that he knew a good deal less about that young man's recent history than I did.

'Yiu-Kuang hardly bears thinking about,' he answered petulantly. 'To tell you the truth, even his parents are no longer kept informed of his whereabouts. Even that much of his filial duty is more than he cares to perform. It seems likely that he has run off with that—that drum-woman! I always maintained that so much indiscriminate reading of novels would throw him off his balance. Was I not right, P'u Hsien-shêng? You can see for yourself. The father of that madman's fiancée feels he has a grudge against us. He goes about saying that the Pao family have ruined the girl's marriage prospects by making her wait so long for nothing. And who can say that Wang Hsienshêng is wrong? Were he to come to Peking, I should not have the courage to face him.'

'Yü Hsienshêng, you do not happen to know where your honoured kinsman has gone?'

'Certainly not. His movements interest me no longer. His unfilial conduct is a blot on my mother's family. Why do you ask?'

'Because the other day I happened to see someone on the street whom, mistakenly no doubt, I took for Pao Hsienshêng. I thought that perhaps——'

'No, I think we may take it for granted that he has had the grace to withdraw from the city. Even he would scarcely flaunt his drum-woman in the faces of his kinsmen. I doubt if the little turtle's egg will dare return.'

Realizing there was nothing at all to be got out of him on the subject of Pao, I tactfully turned the conversation in the direction of goldfish, whereupon a little genuine warmth crept into his voice for the first time that afternoon.

'The fish are responding well to my care. The phoenix-tails have mated and produced progeny. If they grow to resemble their parents, I may even hope to exchange half a dozen pair for one pair of Trailing Clouds. Next time you honour my poor hut with your presence, I may be able to show you such a pair. Meanwhile, I have acquired two pair of . . .'

He rambled on until it was time for me to leave. As he walked with me towards the gate, I thought of a remark which I hoped would horrify him.

'Is it true that goldfish make good eating?'

My plan misfired. Instead of looking at me with eyes full of loathing, he answered placidly: 'Certainly, they are delicious. However, as most varieties taste alike, we generally eat only the commoner sorts. If you would care to try some, I shall be glad to net one or two pair of . . . No? Really not? Then I bid you goodbye, P'u Hsienshêng. Walk slowly, walk slowly.'

•          •          •          •          •

An ordinary human being's desire for novelty is so insatiable that even the peerless Yang Kuei-Fei, for whom the love-besotted Emperor was one day to forfeit the Dragon Throne itself, could not prevent him from slipping now and then into the embrace of some lesser and more artless girl among the cohorts of his concubines. So it happened that I, also, driven by a similar restlessness, would sometimes leave Peking to visit places with attractions of another sort. I would feel drawn by a desire to spend some days in a lonely temple in the mountains, or be lured by the spell of those monuments to high antiquity which lie scattered in profusion across the North China plain—that vast yellow and green expanse which had been tilled by man for twice or thrice the span of recorded human history. Sometimes I went alone; sometimes Dr Chang or (rarely) Professor Lee accompanied me. My opportunities were abundant; for, in addition to the university vacations, there were frequent periods when students and even schoolchildren came out on strike in an angry but futile attempt to force the Central Government to reverse its spineless policy towards Japanese aggression. Professor Lee, who loved his students and felt personally responsible for their safety, never left them except when they scattered to their homes during the normal vacations, but Dr Chang felt free to hand his patients over to his chief disciple whenever the urge to travel came upon him, so I was able to enjoy his company almost as often as I wished.

During nearly three years, I visited almost every accessible part of North China. For several months, as I have written in my *Wheel of Life*, I lived on the sacred mountain of Wu T'ai Shan—that high plateau surrounded by five peaks where wild flowers grow almost as thickly as the grass, and where thousands of Mongol lamas inhabiting over three hundred temples and monasteries used to stage processions and ritual dances with a splendour not to be equalled by anything remaining in the world today. In the winter of 1935 I visited Si-An (or Ch'ang-An), which had been the capital of the T'ang Empire at a time when the Sons of Heaven had surrounded themselves with talent, intellect and beauty on a scale unmatched in Peking even during the days of those scholar-artists, the Emperors K'ang Hsi and Ch'ien Lung. True, little remained of the city's former glory, apart from some stone inscriptions, for even the ponderous walls and incredibly massive gates dated from a later period than T'ang, but the visit did give me an opportunity to climb the sacred mountain of Hua Shan during a season when ice and snow enhanced its normal loneliness and majesty.

Hua Shan, sacred to Taoists and, so it is believed, to their pre-historic ancestors for thousands upon thousands of years, must at all seasons be an impressive sight. Rising from the plain amid a range of relatively low hills, it soars towards the sky, sloping gently on one side but rising so steeply on the other as to form one of the most awe-inspiring sheer precipices in the world. In winter, with its craggy surface blurred beneath drifts of snow and its pilgrim path hidden under iron-hard, blackish ice, it is endued with a hostile personality as tangible as a living being's. Though I was to pit my strength and young man's determination against it, I could not prevail, and had to abandon the climb while still a mile away from the temple crowning its highest point. I do not wish to give the impression that this was a sort of minor Everest expedition. Sacred mountains in China always have flights of steps hewn from the rock, by means of which even old ladies with bound feet (who are therefore forced to ascend on their knees) can, in time, reach the top. No special boots or other equipment are needed; but, for all that, the mountain deities are sometimes able to preserve their solitude inviolate during the winter when the ice-glazed steps become a hindrance rather than a help to climbers.

I had made the journey from Peking to the north-west alone. Now, willy-nilly, I had acquired a climbing companion, a middle-aged peasant who had appointed himself both porter and guide; although, as it turned out, he had never set foot on that or any other mountain. Too poor to own one of the sheepskin gowns worn by most peasants in winter, he shivered miserably when chilly mists enveloped us and gusts of wind raised spirals of powdered snow all about us. An opium addict, he had rashly walked straight out of the field where we met without making any provision for several days' absence from home; and, as the hermitages and temples clinging to Hua Shan's slopes were normally unable to provide him with opium, he was often in a state of near collapse; I had to admire the courage with which he shouldered my luggage and pressed forward in spite of his sufferings. It was not poverty which drove him on, for I should have been glad to pay him well and let him go; but he had undertaken to stay with me until I returned to the plain, and meant at all costs to keep his word. He was a pleasant enough fellow, but as a guide he was useless; whenever we came to a place where the pilgrim path, obliterated by snowdrifts, was not clearly marked by an ice-encrusted iron hand-rail, he gazed around him in despair.

'You offered to *guide* me,' I said sternly.

'Laoyeh, I am a smelly turtle's egg, a criminal, a ne'er-do-well, or anything you choose to call me, but I did not intend to deceive you. I have lived within sight of this mountain all my life; I have known since childhood the name of every temple, hermitage, rock and peak; I have seen old women climbing it on their knees; so how was I to know it would be difficult to find my way through this wretched snow? As it is—well I *am* carrying your luggage, Laoyeh. You cannot say I am a useless burden to you. You would not like to have to carry it yourself.'

He was so right about the luggage that I burst out laughing and never thought to be angry with him again. Towards dusk on the second afternoon of our climb I abandoned hope of reaching the topmost peak, for a blizzard was hurling hard snow into our faces and, if the temple at the top should prove to be locked and deserted, we might not be able to reach another place of safety before dark. So we took refuge from the snowstorm in the hermitage of a chubby, bearded Taoist who welcomed us with a smile that was warming in itself. Lao Ch'ên, my guide, was taken to the kitchen, from which the odour of opium-smoke was soon pervading my own room next door where, clad in a borrowed quilted gown, I sat drinking dark Szechuan tea with the Taoist and warming myself at a brazier filled to the brim with red-hot charcoal. My host seldom broke silence until I looked comfortable and warm enough to be able to give some account of my reasons for climbing Hua Shan in the depths of winter. Presently, reminded of Lao Ch'ên by the persistent sucking noises from the kitchen, I said:

'Lu Taoshih, are you quite sure you don't mind my servant smoking opium in your hermitage?'

The old man looked bewildered. He was too ingenuous to suspect that my question hinted disapproval of a pious recluse who, though he had chosen to withdraw from the world and live in the solitude of this sacred place, was nevertheless able to offer such entertainment.

'Mind? Why should I mind? I took it to him myself. Poor fellow, he is busy sucking back the life he nearly lost in the blizzard outside. Just listen to the wind. It sounds like the moaning of disappointed demons. Would you not like me to bring some opium for you, to help you get over your fatigue?'

'No, I think not, thank you. I have tried opium once or twice, but I am afraid of it. I should not like to become addicted. Do you care for it yourself, Lu Taoshih?'

Suddenly a smile of understanding spread over his calm, chubby face. At last he had sensed my implied criticism. He was vastly amused, and chuckled his pleasure.

'Ah, I see now. A recluse must not permit himself too many indulgences. Is that it? Then I shall confess to you that, in the sixty-odd wasted years of my useless life, I have never chanced to taste opium. When hot, I drink water carried by a bamboo conduit from a nearby spring; when cold, I make myself a pot of tea—do you not find the flavour of this tea passably good? My food is chiefly millet, of which I still require a few handfuls every day. These and the services of my acolyte who is away now are, thanks to the precious inheritance I received from my Master, my only needs. But then, P'u Hsienshêng, I am a hermit from choice. I must not expect many to share my simple tastes. All kinds of folk come in here to rest on their way to and from the Sacred Peak. Some wish for this, some for that. It is my pleasure to do what I can for people, far from shops or the comforts of home, whose piety has driven them to exert themselves performing a tiring pilgrimage. Do you not agree? Hungry and tired, hot or freezing, they need whatever comfort my poor grass hut can provide.'

He swept out his hand in a depreciatory gesture, as though the simply furnished, substantial, grey-brick hermitage were really a mere hut, and continued:

'So I keep a bunch or two of dried fish, a few jars of pickled meats, some wine, opium and a few herbal remedies for simple ills always on hand for emergencies. When you are rested, I shall make bold to offer you some coarse food, indifferently cooked by a hermit's unskilful hands. I cannot hope it will please you, but it will satisfy your hunger.'

The coarse, indifferently cooked food turned out to be three dishes which, had I been less hungry from my climb, would still have been tempting—a soup of winter cabbage and dried shrimps; a plate of peppers stuffed with minced salt-pork mixed with shreds of black mushroom and finely chopped bamboo-shoots; and a plate of smoked fish tasting like kippered salmon. Only the reddish colour of imperfectly polished rice and the fact that all the ingredients of the dishes were smoked, salted or preserved in some other way reminded me that we were eating a meal prepared at short notice near the crest of a remote mountain rising from the heart of snow-bound fields. After my fourth bowl of rice, I felt scarcely able to keep my eyes open, and thought longingly of the bed with its pile of warm quilts which stood just behind my chair; but it would have been heartless to deny the old gentleman any further opportunity to chat with the first visitor to reach his hermitage since snow had begun to fall about two months earlier. So I fought off my fatigue with many cupfuls of the dark Szechuan tea.

'Lu Taoshih, may I enquire what you meant when you spoke of a precious inheritance received from your Master?'

'That would not be easy to put into a few words. Also, I am afraid you will think I am boasting. But you may judge for yourself. You see me here, an old greyhead rising sixty-four with a beard that is almost white. I look my age, but my flesh is still firm, my four elements are harmoniously combined and I have never, so far, experienced serious illness. In summer, when the path is easy and the days are long, I can walk down to the plain and back up to my hut in a single day. My few wants are easily satisfied by what you see around me; I am generally content with my own company and, indeed, have deliberately chosen a poor mute boy from the Chang village as my acolyte. Yet all these things are luxuries which my Master generously added to his main gift—a reasonable expectation of achieving immortality in this life or the next.'

'Indeed? I see that you are a rich man with treasures greatly to be envied. But what exactly is this immortality? Can this very body of yours become immortal?'

'If my power of transmutation is perfected in this life, yes. Why not?'

'But . . .'

'But then my body will no longer be what you see before you. My

flesh will be less solid than the wind and scarcely visible or quite invisible to the untrained eye. It will be impervious to heat, cold, thirst,
hunger, fatigue, illness and deterioration. I shall—— But I am a
garrulous old man keeping you from your sleep. I must not bother
you with my nonsense.'

'No, Lu Taoshih. It is true that I am sleepy, but what you have
said interests me profoundly. Please do not go without first telling me
one thing more. When your transmutation has taken place, will you be
miraculously transported to some Abode of the Immortals, or will you
remain here upon this mountain?'

Rising to his feet, as though to keep from yielding to the temptation of prolonging our chat beyond the limits imposed by a guest's
need for sleep, he answered:

'First I shall remain upon this mountain, rather as a fledgling
keeps to the nest while testing the power of its wings. I shall have to
acquire experience in dealing with a new kind of body—weightless and
therefore apt to leave the ground at the wrong moments—though,
fortunately, the mountain winds will pass through me and not be able
to blow me away. When I have learnt to behave in my new form, with
the propriety becoming to a very junior Immortal, I shall go to rejoin
my Master and His Masters beyond the Jade Pass.'

'Just a moment, Lu Taoshih. One more question, please. Are
there others, *here* on this mountain, *now*, who have already been transmuted and who linger still, testing their new powers?'

'Just now? Only two, I think—no, three,' he answered as matter-
of-factly as a man reviewing his neighbours in his mind to count how
many of them happen to have beards.

'Have you *seen* them?' I asked, almost shouting in my excitement.

'No, P'u Hsienshêng, I have not seen them. That is one of the arts
in which my Master had no time to train me before his transmutation.
But I see traces of them—oh, almost every day. My late neighbour, the
Firefly Hermit, who used to be in charge of the temple close to the
Sacred Peak, was always fond of this kettle. He still borrows it now
and then, when I am not on my guard.'

'You mean his *ghost* borrows it?'

'Certainly not, Hsienshêng. He is not a ghost, though people might
think so, because he is, naturally, invisible to them. He was transmuted
in the autumn of this year.'

'But . . .'

'Sleep well, Hsienshêng. I'll leave the lamp in case you need anything during the night. There, now the flame is too low to trouble you.
Your breakfast will be ready when you wake an hour or so after dawn.'

.        .        .        .        .

Another of my journeys occupied a long weekend in summer,
during which I joined Professor Lee and Dr Chang on a pilgrimage
to the tombs of Masters K'ung and Mêng (Confucius and Mencius),
both of which lie within easy distance of the railway, a night's journey
south of Peking. They lay amidst fields sucked dry by the summer sun
—a featureless, yellow plain where the dust blown by a hot and restless
wind into eyes and nostrils must be thick with particles from the bones
and habitations of the millions upon millions of human beings who,
for untold and untellable generations, lived, toiled and died in that
ancient place. Otherwise the two shrines had little in common. At
Tsohsien, birthplace of Master Mêng, the greatest of Confucius'
posthumous disciples, we found a village beyond which lay a simple
temple surrounded by cedars, with innumerable white herons resting
among their boughs, and three inscribed tombstones protected from
the weather by unlovely structures of brick. These tombstones faced
a bronze sacrificial urn, cold and neglected, with no scarlet incense-
stubs to indicate that pious farmers still bothered to honour the sage
before whose tablet emperors had been wont to prostrate themselves.
Of we three modern pilgrims, only Professor Lee could view it
without sadness, for he said:

'At last Master Mêng rests in peace with no tiresome fellows to
importune his spirit.'

Confucius' temple at Ch'üfu was, on the contrary, large, magnificently appointed and far from showing signs of neglect; for the Sage's
youthful descendant, the Marquis K'ung Tê-Ch'en, whose residence
was close by, still received the stipend paid by successive governments
of China to his family for the last two thousand years, so that the temple
and tomb in this Chinese Holy of Holies might be kept in a state of
good repair. The tremendous upsweeping roofs of the main shrine-hall
rested upon a colonnade of massive scarlet pillars to which clung carven
dragons resplendent with fresh, unblemished gilt. Within, beneath its
gorgeously painted ceiling, sat a larger-than-lifesize statue of the Sage
with a headdress of pearls and fronted by a gilded tablet inscribed:

'*Spirit tablet of the holiest and first of all Teachers, the Master K'ung.*'

The splendour of this temple, and the impressive avenue of statues alternating with archways of elaborately carved stone leading from the temple to the tomb itself, led me to fear that the latter must be an ornate structure unsuited to house the remains of a sage whose attachment to ceremonial forms had been tempered by a strong admixture of austerity. However, Dr Chang, who knew the place well, told me not to have any anxiety on that score. He was right. The tomb had been perfectly conceived. A simple inscribed stone slab, its top-piece ornamented with restraint, stood behind an altar and sacrificial urn of unpretentiously sculpted stone, against a background of cedars and plum-trees. Here were majesty and simplicity combined according to the dictates of an ancient Chinese tradition which, in these days, lingers only in Japan. When he had admired the place sufficiently, Dr Chang asked:

'Shall we spend the night here in Ch'üfu and call on the young Marquis in the morning?'

'Well,' replied Professor Lee, 'we could do that. On the other hand, young K'ung Tê-Ch'en probably finds it tedious to have to receive strangers so often. Any questions we can ask him must have been asked hundreds of times before. Whereas, if we leave by this evening's train, we shall be able to spend all of tomorrow at a little place called Wan Tê.'

'What is to be seen there to make you prefer it to this wonderful place?' I asked.

'Lowish hills, so craggy and jagged that you can imagine you are looking from a distance upon some tremendous mountain range. There is also a rustic temple where, while Lao Chang sits crosslegged contemplating his sins in previous lives, you and I will enjoy the comfort of a clean, well-cushioned sleeping platform.'

'That sounds very tempting,' answered the doctor. 'Antiquities are always worth coming a long way to see, but you can't enjoy looking at them for hours on end as you enjoy walking among hills or mountains. I prefer my pleasures to be as little exacting as possible. John?'

'I agree with you, especially as I want to see Professor Lee in the sort of surroundings he has just described. I have always believed him a Taoist at heart—you can guess that from his fondness for our

English Taoists, Shelley and Wordsworth. Wordsworth's "Intimations of Immortality" is absolutely Taoistic from——'

'Yes, I agree; but we must hurry to catch the train.'

Travelling by rickshaw to the railway station, thence by train, and finally on donkey-back, we reached the Ling Yün Temple about dusk. A modest pagoda and some low, creeper-covered temple buildings with trees all about them stood in a sort of natural cup, with the hills on our right rising to a jagged crest much as the Professor had described. I began to suspect that one of his motives for bringing us there was to take a sly dig at Dr Chang's piety, for it appeared that the only monk then in residence was somehow connected with a thin woman and a brood of children living in a house built in a little wood adjoining the temple walls. If Dr Chang shared my suspicion as to the nature of their relationship, he gave no sign, but greeted the prelate with grave courtesy.

'Hail to the Buddha of Boundless Light!'

'Hail to the Buddha of Boundless Light! Have you gentlemen come to pass the night here? Such a pleasure. Please stay for several nights if you wish, but forgive me for having nothing to . . . I was not expecting . . . Only a country place, you see. Even in the village, they haven't . . . And then, I can provide only vegetarian food. The rules of my Order . . .'

It seemed to me that the monk was flustered only because he doubted his ability to offer us the sort of hospitality he thought city people would require; but the Professor, who had never made a secret of his contempt for monks, looked so meaningly at the woman busy lighting a fire in front of her house that His Reverence blushed.

'My widowed sister and her older children help with the cooking and other things. It is very convenient.

'Widowed sister, my aunt!' exclaimed Professor Lee in very idiomatic English and possibly with intentional humour. 'Anyone can see she is not his sister.'

'Don't be too sure,' answered Dr Chang mildly. 'I think I see a family resemblance. Both have wide foreheads and rather narrow faces. Lao Lee, you mustn't let yourself be prejudiced against real monks by all the nonsense about *flowery* monks you read in those books you hide so carefully from your daughters!'

There was still light enough to see. Unobtrusively, I compared the two faces and decided that Dr Chang was right.

'I would have to agree with you,' I said, 'even if I shared Professor Lee's anti-Buddhist prejudices.'

'As you like, John,' laughed the Professor. 'To both of you, he shall remain a saint—inviolate. To me, he remains a flowery monk and therefore to be congratulated as a reasonable human being.'

Our host's anxiety lest he be unable to provide us with a good dinner was, as I had long before learnt to expect in such cases, entirely unfounded. I had yet to encounter a Chinese who, unless handicapped by desperate poverty, was so unresourceful as to be unable to conjure up a good meal at short notice. In this matter the Pekingese were not exceptional among their countrymen. That night our dinner was of course vegetarian in the strictest sense of that word, for the food served in Buddhist temples must not contain even eggs or milk-products; nevertheless, it was delicious. There were four dishes and a soup, each composed of various kinds of vegetable mixed with such things as mushrooms, the tree-fungus known as 'silver ears', bamboo-shoots, walnuts, flower-petals, ginger and crisp-fried slivers of bean-curd. I doubt whether a foreigner new to the country would have noticed the absence of meat or fish, especially as the ingredients were too finely chopped and blended for the eye to be of much assistance in recognizing them. The soup was especially notable. A giant-size marrow, as broad as it was long, had been beheaded like a boiled egg; then the pulp, the seeds and some of the inner flesh had been removed to make room for a soup containing at least eight ingredients, which was cooked and brought to the table still inside it. When the time came to ladle it into our bowls, we were careful to draw out not only the soup, with its floating ingredients, but also some of the tender flesh from the sides of the marrow itself.

After dinner, His Reverence, who had eaten apart from us, came in for a chat. Even the vaguely hostile Professor had to congratulate him on the excellence of his cooking, but he added with a bluntness which, by Chinese standards, was absolutely rude:

'You must feel very bored here, sometimes.'

'Bored? I am too busy, Hsienshêng. I have to conduct the morning rites an hour before dawn; then follow two hours of meditation, plenty of work to keep the buildings in some sort of repair, a little gardening, another set of rites in the late afternoon and, from dusk to bedtime, further meditation.'

'If that is really your daily programme, how is it that you are not meditating now?'

I had not believed Professor Lee capable of such needless rudeness. Normally, he was a genial person who seldom went beyond gentle irony even in the company of intimate friends; but now his discourtesy was so clearly deliberate that our host flushed.

'If Hsienshêng desires to be left alone with his friends, I can——'

'No, no, no, no!' interposed the doctor, looking sideways at his old friend with something like anger. 'My friend here has a peculiar sense of humour. It is just his way of having fun with me, because he has often heard me say I should like to be a monk.' (This was untrue, but it served the purpose of explaining away the Professor's rudeness.) 'We are delighted to have the company of a *fashih* [Dharma Teacher] and wish to receive some instruction in the Dharma suited to our limited understanding.'

A broad smile of incredulity overspread the monk's face.

'Layman Chang,' he replied. 'How should I dare to instruct you? As soon as I heard your honourable surname and distinguished cognomen, I recognized you as the author of I do not know how many learned articles on Buddhism. I should be happy to become your disciple. May I request you to be my Teacher?'

Professor Lee, who seemed impressed by the monk's modesty and by the fact that he was acquainted with Dr Chang's sometimes abstruse articles, immediately regained his good humour, but was still disposed to be argumentative. While he was speaking, I wondered if his hostility towards Buddhism sprang from a secret and carefully concealed envy of his friend's being able to wander so freely in worlds still closed to him. What he said was:

'I am sure each of you is qualified to teach the other, whereas I am an ignorant fellow who will not be able to follow even the drift of your conversation; so, before you ascend to transcendental topics, will you please answer one very simple question. Since this world exists, and is as it is, and since we are part of it, how can it be meritorious to abandon it for the life of a recluse?'

Understanding that the question was meant seriously, the monk brushed away his memory of previous rudeness and answered with conviction:

'A monk does not *abandon* the world. That would be a crime towards all the myriads of creatures who plunge again and again into the

Sea of Suffering [*Saṃsara*], escaping it at death only to be dragged back here at each rebirth. A monk passes several successive lives striving to open the Eye of Wisdom by which he will perceive the Reality of this universe, to which most men are blind. Having done so, he must devote aeons of future lives to leading others towards that Bliss for which all creatures are born, though few are awakened to it.'

'Very well put,' exclaimed the doctor.

'Yes, indeed,' agreed Professor Lee meekly. 'Yet, in practice, is there a single thing Your Reverence can do for—say—a man like myself?'

'I, personally? Surely nothing at all. I am still a poor ignorant fellow who has failed to discover his Real Self. A monk who had succeeded in doing that would so impress you by his mere appearance that you would accept him as your Teacher without question.'

'Excellent. But can Your Reverence tell me where a single one of these monks is to be found—in all China, in all the world? One, just one, would do.'

'They are not easy to discover, Hsienshêng. This is *Kali-yug*, the age of degeneration. Nevertheless, when a man is ready for instruction, the Teacher will appear.'

The Professor shook his head as though unconvinced and disappointed by this answer.

'I thank Your Reverence for being so patient with me; yet I am bound to admit such an answer does not altogether satisfy me.'

'Is anyone ever altogether satisfied?' answered the monk slyly, whereupon Professor Lee retired from the conversation. Leaving Dr Chang and our host to carry on an abstruse discussion in a language full of bewildering terms, we walked across to the big sleeping platform, unrolled our quilts and fell asleep on pillows stuffed with some sort of fragrant seed.

At some time between midnight and dawn, I happened to awake. I did not open my eyes at once, but presently my ears caught the gentle swish of a Chinese gown, the sound forming a curiously rhythmical pattern as though someone in soft shoes were walking stealthily up and down before the altar facing the main doorway from the farther side of the room. Faintly alarmed, I opened my eyes. A small oil-lamp and three sticks of incense (marked by three glowing points of red) were burning on the altar before a statue of Kuan Yin, a female form of the Bodhisattva Avalokita. Facing the altar and barely discernible in the feeble glimmer of light cast by the lamp was a figure in dark clothes, engaged in slow but almost continuous motion. Rising from the ground as I watched, it stood straight for a moment, raised its hands which glimmered whitely where they emerged fom the long sleeves, fell to its knees and placed its head upon the floor, then rose again and went slowly through the same series of solemn motions again and again and again. For a long time I kept my eyes fixed upon it, certain in my mind that it was the monk engaged in his nightly devotions; but, when my eyes had become better accustomed to the near-darkness, something familiar in the figure's outline told me that it was not our host, but Dr Chang! Though I had always known him to be a sincere Buddhist, it had not occurred to me that his piety went so deep. For two days we had been tiring ourselves with travelling and sightseeing; moreover, it had been arranged that we should get up at dawn to walk in the hills before the sun's heat grew too strong. All of us were tired, and yet this was how the doctor chose to pass several hours of the night! Now I realized how little, in almost two years of fairly intimate friendship, I had got to know what kind of man he really was. Of his visits to the willow-lanes, his intimacy with Spring Fragrance, his pleasure in food and drink he had made no secret; his piety had, on the whole, been veiled from his friends. If Professor Lee had awakened just then, he must have been impressed.

During our walk in the hills, which began soon after dawn, my friends were at one in their enjoyment of the scenery. The Chinese, fond of observing every one of nature's aspects, prize above all other natural phenomena the beauty and suggestive shapes of unusual rock formations. Where I, unaided, could see nothing but a panorama of jagged or undulating hills, my Chinese friends would see lions, tigers, dragons, phoenixes, griffins, hermits, mothers with their children, monks with billowing robes, fleeing warriors, hermits performing magic feats, avenging swordsmen—all sorts of living beings in every conceivable position. It was as though they had intuitively grasped the kinship of sentient beings and so-called inanimate objects; as though for them the chief point of difference between the configuration of a wrestler's arm at a particular moment and the silhouette of a mountain range was that the latter occupied a slightly larger segment of beginningless and endless time. Throughout China, there is scarcely a peak or an isolated rock which does not bear a fanciful name suggested by its contours; nor a noted garden without a cunningly constructed rockery built to suggest a mountain chain in miniature or a series of grottoes, or to recall those weird rock formations which writhe upon the enchanted plain around Kweilin and Yangsu.

My two friends, so often at odds as to the respective merits of traditional and semi-modern ways, were entirely in sympathy as regards their feeling for rocks and hills, whereas I preferred taking in the scene as a whole. While they were discovering unicorns and giant turtles, I stood with my back to the line of jagged peaks, staring down towards the plain. Below us were wooded slopes rising from the grove of trees which now concealed all of the temple except the tip of its pagoda. At some distance beyond the trees stood a huddle of yellow walls and thatched roofs, bounded on one side by a turgid stream and on the other three by orchards of peach, pear, apple, plum and cherry— for we were well within the borders of Shantung Province where, provided there is plenty of water, fruit-trees flourish as thickly as palm-trees on a Pacific island. Stretching from the village orchard belt to the horizon lay mile after mile of fields, forming irregular patches of green and yellow where different sorts of crops stood ripening in the hot sunshine. Here and there were blue-clad farmers, cattle and donkeys. With a few minor changes, the scene would have resembled some of the especially delectable spots in the sunny, fertile parts of Italy or Spain.

As soon as we got back to the temple, Dr Chang produced from his luggage an ink-stone and brush with which to dash off the following poem. Its Chinese original consisted of eight vertical columns of impetuously flowing grass-characters:

> 'The sun impaled upon these jagged peaks
> Lays bare the secrets of the cedar grove;
> The blue smoke rising from a sea of roofs
> Ascends too late to guard its mystery.
> Three friends grown drunk on sharp pine-scented air,
> With loosened robes and scholars' caps awry,
> Unable still to emulate the birds,
> Laughing like madmen, flap their sleeves in vain.'

'Excellent!' cried the Professor. 'After breakfast you must certainly write another.'

'After breakfast,' Dr Chang answered, 'I am going to enjoy a long summer morning's sleep. You may wake me for lunch.'

The following winter Dr Chang was called to the bedside of a sick warlord in T'ai Yuan, the capital of Shansi Province, of which the old man had been virtual dictator for a great many years.

'You might as well go with me, John. If the warlord dies on my hands, you are scarcely likely to see me again in this life. And, who knows? My travelling in the company of a foreigner may afford me some protection. I shall tell them that, in spite of your youth, you are an eminent journalist with connections in England, America and Japan. The Marshal's henchmen are arrogantly careless of Chinese public opinion, but they would scarcely wish the whole world to know them for what they are; because that might stir the Central Government to eliminate a few of them.'

So we went by train to T'ai Yuan, where Dr Chang's wisdom in taking me along was proved within five minutes of our arrival. Old Yen, the warlord, had arranged for Dr Chang to be accommodated within the compound of his palace, where he could easily have been made away with, without any fuss. However, the men he sent to meet us had no desire to introduce a foreign journalist into that sacred enclosure, so they made no difficulty about our putting up at T'ai Yuan's best hotel. It was not exactly a smart place: prostitutes swarmed there like mosquitoes; they were so extremely numerous and persistent that the most chaste traveller was likely to be browbeaten into accepting the favours of one of them, just as a wise man journeying through bandit country employs one bandit to keep the others away. I was not surprised to find that Dr Chang shared my distaste for casual encounters with prostitutes, but in the end we were forced to compromise with them. After submitting to a great deal of annoyance, we chose two girls at random and made them sleep together on one bed, while we shared the other. The arrangement suited them even better than it suited us; they were overjoyed. By selecting them, after refusing so many others, we had given them considerable face; they were to be paid for their services at the ordinary rate; and they were to enjoy the unusual experience of a night's unbroken sleep. In the morning we were so touched by their gratitude and so grateful to them for ensuring no further disturbances that we engaged them to come every night until the end of our stay. They were a slovenly pair, one of whom did not even bother to attend to her running nose, so neither the doctor nor I was in danger of succumbing belatedly to temptation. Nothing marred the peace of our nights, apart from the expected army of bedbugs, against which, in those pre-D.D.T. days, we had no adequate defence.

By good luck the Marshal had almost recovered by the time the doctor reached his bedside. The latter returned to our hotel after his first visit to the sacred presence, fingering his throat as though to emphasize his good fortune in finding his head still on his shoulders. He told me we could hope to leave after three or four days.

'That,' he added, 'will give us time to visit a place I have always wished to see—the temple of Ch'in Ts'û with its hot springs.'

A few miles from the city walls stood an ancient temple with hot streams, fed by natural springs, meandering through its main courts. These were especially worth seeing in winter, for the clouds of steam rising from the flowing water made a novel contrast with the thick snow lying to either side, so I was not surprised to hear my friend mumbling snatches of extempory poetry as he busied himself fitting his impressions into metrical form. Suddenly he lost all interest in the poem and cried delightedly:

'I believe I can smell something cooking. Who would have thought it? The place seems deserted.'

Guided by his nose, we entered an unfurnished but excellently preserved building. A thin, middle-aged man in an old-fashioned skull-cap and an unquilted gown unsuited to the weather was kneeling on the floor, vigorously fanning no less than three portable charcoal stoves. The doctor, recognizing him as one of the Marshal's personal aides, stared at him in astonishment.

'Lao Ts'ai! Whatever are you doing here?'

'Cooking your lunch, Chang Taifu!'

'Excellent! But we didn't know ourselves until this morning that we were coming here today, so how could you . . . ?'

Lao Ts'ai laughed sardonically. 'The Marshal always does know what everyone is going to do before they know it themselves. How else could the old gentleman have managed to remain father and mother of this province during all these years? Among the great, little slips extinguish lives. He was kind enough to send me by car. I was in the black sedan which passed your bus an hour ago.'

'Good, good. But why does the Marshal specially honour us just for today? Yesterday, and the day before, we were allowed to get our own lunch and dinner.' Then, thinking perhaps that we were going to be poisoned in that lonely place, he added anxiously:

'The Marshal's health? It is not worse, I hope, since my visit after breakfast?'

Again Lao Ts'ai laughed in a way I did not like. No doubt he had been quick to see the doctor's point. His words, however, were reassuring.

'The Marshal is well enough, thanks to your brilliance, Chang Taifu. But this deserted temple is a lonely place in winter, is it not? The old gentleman was afraid you might come to some harm here. As soon as he heard you had taken the bus in this direction, he gave me orders to protect you.'

'What sort of harm?' I asked, speaking for the first time.

'Many sorts,' he answered ominously. 'I think the Marshal chiefly desired that Chang Taifu be protected against malevolent characters who might mislead him into thinking evil of the father and mother of the province. So he sent me to protect you.'

'With a lunch?' exclaimed my friend, laughing rather hollowly at his own little joke.

'With *this*, Taifu!'

Lao Ts'ai's hand swept under his gown and came forth grasping a heavy automatic pistol. Then he informed us that there were three of his comrades stationed unobtrusively in various parts of the temple. If any strangers had come along just then, it might have gone hard with us; we could scarcely doubt that the Marshal, disbelieving in our fondness for sightseeing in the depths of winter, supposed that we had an assignation with some of his enemies. Fortunately, no one else appeared and the lunch—need I say it—was delicious, though neither of us was able to do justice to it from a lingering fear that it might be poisoned after all. By the time it was ready, our fingers were too cold to manipulate the chopsticks properly, so we went out into the court- yard and plunged our hands into the hot stream. When it was over, Lao Ts'ai indignantly refused a small present of money, but insisted that I take his photograph and send him several prints. I have one of them still and can never look at it without remembering how my tongue tested each mouthful of the food he had cooked, trying to detect an unwonted bitterness, before I swallowed it!

·        ·        ·        ·        ·

All I have said up to this point is intended to give an unexaggerated picture of how I enjoyed myself during the three years of my first stay

Statue of Confucius at the temple in his native city

My Taoist host on Hua Shan

Yang. the Taoist

in Peking—years which undoubtedly formed the happiest, if not the best-spent, period of my life. Almost to the end, I believed that nothing could induce me to leave a place so marvellously congenial to me in so many different ways. Chinese New Year (February) in 1937 marked the peak of my contentment, for soon after that it became no longer possible to disregard rumours that the Japanese snake was coiling to strike again.

Bang-bang-bang-bang-bang! Chinese New Year's Eve! Fire-crackers exploding all over the city and countryside—small crackers, big crackers and super-gigantic crackers. For days beforehand, incoming trains, buses and carts had been crowded with laughing, chattering people hurrying in to rejoin their families for the period of the festival. Throughout Peking (and every other part of China), debts had been hastily settled, even at the cost of selling off treasured possessions or engaging in a bout of banditry; while shops and restaurants, after a sudden crescendo of business, had closed and barred their doors for anything up to fifteen days to come. That night, reunited families were sampling the first fruits of many days or weeks of preparation in the kitchens; and the Kitchen God in every family, being about to ascend to Heaven to make his annual report upon the conduct of each family member, had had his lips carefully smeared with honey. The smoke of incense, the savour of roast pork and the fumes of wine ascended to the spirits of the ancestors from altars placed before their spirit-tablets or, where these were lacking, scrolls inscribed with their names and titles in the form of a family tree. Eating, drinking, prayer, sacrifice, music and gambling were going forward simultaneously in every nook and corner of that far-flung realm; and I, a stranger with no family altar to serve, had become for that evening a guest of the noble Manchu clan of Chu.

Bang-bang-bang-bang-*bang*! Chinese New Year's Morning! Fire-crackers exploding as continuously as shells in a major bombardment! Red and gold inscriptions of good omen, above and to the sides of every door. New effigies of ferocious demon-scaring Guardians upon the gate-flaps. Temples so crowded with worshippers that there was scarcely room to move, their halls and courts blurred by blue mists of incense-smoke. Tables in every house laden with vegetarian fare, that even the animals might rejoice and live that day. Peals of laughter, rattle of majong tiles, clink of coins, tinkle of winecups, screech of fiddles, clash of cymbals, throb of drums, perfume of incense, scent of cooking, tang of garlic, fragrance of indoor flowers, sulphurous whiffs of exploded crackers—exciting noises, exciting smells, everywhere. New silk brocades clothing the rich, new sky-blue gowns for shop apprentices, new scarlet jackets for babies; new garments here, new garments there—all evils, vices, demon-plagues and sad misfortunes discarded with the old.

Bang-bang-bang! The next day and the next and the next. Diminished, but not *much* diminished, noise. Streams of gift-laden visitors passing in and out of the houses of relatives and friends.

On *Ch'u San* (the third day) no less than thirty of my students called to present gifts and New Year greetings, their gestures of courtesy ranging from a swift bobbing of heads to low bows with bodies bent at right angles; and, in the case of Chu Tê-Ku, an attempt, frustrated just in time, at head-to-floor prostration.

'Really, Chu! That's absurd. I am younger than you are.'

'You are my teacher.'

If, during those fifteen joyful days, someone had prophesied that long before the Mid-Autumn Festival that year I should have left Peking, perhaps for ever, I should have thought him mad. Yet that is what occurred. Months before that festival came round, Tientsin fell to the Japanese invaders, who marched from there upon the undefended city of Peking. The Central Government in Nanking, chiefly composed of southerners, was prepared to sustain any losses in the north as long as it could retain its hold over the rest of China. If the Japanese had abstained for a while from warlike activities in the region of Shanghai, they could have taken all North China without risking a single major battle!

The Pekingese, with set faces, tried to restrain their tears as the dread army of the Island Dwarfs clanked into their city. The long period of uneasy twilight had given place to a darkness unthinkable. For eight bitter years they had to suffer whatever indignities and pains the Imperial Japanese Army chose to inflict. These, besides such routine matters as face-slapping and public stripping; besides such commonplace atrocities as rape, mutilation, head-chopping and so forth, also included such amusing spectacles as burial alive in pits dug by the victims' hands—all of which provided the Japanese officers with pleasant opportunities to indulge their fondness for amateur photography.

It was my marvellous good fortune to be absent from Peking

on a brief, unexpected visit to England when this black misfortune befell my friends. Had I been present—though up to 1941 I need not, as a neutral, have had to suffer anything worse than a face-slapping for forgetting to bow to a Japanese sentry—I am not sure I could have controlled my fury at seeing Pekingese so horribly illtreated. Unless prevented by cowardice, I should sooner or later have committed some crime against the Imperial Japanese Army punishable by imprisonment or death.

As it was, I decided I could not return to Peking until the end of the war. Abandoning my curios and most of my clothes, leaving my faithful Lao Chao and Chao Ma to a fate I was powerless to avert, I made my way via Hong Kong to Kunming in China's far south-west. There, to my joy, an ever-increasing stream of my Peking friends and acquaintances came to join me in exile—bringing with them no property beyond what they had carried on their backs for close on a thousand miles, but sucking greedily at the untainted air.

# 11

# Darkness

FROM the middle of 1937 to the spring of 1945 the Pekingese
walked helplessly beneath the Japanese yoke, yet they were
spirited enough to treat with silent contempt the few traitors
who served the Japanese as puppet officials. Not all the invaders
behaved savagely and, being Japanese, they seldom damaged temples
and ancient monuments; so the city's outward appearance, though
shabbier than before, remained otherwise unchanged. Apart from the
legal torture and execution of Chinese suspected of the crime of
patriotism, and from the indignities suffered by individuals (including
rape and unauthorized violence, which were *sometimes* punished by
the Japanese authorities), life went on; but gaiety was precluded by
conditions of increasing austerity and by the oppressive clouds of
darkness which lay upon the people. Gradually, those who had no
binding family responsibilities—especially students—vanished one by
one from their homes and dormitories, to reappear months later in one
of the cities deep in the interior of their vast country. Of those who fled
the Japanese occupation, some set out for provinces still under the
Nationalist Government's control, while others preferred to make for
the Communist centre at Yennan, a small town in the north-west. The
latter threw in their lot with the Communists, less, I fancy, for ideo-
logical reasons than because the Communists had shown a much more
aggressive spirit in combating the enemy.

During all the years I lived away from Peking the city was never
far from my thoughts. First in Kunming, where I lived in a Buddhist
monastery overlooking the Êrh Hu Lake, then in London as an officer
working in Military Intelligence, and later in Chungking as Cultural
Relations Officer to our Embassy, I thought of Peking by day and
dreamt of her by night.

At last the war was over and I rushed back with the eagerness of a lover racing to the side of an adored mistress. With foolish optimism, I expected to find the dark storm-clouds reeling back before a dawn as brilliant as the sunrise which had inspired Dr Chang's poem at the Ling Yün Temple. Instead, I found scarcely diminished darkness! To the crippling effects of the weary occupation years, and to penury caused to the middle-class and formerly prosperous artisan-class by the current inflation, was added the incredible behaviour of the Nationalist Government officials. Their treatment of the Pekingese hardly differed from that of officials administering conquered hostile territory! The liberators, welcomed delightedly as friends and fellow countrymen, behaved only a degree less harshly than the Japanese! Nor were cruel monetary and property exactions the only cause of fear; for the Communists, their strength augmented by popular disgust with the Nationalists and by Russian assistance in allowing them to occupy most of Manchuria at one swoop, caused such alarm in high places that a sort of 'White Terror' set in. Spies and secret police were ubiquitous; all criticism of the Government, however disinterested or well justified, was met with savage reprisals—torture, imprisonment and death. With university professors and students especially liable to arrest (often for vague, insufficient reasons), the university authorities were too browbeaten to protect even the wholly innocent.

Such was the scene I returned to. Yet none of these horrors, except omnipresent poverty and shabbiness, was immediately apparent. For a while we all believed that the good life would return. Naturally the first thing I did, even before setting about the pleasant task of house-hunting, was to visit or seek news of my friends. Pao was still un-traceable; the Imperial Tutor Yü had died of heart-failure during the occupation, leaving his elusive wife to return to her own family in Tatung; and Layman Têng had been caught and beheaded by the Japanese. Dr Chang was in good health and relatively prosperous, for the Japanese had regarded Chinese-style doctors as a class too con-servative and too unpolitical to be dangerous; moreover, he had had the forethought to convert his occupation currency into gold bars just before its value plunged to nil. Professor Lee, who had spent most of the war years in Kunming, teaching in the reconstituted university there, was inwardly his old self; but his gowns were old and tattered; most of his furniture and possessions had been pawned or sold to supplement a salary reduced to infinitesimal proportions by the inflation; and he and his family now ate thin rice-gruel or coarse millet bread as their staple food. Though Dr Chang was often host to us again, the Professor made no false pretence of being able to return his hospitality.

Several of the Chu family were dead. Old Mr Chu himself had died like a hero (presumably under torture) in a Japanese prison. As a Manchu nobleman dispossessed by the Chinese at the fall of the dynasty, he had seemed just the man to be given a high post in the puppet government. This would have afforded him wealth, protection and opportunities of dizzy promotion without encumbering him with anything so distasteful as actual duties to perform. The post must in many ways have seemed the answer to his prayers, but he had preferred imprisonment and death to the shame of lending his distinguished name to enemies and traitors. His son, Chu Tê-Ku, married now and a petty official, was still smiling and elegant in his poverty, but openly ashamed of his involvement with the Nationalist authorities. He had seen property confiscated from wealthy Pekingese whose only crime was that they had been *forced* on pain of death to lend it to the Japanese during the occupation. Such injustice disgusted him.

Shura and Father Vassily had both disappeared without trace. My faithful servants, Lao Chao and Chao Ma, had not ventured to return to Peking from their native village, where they were managing to eke out a living by farming a tiny piece of land. Lao Chao wrote that they now had three children, all girls. Bill Luton, now back at the university, had made one of a party of teachers and students who had fled to Kunming carrying an important section of the university library on their backs! The garden of his new house having been a crematorium for Japanese troops, he took a grim delight in the beauty of the flowers he grew from soil fertilized with the ashes of the dead. The Singing-Master had transferred himself and his four female attendants to a theatre in Shanghai, where Little Wang was now a young female-impersonator on the brink of fame. Yang Taoshih, having vanished from Peking, was variously reported to have been shot by the Japanese or entered seclusion upon the mountain of Nan Yeo (Hêng Shan) in the south; but I like to think he had quietly achieved trans-mutation! The Hermit of the Peach Garden I was to encounter later —still happy and content, but laughing only when there was something to laugh at. Apart from those old friends and acquaintances whom I took the trouble to seek out, there were some I encountered by chance, including—Jade Flute!

We met one afternoon when I was strolling through the Tung An Market to buy toffeed grapes for the children of my new servants. On my way to the sweet-stalls I had stopped to browse among some book-shops and second-hand-book stalls where, presently, a good-looking woman wearing a shabby cloth gown accosted me.

'Third Father Wang! Is it really you? The Dwarfs didn't finish you off? Oh, I *am* glad!'

Had she addressed me by my real name I doubt if I should have recognized her; whether it is for better or for worse, a seventeen-year-old girl changes a good deal in nine years, even if her life has been an easy one. Happily, that special name, as well as something familiar (and still charming) about her smile, enabled me to answer promptly:

'Jade Flute! What lucky chance brings you here?'

'Lucky chances don't come my way,' she answered, laughing. 'It must be Third Father Wang who brings the luck.'

'Well, anyway, do let's sit down somewhere for a chat. Have you time?'

'Time is the one thing I am rich in, Third Father Wang.'

Soon we were facing each other across a table in a teahouse which specialized in Western-style cakes; but when I noticed how hard she was trying not to eat too fast and too much, I pretended I was hungry, too, and easily persuaded her to go round the corner with me to a restaurant where we ordered big bowls of chicken noodles and some stuffed dumplings as well. Waiting until something of our old intimacy had re-established itself, I said:

'In the old days you would never tell me much about the real circumstances of your life; you were always pretending to be happy, so that no one need feel sad for you. Do you still object to telling me how you came to be in a flower-house?'

'Not at all, Third Father Wang; my story is easily told. I'm from a farm in Shantung Province. When I was six there was a famine, and my parents, unable to feed all of us, sold me to a married man who promised to treat me well. He took me home with him to T'ai An and presented me to his wife as a *ya-t'ou* [unpaid servant girl]. For years they were very kind to me—that is, until I was nearly fifteen, when the husband began trying to bribe me to sleep with him. He had a right to that, I suppose, but I didn't want trouble with his wife, so I refused as politely as I could. He became so unhappy that his wife noticed the cause and, after sending him off to Tsingtao for some business, took me to Peking and sold me to the flower-house where you met me. There, while waiting for a customer who would pay a special price for a virgin, they fed me well, gave me lovely clothes and taught me a lot of tricks. I had to learn how to please every sort of patron and how to pretend I liked each one better than all the others. I can't say they treated me badly. I was whipped only twice and occasionally given no food for a day. Oh, don't look so sad. I had done plenty to deserve it.'

'What sort of crimes could a little girl commit?'

'For instance, the patron who bought my virginity was a gross man, with filthy tastes. Every time he touched me the hairs on my arms stood on end. So in the middle of the night I ran out of the bedroom and hid myself in the lavatory until morning. Naturally they whipped me. The man had paid forty *yuan* and had the right to do exactly what he liked with me that night.'

'*Kai ssŭ!* [He deserved to be shot!].'

'That's what I thought. But I got over it. Most of the patrons were really quite nice. Some were even gentle and understanding— like Third Father Wang.'

'Jade Flute, once something you said about jade and bamboo made me wonder if you loved me a little. I felt so ashamed of myself for having kept away from you. I suppose you didn't really love me, did you?'

'Oh, I don't know,' she answered carelessly. 'Perhaps I did. I think I loved everyone who was nice to me. Even the hateful ones had to be made to think I loved them. I couldn't always manage that, though I tried hard—after that first time. With virgins, it's different. They are frightened when their turn comes, but they never seem to find a nice man. If a man is nice, he won't demand a virgin, you see.'

'Poor Jade Flute! And then?'

'And then the occupation. The Dwarfs treated us like ordinary prostitutes. They used to queue up for us! I ran away.'

'Where could you go?'

'I had nowhere to go. I just walked to the Tung Ssŭ Archway and stood there half a day, accosting elderly women with kind faces. Most were too frightened to help me, but one poor old T'ait'ai took me home and allowed me to work for her in return for my food. Sometimes she even managed to give me clothes or pocket-money.'

'And then?'

'Last year she died. Her widower son came home for the funeral and, as he had decided to stay on in the house, he said I might as well stay to look after him. Around Ch'ing Ming [the Spring Festival] this year we were married.'

'Married! I didn't know! Why didn't you tell me? I'm delighted— or I shall be if you go on to say that you are happy with him.'

'Happy?' She paused to consider this, and I could see that the matter of happiness had never occurred to her. 'Yes, I think I am happy. My husband is good to me—elderly men often do treat girls kindly. If my child turns out to be a boy I am sure I shall be happy.'

'Child! Congratulations! When?'

'Some six months from now. It's a long time to wait, isn't it?'

'What if it's a girl?'

'That would be a misfortune—for the child. We are poor, you see. But I'll never sell her. You can be sure of that. It's only that very poor girls have such little hold over their husbands. That's why I'm glad my man is old and rather ugly. He stays faithful.'

'May I come to see you and your husband? Oh no, that would be too indiscreet, wouldn't it?'

'Indiscreet? Why? He knows what I was. He's not from a scholar-family. Why should he mind? Bring him a bottle of wine and he will welcome you.'

A few days later I did go to see her; and when her son was born in the winter I attended the *manyüeh* ceremony which marks the first compete month of a child's life. Jade Flute had analysed her feelings accurately. On my first visit I found her not unhappy; on my second she was beaming with joy. Her elderly husband, who really was an ugly man but a kindly one, could scarcely believe his good fortune; his first wife had produced no children and he had long ago resigned himself to entering the world of spirits with nobody to soften his fate there by means of sacrifices. Now he could not contain his excitement. I am afraid the evening ended with all of us, except the baby, getting drunk.

.     .     .     .     .

As the Communists continued building up their strength in the north-east the Nationalist authorities grew wilder and wilder in their reprisals against whoever was suspected of being critical of the Government on any grounds whatever. One morning came tragedy. I was on my way to see Professor Lee in his office at the university where, as I now held a Chinese Government research scholarship, I no longer taught. It was about ten in the morning; the university grounds, which should have been deserted except for those hurrying to and from lectures, were dotted with small knots and large groups of angry, gesticulating students, some of whom were unashamedly in tears. They were too excited to notice me, so when I shouted questions I received no answers. At last I could bear the suspense no longer.

'What in heaven's name has happened?' I cried, seizing one of a knot of students by the elbow and swinging him round to face me. Instinctively he raised his hand in self-defence and the others, with angry exclamations, closed in around me. Then, as though suddenly realizing I could not be an enemy, they dropped their hands and began shouting explanations in two languages at once.

'Please, please. I can't make out what you are saying. Please let this man explain. I'm a friend. I used to teach here before the occupation.'

Gradually the other voices subsided and the youth whose elbow I had so imprudently grasped panted out:

'They've smashed up everything and beaten our classmates! Sticks tipped with nails, bludgeons, fists! They beat them and tore at them and stamped on them—even girls! Some are dead! When the ambulances came I had to carry a girl with her face all cut to pieces and—and a bloody hole where her eye had been. There was a boy who——'

'But wait a minute, please. Who beat up who? Why? I don't know anything yet.'

It took time to piece together a coherent story. Earlier that morning several closed vans had driven up at speed, halted close to the dormitories and disgorged a crowd of men who looked like professional thugs. Besides carrying brutal weapons, they had mostly been dressed in a way typical of Chinese gangsters—soft felt hats and black cloth gowns worn to display several inches of shabby white underjackets at sleeves and neck. Without provocation, they had rushed two of the dormitories; smashed windows, furniture and personal possessions; seized whatever students they happened to find, including some girls passing by on their way to an early-morning lecture, and treated them with savage brutality. Some had certainly been left unconscious and it was possible that some were dying or already dead. Then, when horrified students from the other dormitories came rushing to the rescue, the attackers had bunched together, run back to their vans and made off at high speed.

Why, why, why?

As nobody could answer, I ran across to Professor Lee's office, where I found him surrounded by the same sort of shouting, gesticulating people as those I had just left; only these seemed to be lecturers and assistants rather than students. Decorum had been swallowed up in flames of anger. For nearly an hour I sat by myself in a corner, trying to make some sense of what they were saying. Then bells started ringing and they all rushed out like a garrison answering the call to arms. Professor Lee, the only elderly man present, began hastening more sedately in their wake.

'Sorry, John. No time now. A meeting. Please understand.'

'But I *don't* understand!' I shouted, determined to follow him to the place of the meeting and extract at least a sentence or two of information that made sense. 'Who were they?'

'We shall find out,' he said grimly, as I hurried by his side.

'But what do you *think*? Whom do you suspect?'

'I think some blundering fools in the Government are afraid of our students and thought they could be cowed by an outrage like this. Idiots! You know how ordinary people here look to the students for a lead, and you must have discovered that the students have plenty of reason to be vociferous in their criticisms of the régime. So——'

'Yes, yes, I see. But what have those gangsters to do with the Government?'

'Who, since the war, has been able to get hold of *new* motor-vans? Those were pretty surely *T'ê Wu* [secret police] vans, as we'll soon prove. Thank God someone had the sense to note down their numbers.'

With that he stalked into the hall where the meeting had just begun.

The next day the Government-subsidized section of the local Press contained an interesting news item. Apparently, a patriotic group of Chinese citizens, unable to put up with shameless demonstrations organized by Communist elements among the students, had (regrettably, but understandably) taken the law into their own hands. Driven by their righteous indignation, they had entered the university compound in force and given the criminals a well-deserved lesson.

Communists? Criminals? There had indeed been recent student demonstrations. They had carried banners with slogans demanding heating for classrooms and dormitories during the bitter winter months, better food for the pitifully undernourished students whose poverty left them dependent on Government subsidies, and more pay for their wretchedly poor teachers. The only 'political' slogans had been those calling for heavy punishment to be meted out for corruption!

True enough, a lot of students and some teachers did go over to the Communists at about this time, or shortly after; but their professors maintained that the reasons for their switch of allegiance were poverty, malnutrition and the frequent arrests of students and teachers (some guilty, many innocent), coupled with blazing resentment at the Government's abominable treatment of those Pekingese who had been forced to stay behind and endure the Japanese occupation.

'How are you personally affected by all this? What are you going to do?' I once asked Professor Lee, when we had been talking over these defections to the Communists.

'I shall stay on and run my department so long as this or any other régime allows me to do so. I cannot see that Communism is the right way out of our difficulties, but it is very sure that things can't go on much longer as they are now.'

.     .     .     .     .

On a summer's afternoon in 1947 I thought to get a breath of air by going to sit at the top of Mei Shan (Coal Hill), a pavilion-crowned eminence north of the Forbidden City, from which I could look down into the very heart of that prodigious nest of dark-red halls and golden-yellow roofs. The highest of Mei Shan's pavilions stood upon the most exposed and therefore coolest spot in all Peking. According to legend, the hill was a gigantic mound of coal which owed its existence to a siege-conscious Ming emperor who reigned some six hundred years ago; in reality, it was one of two hills laboriously built up to a height of several hundred feet from earth dug out during the widening of the chain of palace lakes. It was besides a lovely place to spend a summer's afternoon: there was a choice of five lacquered pavilions, built each in a different style, which stood out above the trees like a dragon's vertebrae; and, for those romantics who like their pleasures to be tinged with melancholy, there was the memory of the last Ming emperor who had hanged himself on Mei Shan as soon as the conquering Manchu army entered the city.

When I had spent a long while sitting alone in the topmost pavilion, I heard soft footsteps and the swish of a robe coming from behind me. Turning to glance at my chance companion, I found myself face to face with a friend from long ago—the laughing Taoist! I am sure my expression must have registered intense delight, but I received from him only the sort of half-smile that well-disposed people bestow on strangers. He had forgotten me, or else the war years had changed me beyond recognition. The Peach Garden Hermit had also changed, but in a different sense. Though he had not discarded his Taoist's robe, he managed to look as decorous as a Confucian scholar; the well-remembered cascades of boisterous laughter were but faintly echoed by the mocking, good-humoured expression in his eyes.

'The Peach Garden Hermit! Don't you remember me? I came more than once to your island hermitage and drank who knows how many cups of your precious tea. My insignificant surname is P'u.'

A slow smile touched his lips and suddenly leapt to his eyes, followed by a bubble of laughter.

'Ha-ha-ha. *Such* a rude fellow I was! Have you forgiven me for making a demon out of you? How could I help it? You appeared from nowhere just as the incantation left my lips. Ha-ha. Really!'

'Forgiven you? After all that wonderful tea, which gave off its fragrance at the moment of touching the tip of the tongue—wasn't that it? I loved your frankness and the way you trampled conventions. It was like a breath of air from the Realm of Immortals.'

'Truly so? It struck you like that? Ha-ha. An affinity from former lives made us feel familiar from the first. There! That was a beautifully conventional sentence. I'm learning, you see.'

'Why *should* you learn? No one expects convention from an Immortal! Your mission is to shock some understanding into us, isn't it?'

Readily he answered:

> 'Of grave missions I've none.
> Neither scholar nor saint,
> I've no single excuse
> For encumb'ring the earth——

'No, that's wrong! My one excuse shall be offered immediately. Look!'

Groping under his robe, he brought out a squat earthenware bottle with a scarlet paper seal bearing a mystic diagram.

'What is it? Surely you are not old enough to have discovered the secret of manufacturing the elixir of immortality?'

'Ha-ha-ha-ha! The effects of this elixir don't last so long. Their virtue lies in their intensity. But we cannot drink it virgin; it needs a mate—Yunnan ham or Cantonese smoked sausage would do. I suppose you carry something for emergencies?'

'No, I can't say I often do that. My pockets are not so capacious as your robe.'

'Nonsense! You foreign devils have as many pockets as a centipede has legs. I have always wondered what delicacies you hide in them. Never mind. If yours are too precious to be squandered, we shall find a restaurant in the Pei Hai with tables under the trees.'

The wine, distilled from tiny yellow flowers growing from inaccessible crags in the wilder mountains beyond the Western Hills, had a rare fragrance and was wickedly smooth; three small cupfuls, swallowed as easily as cupfuls of harmless syrup, made me feel as if I had been steadily boozing since lunch-time. The Hermit, though red in the face, seemed otherwise unaffected.

'You have an oceanic capacity,' I laughed.

'Wrong again! A man born half-witted and kept intoxicated by too much sunshine and rain is impervious to wine. Take more to eat and you will feel better. You are not a Japanese to get drunk on three cups.'

'Ah yes, that reminds me. I haven't asked you how you managed during the occupation.'

'At first I flourished. The Japanese brought me presents of cakes made with seaweed, as well as fried octopus tentacles and radishes as big as cucumbers. My island hermitage became famous. The Dwarfs brought their girls there and held drinking-parties by moonlight, treating me like a popular innkeeper. I did not object, especially as the best of them could write classical Chinese poems that were really quite witty. Some of them called me *Sensei*, which is their pronunciation of the word for Teacher. They were kind enough to say I had been born after my time, that I belonged to Old China and was not a bandit and a spy like most Chinese!'

'But you said this was only at first. What happened after?'

'Ha-ha-ha! Later they said I was a bandit and a spy. They shut me up in prison.'

'I'm sorry to hear that. Was it frightful?'

'No, prison was a joy. It gave me a holiday from having to drink with them and endure night after night of their drunken loquacity. Now I enjoyed solitude and a supply of rice and salt vegetables twice a day. In short, they provided me with all the advantages enjoyed by a mountain-dwelling recluse, while sparing me the worry of having to search for food. I was grateful.'

'Had you really been spying?'

'What a question to ask. I shouldn't know how to spy. The Chinese girls brought by the Dwarfs to their moonlight parties used to whisper little things when their whore-masters were drunk. In the mornings it might happen that a fisherman found his boat drifting close to the willows growing by the shore of my island. If sometimes he heard me singing, and liked the impromptu verses I composed, I could not very well order him not to listen.'

'You are lucky. I should have thought they executed people for less than that.'

'Right. Ha-ha. They were going to make me sit in the sun with an empty petrol tin on my head, which would presently have become so hot that I should have smelt my own flesh roasting. But then the war ended so abruptly. In those last few days they grew afraid of teaching us such tricks, in case our people thought of practising on them later. Some wanted to make sure by finishing us all off; but there were so many of us that, before they could manage more than a few hundred, we had changed places.'

'You mean the prisoners became jailors?'

'No, that was my vague way of talking. I went off into the hills, where I met the Hermit of Cedar Grove Library, who instructed me in the secret of the little yellow flowers. As you perceive, I became an adept.'

When dusk began to fall, he helped me as far as the rickshaw-stand outside the park gates and lifted me into my seat. His last words were an injunction to visit him soon, but my fuddled state then prevented me from ever seeing him again.

A week later I hurried full of anticipation to his island hermitage, to find it occupied by a Buddhist monk absorbed in a mountain landscape he was painting from memory, as Chinese landscape artists always do. Without halting the sweeping movements of his brush, he assured me that the Peach Garden Hermit had never returned after his imprisonment. Characteristically, he had left many of his things there and never thought of coming back for them, for he was one of those men who are born to travel light; but the monk knew nothing of this and was surprised to hear he was still alive. I apologized for disturbing him and walked back over the bridge separating the enchanted island from the ordinary world of mortals, angry with myself and cursing the little yellow flowers. No doubt the Peach Garden Hermit had told me his new address at a moment when I was too befuddled to take in what he was saying. A recent snapshot of himself, which he had pressed into my hand before saying goodbye, was lying somewhere at home. Pinning my faith on this, I hurried home to examine it. There was nothing written on the back at all!

.        .        .        .        .

In the autumn of the same year Dr Chang gave a party in his courtyard, specially in honour of the chrysanthemums. If the poems written after the dinner had not obliquely reflected Peking's undercurrent of anxiety about the future, it would have seemed like old times. Each of the guests was invited to compose a poem inspired by the individual charms of whichever of the fifty or sixty varieties of chrysanthemums on view seemed to him loveliest; and, as Dr Chang had remained loyal to his old affection for the metrical forms of the T'ang Dynasty, all the poems were to consist of four lines with the first, second and fourth lines rhyming. The only choice allowed was between lines of five syllables and of seven. Approximate renderings of two of the resulting poems are as follows:

> 'These smooth, thin petals, burnished sunset bronze,
> Drive from your courts the chill of autumn's breath.
> We raise our goblets, drinking deep and long,
> Lest warmth depart when icy winter strikes.'

And (referring to the traditional symbols of joy and sorrow—red and white respectively):

'Crimson and white spring forth from mingled stems
Like jewels clustered round their orbs of gold.
Gladness and woe commingle in our lives—
But crimson petals fall before the white!'

Dr Chang avoided competing with his guests by making his poem
refer not to the chrysanthemums but to three trees known collectively as the Three Friends of Winter, because they flourish impervious
to wind and snow:

'With wine and flowers we pass an idle hour
Recalling years when these were friends enow.
Today we stand in need of sturdier folk
With hearts like bamboo, pine and winter-plum.'

Not all the poems were melancholy. Indeed, one grey-headed old
satyr produced roars of laughter by lines which made only the merest
pretence of referring to the display of chrysanthemums:

'Dark, fair and pale are all the same to me;
Rounded or slim, they please me just as well—
The willow-thin delight the roving eye;
The round best satisfy the sense of touch!'

When the other guests had gone, and the tables were being
carried away, I followed Dr Chang into his library where, as so often
happened in those troubled years, our conversation drifted round to
politics.

'Dr Chang, you seem very sure the Communists will take over the
city.'

'Certainly they will. I give the Nationalists another year or two at
the most.'

'How do you feel, yourself? If the Nationalists can hold on to
South China, will you follow them there?'

'No, why should I? The Communists need doctors—Western or
Chinese style—as many as they can get. Since I can be useful to them,
why should they harm me?'

'Suppose freedom of thought is suppressed and everybody is forced
to work, live, breathe in ways pleasing to the followers of Communist
ideology. What then?'

'Freedom of thought? What does it mean? We are always free to *think*. If you mean freedom to say what you please, we lost that long ago—first to the Japanese and now to the Nationalists. The wisdom of keeping our thoughts to ourselves is not something we have yet to learn—have you seen, by the way, that yesterday they arrested seven more students? As for having to live as they order us to live, every man's actions always have been circumscribed by karma, arising from this and past lives and by countless circumstances seemingly out of our control. Even hermits are not free, because they have to eat.'

'But if the Communists suppress the old Chinese way of life altogether, you will feel so sorry. You are a man deeply attached to the past.'

'Yes, I shall feel sorry and sorry and sorry for the loss of some things, glad for the loss of others. Soon, now, I shall be an old man. Old men live more in the past than in the present. No one can take away my memories of the days when I wore a plum-coloured robe beneath an embroidered jacket and rode my father's horse with its jewelled harness. The colour of those days has already faded to near-grey. Decay is inherent in all things, as Shakyamuni Buddha bade us always remember. Death swallows all that has been born; rebirth or re-creation follow in their turn, as spring follows winter. Things rise and wane in unceasing flux. Can you run away from flux? Regret for the past is so foolish, though we may not be able to avoid it now and then. It changes nothing, restores nothing, helps no one. Though, in one sense, most old people live in the past, the wisest of them have learnt to smile where young men would feel compelled to weep. If you have to leave us, John, as may well happen, we shall say our goodbyes still smiling, I think. You will never have to think of me as in jail or suffering death before my time. Unless my Buddhist training has all been in vain, I ought to be able to get along much the same in any company—come devils, gods, hungry ghosts, Nationalists, Communists or any other sort of transient being. The one Life-Force informs them all; there is not one of them to whom I cannot bow, for I have learnt to see them all as potential Buddhas. For example, all men who knew my late wife loved and admired her as I did; some of them cannot understand how I could *descend* from her to Spring Fragrance—an ex-flower-girl. To me, both of them have this in common, that they are World Transcending Buddhas-yet-to-be! How can there have been a *descent*? The Communists might not feel flattered if I told them they are all potential World-Transcending Buddhas, but their feeling otherwise does not make them less so.'

Though I was to see Dr Chang again and again right up to the early summer of 1948, and though he was then to give me a never-to-be-forgotten farewell party, I think our talk that night was his real farewell to me. Never a boastful man, he meant what he said about being at home in the company of gods and devils. I am still able to think of him without sadness. If he is alive, he is surely content with his lot, however hard.

.        .        .        .        .

One of my servants at the new house I had taken in the east city had a twelve-year-old brother called Little Kang, who now and then came in from his village home to spend a few days with us. In 1948, shortly before Chinese New Year I took Little Kang to the neighbourhood of the Heavenly Bridge outside Ch'ien Mên, to enjoy the feats of the jugglers, magicians, wrestlers and mock-gladiators who performed there in the open air at all times of the year. The day was cold enough for beads of ice to form on our eyebrows and lashes, but was made cheerful by a red winter sun shining from an unclouded sky which could almost be described as dark blue. Driven from booth to booth, as much by the little boy's eagerness to see everything as by the cold, we came to rest for a while near the brazier of a chestnut vendor. The air around us was warm and fragrant with the smell of roasting chestnuts. I bought two large bags of them and, while munching them, we kept our eyes fixed on two remarkable swordsmen who managed to give a lively impression of a life-and-death combat, in spite of an agility in dodging blows which left both of them unscathed. Presently, someone in the crowd of bystanders, his face largely concealed by a scarf so worn that only his eyes were visible beneath his cheap cat's-fur hat, pressed close to Little Kang and, bending so that his lips almost touched the flap protecting my right ear, called me softly by name. It was Pao Yiu-Kuang!

'Good heavens!' I answered, straining to prevent my voice rising with excitement. 'What a fright you gave me; but how wonderfully good it is to see you again after—— Why, it must be ten years or more! Do be a good fellow and come to my house for a long, long chat. I am living now——'

'Better not,' he whispered, still carefully directing his eyes towards the fight.

'Well, you know best, of course. But you must tell me your news—especially about Kuei-Hsiang. How is she?'

'Everything is going well with us. Kun, as we call her now, has stayed behind at—in the country, because she is expecting again. Did you know we have a son of nearly five and a daughter of two? How I wish you could see them, John. Perhaps next year, or the year after —if you are still here—we shall be able to visit you openly. As it is, either of us might do you great harm by going to your place now.'

'Then, are you . . .'

'Please don't. You know how to put two and two together. I ought not to be talking to you now. There are spies everywhere—theirs and ours. Only, before I go, I must tell you something of great importance. If you think that, when the change comes, you could get along with our people, *please* stay. We shall need teachers. English will still have to be learnt for all sorts of reasons, so do please stay. I shall be very much in a position to guarantee no harm will come to you. But, my dear friend, if you are still the same old John—lovable, but selfish, individualistic, romantic, a Buddhist and all that—then, for your own sake, don't be here when we come. Our people will not understand you or know how to appreciate you. English Buddhist? Ha, spy! Naturally they'll think that way. If you are still like that, and also wise, then *leave Peking before—oh, before autumn of this year!*'

'Oh *no*! No, no, no! Is there really such . . .'

The place beside Little Kang was vacant. Pao had vanished as completely as a bungling Taoist who, accidentally dropping a phial into his experimental brew, is instantly transmuted!

'Laoyeh!' exclaimed Little Kang just then, fixing on me a gaze discomfortingly full of precocious wisdom. 'Who was that gentleman?'

'A Taoist,' I answered hastily. 'A Taoist with marvellous powers of transmutation—you know, of vanishing.'

'He smelt of garlic, Laoyeh, and vanished simply by walking into the crowd. Was he a *Palu?*'

I shivered. *Palu*, short for Eighth Route Army, had become the usual colloquial term for Communist.

'How should I know if the Taoist gentleman is also a *Palu*, you rabbit-child?'

'You seemed to know him well, Laoyeh. But do not fear. I am going to be a *Palu* myself when I'm old enough to fight. I'm going to——'

'*Silence*, little turtle's egg. How dare you talk such wicked nonsense! Do you want to get your whole family into trouble, and me as well?'

The wretched child, popping a couple of chestnuts into his mouth, gave me a conspiratorial smile which exactly corresponded to a Western child's wink. It was a smile which frightened me more than if he had run off to call a policeman. After all, I had done nothing subversive, and ought to be able to clear myself of a specific charge without any difficulty; but if a twelve-year-old child could take it so absolutely for granted that someone he liked—a man whose friends were chiefly *teachers and students*—must necessarily favour the *Palu*, and be glad to hear the little wretch confess his intention of joining them, then Peking was no longer a place admirably conducive to peace of mind! In those last months of Nationalist power an accusation of that sort was treated as tantamount to proof of guilt! Neither a Nationalist prison nor a Communist régime held much promise of attractions for me. During a civil war, when child turns against father and brother pits himself against brother, if a man is lucky enough to be a foreigner, with somewhere else in the world to go, it is wiser to go without much delay. The one Christian doctrine which seems to have been universally accepted these days is, ironically, the chilling sentence: 'He that is not with me is against me!' Around the neutrally minded, prisons yawn!

Soon after that, I decided that I clearly recognized the writing on the wall. Deeply though I sympathized with the hungry students, undernourished professors and all the other victims of war, inflation and misgovernment, I felt by no means inclined to accept Pao's kindly invitation to stay behind and take up a teaching post under the new régime. I had no desire to live in a Communist-controlled Peking where, however salutary some of the changes might be, the traditional ways I had learnt to love would certainly have vanished. As the horribly fratricidal struggle swept down the railway line from Manchuria, to within earshot of Peking, my hopes of living out my life in that loveliest of cities came thundering to earth.

Naturally I did not have to tear myself away at once. There was not that much urgency. Indeed, it would have done me no harm to

have remained with many other foreigners to witness the Red Army's
triumphal entry and waited for the expulsion which overtook most
Westerners in the year which followed. However, for a number of
reasons, I decided to leave in June. From Chinese New Year until then
I set myself to enjoy every delight which the city still afforded. At
about this time, Chin P'ei-Shan,[1] an elderly Manchu scholar whom I
had come both to love and revere, assented to our placing the seal of
blood-brotherhood upon our friendship; thereafter, I spent many an
enchanted hour listening to him as he relived the colourful days of his
youth, which had been passed during the time of the Empress-Dowager.
I was also busy acquiring the Pekingese wife who was to lighten the
burden of my coming exile. Moreover, in the spare time left by my not
very arduous research work on T'ang Dynasty Buddhism, I wandered
nostalgically through the temples, palaces and gardens which had so
often been the scenes of the various sorts of happiness I had enjoyed
in the pre-war years; I mingled with the good-natured crowds at
markets, flower-shows, goldfish contests and temple fairs; I revisited
my favourite bath-houses and curio-shops; and I passed many gay
evenings with my friends in restaurants and at the theatre, for I was by
then addicted to the modern straight plays—a Western art-form which
the Chinese had successfully adapted to Chinese needs. Often, in my
search for renewed happiness, I found what I was looking for; but, as
the bitter day of parting drew nearer, I was oppressed by the thought
of having to say farewell to so many people and things closely
entwined with my life.

Towards the end, I found myself guest of honour at a dinner-party
almost every evening. My wife, however, was less fortunate; for,
though the sexes now mingled in public more often than in pre-war
days, full-scale dinner-parties in restaurants remained as sacrosanct to
males as most of London's more famous clubs. The party I remember
with particular pleasure was given by Dr Chang at a duck restaurant
and attended by ten of my oldest Peking friends. Professor Lee was
unfortunately ill that day, his health having suffered a good deal from
the anxieties arising from the increasing political ferment within the
university; but many of my former colleagues including Ouyang, as
well as Bill Luton and Chu Tê-Ku, were there. Chu, now one of the
poorest of all, having resisted eking out his inadequate official salary
by the usual corrupt means, was still fond of doing things in the grand

[1] See my *Wheel of Life* (Rider), page 197 ff.

manner; as I had refused to let him put on a special farewell dinner for me, he tried to play host at this one. Towards the end of the feast, Dr Chang, warned just in time, hurried down to the cashier's desk at the bottom of the main stairway and caught Chu in the very act of handing over a wad of notes which must have amounted to more than he earned in a month!

The dinner was much more elaborate than the simple affair consisting of two or three roast ducks, a duck omelet and soup at which I had once played host in a rival duck establishment across the lane. This time we had a full-scale feast, with sixteen main dishes supported by a large number of subsidiary courses; Peking duck, as the *pièce de résistance*, came somewhere in the middle. The famous Shantung Cold Plate, with which all such feasts began, was followed by shark's-fin soup made with fins then worth their weight in gold because of the Communist disruption of the railways—indeed, only a few ounces of fin had been used, and both the flavour and texture of the soup depended largely on the other ingredients, but the solemnity of the occasion was such that Dr Chang had refused to dispense with a delicacy traditionally essential to the composition of a major Chinese feast. The other dishes were mostly old favourites of mine, some of which have been described elsewhere in this book. Even in Peking, after enjoying a hundred or so separate feasts, it was difficult to come across completely novel dishes; however, as each restaurant prepared them according to its own secret and well-guarded recipes, and as at least some of the ingredients varied according to the current inspiration of the chef, an exact duplicate of some especially delectable dish was hard to get even when desired. Only straightforward dishes with a minimum of separate ingredients, such as Peking duck, roast sucking-pig or crisp-fried Yunnan ham, were more or less constant in flavour, texture and appearance. Like accomplished piano soloists, the *tashihfu* (maestros) of the kitchen knew how to apply infinite variations to a single theme.

During dinner that evening, we drank a good deal of my favourite Shaohsing *huang chiu* and grew boisterous over such drinking-games as finger-guessing, the object of which was always to make your opponents pay the penalty of draining yet another cupful. With experienced players, wild guesswork gave place to a duel of wits depending upon a psychological and mathematical assessment of possibilities—so much so that a master-player could drive a whole succession of opponents to the stage where they begged for mercy without himself becoming noticeably intoxicated. Presently I suggested another sort of wine-game involving the composition of extemporary poems at speed. The toastmaster produces an opening line at random, whereupon the three other players have to compose suitable second, third and fourth lines in turn. This must be done within an agreed length of time and with proper attention to content, rhythm and rhyme. He who hesitates or fails has to down three cupfuls of wine as a penalty. It was a classical game which had been out of fashion since the passing of the days when every Chinese gentleman was so steeped in traditional poetry as to be able to compose fluently and well at a moment's notice; so my proposal met with a chorus of dissent; yet, to please their guest of honour, four people reluctantly agreed to have a try. Dr Chang, the only expert among us, was politely kept out of the competition by being appointed toastmaster, whose business it was to produce the initial line. Ouyang, Chu and another friend, Professor An, agreed to follow on.

'Why should not Professor Luton set the first line?' asked the doctor. 'His Chinese is better than ours.'

This compliment, which the Chinese often pay to foreigners though it is seldom, if ever, deserved, brought a quick disclaimer from Bill.

'Thank you, thank you, Chang Taifu. Your praise is more kind than accurate; stupid fellow like myself is bound to find it embarrassing. Allow me to decline the honour.'

I gave Bill a quick smile. By answering readily in idiomatic Pekingese he had passed muster, and was allowed to escape a task too difficult for a foreigner at such short notice. So Dr Chang, holding up his hand for silence, intoned seven Chinese syllables meaning something like:

'We speed our guest beyond the ancient walls.'

Ouyang, who had guessed the doctor would lead off with something very simple concerning a parting, was quick to add a line with a classical reference to tears in it.

'Sadly we turn our horses, moist our sleeves.'

Chu hesitated much longer, recovering only just in time to avoid the penalty of draining three cupfuls.

'Ten thousand *li* of lonely mountain road.'

So far the results had been trite and the rhythmic correspondences barely passable. Everything depended upon the last man, the humorous Professor of Western Literature, who brought out:

'Why lonely? See the chariot follows close.'

This reference to my wife caused some mild applause; otherwise, the experiment had failed, so Ouyang asked Dr Chang to complete the whole verse by himself. Within three minutes our host produced lines which, if less than poetry, were at any rate technically faultless—though this does not appear in my rough English rendering—and which hinted at genuine feeling:

> 'We speed our guest beyond the ancient walls;
> As distance widens, words dissolve in smiles.
> Now, lost to view, he skirts the cloud-capped peaks,
> But thoughts from heart to heart unite us still.'

'Our doctor, reared amidst the fragrance of books, still keeps a store of volumes locked in his belly!' shouted Ouyang admiringly, his voice rising above the sound of general applause.

Later in the evening, Ouyang made a half-hearted suggestion that we should, for old times' sake, pay a visit to the willow-lanes; but the flower-houses had become so impoverished and degenerate during the war that scholars no longer regarded them as either respectable or amusing. The gay after-dinner gatherings held in the company of girls whose wit and talents matched or exceeded their youthful beauty had become things of the past. As for me, I had an objection of another sort.

'But I am married now!' I exclaimed, the words leaving my mouth before I had time to recollect that many of my old companions in the days of our willow-lane evenings had often been men with one or two wives and several children.

'What has marriage got to do with it?' asked Kuan Hsienshêng, another of my former colleagues, in justifiable astonishment. 'You surely do not plan to take your wife along?'

'No, of course not,' I laughed. 'But she would dislike my going—I think.'

'Ah, a modern girl! Lao P'u, you ought to have chosen better. Modern girls are sadly tiresome in these matters. *My* wife encourages me to visit such places. She says the reason I make a considerate husband and father is that I spend my surplus affection on flower-girls and professional dancing-girls instead of staying at home and growing bored or irritable. So I try to please her in this way as often as I can. Though I ought not to say it of my own wife, I don't mind telling you she's a sensible woman.'

It was Dr Chang who solved the dilemma. 'It's a beautifully moon-light night and quite warm enough to go boating. Rather than jeopardize our guest's married bliss, let us go boating in the Pei Hai. But first look out of the window. If the moon has hidden herself, then I agree that P'u Hsienshêng must be made to risk P'u T'ait'ai's dis-pleasure.'

Two or three guests, hurrying over to the window, reported favourably on the state of the sky, so I was spared the necessity of having to make an awkward confession within the first month of my married life.

'Good!' exclaimed Dr Chang. 'I am going to arrange a pleasant surprise for you,' and he hurried out to a telephone on the landing. When he returned, we all got up to go. Arrived at the Pei Hai, we found all the boatmen had gone home, so we wandered over the marble bridge and strolled round to my favourite spot—a long wooden gallery on the farther side of the island. Flanked by a pair of battlemented towers, it ran for a little way along the margin of the lake, directly below the hill where the Tibetan-style *chorten* now glimmered above the darkness of the hill itself. Across the oily black water flecked with moonlight were the lights of the Five Dragon Pavilions, which brought back a vivid memory of my encounter with the solitary eunuch at a spot immediately above us over thirteen years before.

The night was deliciously warm and fragrant. It was easy for a party of old friends, mellow after a feast, to slip into a mood of quiet contentment that harmonized with the near-silence of the softly illumined trees and water all around us, so that some of us had soon forgotten all about the surprise which Dr Chang had promised. Presently he slipped away, to return later in the company of two other people. One was Spring Fragrance and the other a fat old man who seemed, at first, to be a disembodied head, for his rusty black gown merged with the surrounding darkness. He was tenderly nursing a silk-wrapped bundle which turned out to be an antique metal-stringed lute.

Spring Fragrance, who was now about forty, had long ago risen from the humble status of flower-girl. Thanks to her remarkable talents, her charm and (no doubt) Dr Chang's energetic patronage, she had become a much-sought-after professional singer, able to command double or treble the cost of the sort of feast we had just enjoyed for a single performance. Even the well-to-do Dr Chang could hardly have afforded such expensive entertainment for his guests, but it could be taken for granted that Spring Fragrance, in her present state of affluence, would not dream of accepting payment from her faithful sweetheart and benefactor. Like many Chinese, she placed personal loyalty to friends above any other sort of obligation; on this occasion she had broken a long-standing engagement to sing at a huge party given by General Shen to his mother-in-law on her seventieth birthday, rather than answer Dr Chang's unexpected telephone call with a refusal. His message had been relayed to her at the general's mansion, where, to everyone's disappointment and chagrin, she had made some excuse and left immediately. By doing so, she had forfeited a large sum of money, lost the patronage of one of Peking's richest dignitaries and damaged her reputation for dependability, without pausing to think twice. When the doctor heard what had happened, he gave her a good scolding in front of us all, to which she replied:

'If I were going to be married, I would leave my own wedding-party to come and sing for you.'

I like to believe that the events of that evening were Peking's farewell to me, made in her own inimitable fashion. There, in the lovely gallery where the Empress-Dowager and her ladies had so often rested after a colourful excursion on the lakes, with the black silver-flecked water before us and the *chorten* glimmering above, we listened to the beautiful voice of Spring Fragrance soaring above the small noises of the night. The fragrance of Turkish tobacco from Bill Luton's pipe became a tangible expression of the friendship and peace uniting us in a cloud of happiness. I can still remember every word of one of the songs she sang. It was a modern Chinese song of no literary merit, its tune neither more nor less beautiful than a hundred others, but I know that Spring Fragrance had specially chosen it to convey Peking's parting message to me:

> 'Spring's beauty lingers yet,
> With freshness of spring flowers;
> Spring breezes from the lake
> Strike softly on our cheeks.
> This silence in our hearts—
> What need for speech remains?
> Twin hearts now merged in one!

Though spring must surely pass,
Though petals fall to earth,
For us the joy remains
Unchanging and unchanged.
I charge you to recall
For ever and for ever
This loveliest of days
Too precious to forget.'

Originally, the words had expressed the mood of a pair of lovers; yet it was so easy to apply them to the circumstances of that evening. The scent of spring flowers, the breeze from off the lake and the silence of perfect contentment were actually present to our senses while the words were being sung. Spring's approaching end, the falling to earth of the petals, suggested my coming exile; and the final admonition was an injunction never to forget the enduring friendships and miraculous happiness which Peking had so lavishly bestowed in return for my affection.

Towards midnight, while we were saying our goodbyes near the rickshaw-stand outside the park, I whispered to Bill:

'It's *so* hard to leave. I suppose you'll be the next one to be given a farewell party.'

'Me leave Peking? Never! Old trees die when they're transplanted. I'll have to die, anyway, within the next ten years or so, but let it be where I have lived so well.'

'The Communists may *force* you to go, Bill.'

'I don't believe it. Not me—Bill Luton. Why, I guess a good few of their leaders have been my own students at one time or another. If they tried throwing me out, it would be all up with me. I couldn't take it. But it's not in Chinese nature to be ungrateful to an old teacher. They'll let me stay, all right. You'll see.'

It may be hard to believe, but he was right. Alone among the frankly non-Communist foreign staff-members of Peking's universities, Bill Luton has received indulgent treatment until today. The Communist professors, heads of departments, commissars and so on who were once his students still show him kindness and even generosity. Can it be that the Pekingese have, in spite of themselves, retained some of their old lovable, humanistic qualities? The rare news I receive from Peking is very conflicting.

In any case, come what may, I have my memories. In the scenes I recall, the Pekingese live on smiling, tolerant, kindly as ever. However harshly others may now be forced to judge them,

> *For me the joy remains,*
> *Unchanging and unchanged!*

# 12

# Dawn?

I HAVE not visited Peking since the Communists entered the city in triumph more than ten years ago. From all I hear and read, I cannot doubt they have accomplished much that was desirable and even more that seemed desirable to them. Factories, kindergartens, crèches, clinics and modern hotels have sprung forth like mushrooms; streets are cleaner; temples and palace buildings shine beneath new coats of lacquer; lakes and moat have been purged of century-old deposits of silt. The former inmates of flower-houses and brothels have been re-educated to serve society in less intimate ways. Even flies, they say, have been abolished.

Massive concrete blocks of workers' flats and government offices soar above the low grey roofs of mediaeval dwellings—relics of a feudal past scheduled for gradual elimination. Space-wasting courtyards, once cluttered with anti-social trees and rocks, pots of flowers and goldfish ponds, are being opened up to make room for useful things like garages or blast-furnaces. The ghosts of Confucius and Mencius have fled to escape chastisement by sages Marx and Mao.

No one starves or freezes, which was, alas, not always so. No one eats or plays too much. No one sits idle like old Mr Chu, thinking out new ways of refining old pleasures. The houses of Peking opera flourish; the traditional operas, purged—of course—of feudal sentiments and converted to 'serve the people's interests', are now applauded with civilized handclapping instead of the old feudalistic shouts of 'Hao'. Peking duck, Mongolian mutton, tribute silks and fine porcelain are still there for those who can afford them—foreign advisers and the staffs of foreign embassies from friendly powers. Prices are fixed, beggars banished and hawkers firmly regulated. No whiff of opium taints the northern air. Gods and Buddhas, monks and lamas—ranks thinned, but not entirely liquidated—exemplify to Asian visitors the extent of the new Freedom. Doubtless the more time-consuming items of bath-house ritual have been abolished, lest bathing be re-garded as a pleasure rather than a civic duty. Dr Chang, if he still composes poetry, doubtless writes on improving subjects, such as heroic factory-workers over-fulfilling their norms; no doubt he realizes that scholars should not allow the fragrance of the pines to intoxicate them to the point of flapping their sleeves in emulation of the birds, for birds must still display a tendency towards reactionary, anti-social behaviour.

In all seriousness, who can doubt that much of this is for the good? That no one starves or freezes is a change that even the sternest of the régime's critics dare not refuse to welcome.

And yet?

The world must be in some sort poorer for the loss of 'Old' Peking. The traditional Pekingese way of life was, despite the wide-spread suffering it failed to cure, a living flame from the ancient fire of a civilization as unique as it was venerable. Granting that this culture had serious defects, that callousness towards poverty and illiteracy should not have lasted so far into this century, it remains true that the Pekingese I knew had rare virtues. For wisdom, urbanity, moderation, decorous behaviour, skill in arts and joyous appreciation of beauty in all its forms, they remain unequalled by the inhabitants of any city in the world today.